T0208501

What Should Legal Analysis Become?

What Should Legal Analysis Become?

ROBERTO MANGABEIRA UNGER

VERSO

London • New York

First published by Verso 1996
© Roberto Mangabeira Unger 1996
All rights reserved

Verso
UK: 6 Meard Street, London W1F 0EG
USA: 20 Jay Street, Suite 1010, Brooklyn, NY 11201

Verso is the imprint of New Left Books

ISBN 1–85984–969–5
ISBN 1–85984–100–7 (pbk)

British Library Cataloguing in Publication Data
A catalogue record for this book is available from the
British Library

Library of Congress Cataloging-in-Publication Data
Unger, Roberto Mangabeira.
    What should legal analysis become? / Roberto Mangabeira Unger.
    p.   cm.
    Includes index.
    ISBN 1–85984–969–5 (hbk). — ISBN 1–85984–100–7 (pbk).
    1. Law—Interpretation and construction.   2. Law—Methodology.
3. Law—Philosophy.   I. Title.
    K290.U54   1996
    340'.1—dc20   96–6000
                                                             CIP

Typeset by M Rules
Printed in the United States

Contents

SUBJECT AND PLAN OF THIS BOOK

The conflict over the basic terms of social life, having fled from the ancient arenas of politics and philosophy, lives under disguise and under constraint in the narrower and more arcane debates of the specialized professions. There we must find this conflict, and bring it back, transformed, to the larger life of society.

To gain the freedom to make alternative futures for society with clarity and deliberation, we must be able to imagine them and to talk about them. To imagine them and to talk about them effectively, we must enter specialized areas of thought and practice. We must transform these specialties from within, changing their relation to the public conversation in a democracy. We must bring the specialists to renounce some of the higher authority they never properly possessed, exchanging this false authority for a new style of collaboration between technical experts and ordinary people.

This book offers an example of the effort to penetrate, and reshape from within, one such technical domain – law and legal analysis. It asks how we can change legal analysis so that it may fulfill its primary vocation in a democratic and enlightened society: to inform us, as citizens, in the attempt to imagine our alternative futures and to argue about them. The subject is crucial, and the moment is daunting.

Law and legal thought have been, in the contemporary Western industrial democracies as in many societies of the past, the place at which an ideal of civilization takes detailed institutional form. In law and legal thought, ideals must come to terms with interests, and the marriage between interests and ideals must become incarnate in practical arrangements. Legal doctrine supplies a way of representing and discussing these arrangements that makes it possible to sustain and develop them from day to day and from controversy to controversy. How can we grasp an established institutional and ideological settlement in a manner that acknowledges its transformative possibilities, giving us power to make the future and freeing us from superstition about the present?

This question has now gained added force. We live at a time when the idea of social alternatives risks being discredited as a romantic illusion responsible for historical catastrophe. We no longer attach secure meanings to the fighting words of the past. We must then rediscover in the small variations on which legal thought has traditionally fastened the beginnings of the larger alternatives we can no longer find where we used to look for them.

The intention of this book dictates its plan. The book begins by developing an experimentalist and democratic vantage point from which to judge the intellectual and political opportunities of the present. It discusses why the institutional imagination needs new tools and what work we can hope to do with them. The book then turns to law and legal thought as a source of such tools. The initial step is to show how the original genius of contemporary law, with its unrealized democratizing potential, has remained caught within the constraints imposed by institutional structures and superstitions. To contend with these structures and superstitions, the argument then sets out to explore what is fast becoming the most influential method of legal analysis throughout the world – what I here call rationalizing legal analysis. The book considers the character, consequences, and transformative possibilities of this method from several perspectives, and by means that are cumulative and dialectical rather than systematic and linear. As our understanding of this analytic practice deepens, we begin to see how to reorient it so that it may do fuller justice to the genius of contemporary law and better service to our experimentalist and democratic commitments. The final part of the book suggests how we can put a reoriented practice of legal analysis to work, tracing divergent trajectories along which to advance, through cumulative institutional change, the democratic project.

In a sense, this book is about the translation of hope into insight. The relation between insight into society and hope about people is therefore a good place to start.

INSIGHT AND TRANSFORMATION IN NATURAL SCIENCE AND SOCIAL STUDY

Institutional possibility in social theory and social science

The practical experimentalism of democratic politics and the cognitive experimentalism of the social sciences have something significant in common. The theorist and the practical reformer share a stake in putting actual institutions in their place by understanding and judging them from the vantage point of suppressed and unrealized possibilities. We can keep this freedom-giving and superstition-subverting idea alive today only if we recast both legal analysis and political economy as institutional imagination. With the help of this reformed practice of legal and economic study we can then rethink the established institutional forms of representative democracies, market economies, and free civil societies. We can breathe new meaning and new life into the democratic project.

Transformative opportunity is the key to the scientific exploration of the natural world: we understand how things work by discovering under what conditions, in what directions, and within what limits they can change. The subsumption of actual phenomena within a larger field of unrealized opportunities is not, for science, a metaphysical conjecture; it is an indispensable enabling assumption.

What is true of natural science holds in spades for the whole range of social and historical studies. Largely implicit judgements of counterfactual possibility inform our vision of actual sequences in historical change and of actual forces in social life. A summary statement of our troubling predicament in social and historical study is that we no longer have available to us a credible account of structural change – that is to say, of change in the institutional arrangements and the associated enacted beliefs that shape the practical and conversational routines of a society.

The large explanatory projects of classic nineteenth-century social theories such as Marxism, with their characteristic belief in a predetermined sequence of indivisible institutional systems driven forward by lawlike forces, have fallen victim to both the growth of academic learning and the disappointments of political experience. We nevertheless cling to their left-overs, confusedly using the vocabulary of theoretical systems we claim to have renounced: concepts like capitalism that presuppose the existence of a single, typical economic and legal regime with an institutional logic of its own, or distinctions between the reformist humanization and the revolutionary substitution of the established order. The positive social sciences, for their part, dispense with the idea of structural change altogether, treating basic arrangements and preconceptions as the cumulative residue of countless past episodes of problem solving or compromise, or as the outcome of trial-and-error convergence toward the best available practices. In such an intellectual climate, the transformation and invention of the formative structures of a society become literally unimaginable. As a result, we find ourselves driven back to an understanding of political realism as proximity to what already exists.

The failure to imagine transformative possibility that has come to vitiate the dominant practice of social and historical study infects normative political philosophy as well as the shared language of practical politics.

Institutional possibility in political philosophy

This failure has helped shape, especially in the English-speaking world, a dominant style of political philosophy. It is a way of thinking that disconnects the formulation of principles of justice from the problems of institutional design, refuses to acknowledge the effect of established institutions and practices upon desires and intuitions, and treats the social-democratic compromise of the postwar period as the insuperable horizon for the pursuit of its ideals. The first and second characteristics of this political philosophy connect through their joint dependence upon the third. Together, they result in a paradoxical dependence upon the historical context the philosopher wanted to transcend.

The philosopher may imagine that principles of right – in particular, principles of just distribution – can be first formulated in an institutional vacuum. Technical disciplines of institutional design can then deal with their practical application in the light of empirical knowledge and changing circumstance. Thus, he trivializes the problem of institutional design as one of circumstantial social engineering.

The problem of institutions, demoted by the philosopher's method, strikes back to compromise the authority and the reach of his claims. It does so in one of two ways. The philosopher may frankly identify his method for selecting the principles of justice – for example, contractarian or utilitarian – with the familiar forms of the market economy or of representative democracy, treating these institutions as if they were a credible proxy for a practice of collective choice by free and equal individuals. In this procedure, however, the philosopher fails adequately to reckon with both the defects and the contingency of the inherited political and economic institutions. He fails to recognize that the idea of a society of free and equal individuals might develop in different institutional directions, with different consequences for the character of relations among people as well as for the distribution of wealth and power.

Alternatively, the philosopher may reach behind the institutional façade of the contemporary industrial democracies to a preinstitutional moment in the application of his method. He may appeal to the raw material of desires and intuitions, purging them of their partiality, or balancing them against one another, so that the institutional framework appears among the conclusions rather than among the premises of the argument.

However, he can give his method the requisite power to generate determinate results only by suppressing a crucial internal dialectic in the material of desires and intuitions: the conflict between those of our tendencies that take the established order of social life for granted and those that, as longing, fantasy, or resistance, rebel against that order. This duality of human wants reflects the fundamental two-sidedness of our relation to the discursive and institutional worlds we inherit, remake, and inhabit: we are them, and we are more than them. There is always more in us than there is in them.

If he is to arrive, at the end of the day, at institutions like ours, the philosopher must not merely presuppose people who have our desires and intuitions, shaped as they are by the structure within which we live; he must presuppose people whose life of longing is more one-dimensional than ours in fact is. His imaginary Benthamite or his hypothetical party to the social contract must be us minus one rather than us plus one.

At the heart of these illusions of academic political philosophy lies the failure to do justice to what will be one of the central themes of this book. Call it in one vocabulary the internal, and in another vocabulary the dialectical, relation between thinking about ideals and interests and thinking about institutions and practices. Thinking about ideals and interests and thinking about institutions and practices are not two separate moments or activities: each incorporates the other without being reducible to the other. Thus, each social ideal and each group interest gain part of their meaning from the familiar social arrangements that we imagine to represent or to fulfill them in fact. At the same time, however, there is something in the indistinct longing within our ideals and something in the brute force within our interests that fights, impatiently, against the limits imposed by present arrangements. We take account of this duality when we develop our understanding of our interests and ideals by tinkering, in imagination and in practice, with their practical forms of realization. The central importance of that tinkering is the most important sense of the internal relation between thinking about ideals or interests and thinking about institutions or practices.

We can now understand what would otherwise remain a paradoxical feature of the dominant political philosophy. It wants to transcend its historical situation, sometimes more, and sometimes less (as my later discussion of the campaign to split the difference between historicism and rationalism suggests). However, it wants to accomplish this liberation from the moment and the circumstance at the outset of its arguments, by a methodological move, rather than at the end of its arguments, through a patient labor of the imagination. It therefore fails to recognize the ideological ambiguities and the transformative opportunities that live in the internal relation between our ideals or interests and our institutions or practices. Not to see these opportunities and ambiguities is to squander the means for real distance from real institutions. That is why so much of the speculative political philosophy of today turns out in retrospect to give a metaphysical gloss to the tax-and-transfer practices of established social democracy. A pessimistic reformism, skeptical of institutional alternatives and resigned to compensatory measures, directs the seemingly abstract campaigns of this speculative political philosophy. The philosopher is betrayed by his method into the hands of the historical context that he, out of fear of relativism, had wanted to transcend. He becomes, alas, the unwitting and self-appointed victim of the history he had planned to escape.

DEMOCRACY AND EXPERIMENTALISM

Democratic experimentalism and institutional fetishism

One reason why the weakening of the transformative imagination matters is that it breeds superstitions hostile to the advance of the democratic project: the most powerful and persistent set of social ideas in modern history. To grasp the power of this project – the common coin of liberals and socialists for the last two centuries – we must understand democracy as much more than party pluralism and the electoral accountability of government to an inclusive electorate. Viewed in broader and more revealing light, the democratic project has been the effort to make a practical and moral success of society by reconciling the pursuit of two families of goods: the good of material progress, liberating us from drudgery and incapacity and giving arms and wings to our desires, and the good of individual emancipation, freeing us from the grinding schemes of social division and hierarchy. Such schemes prevent us from dealing with one another as inexhaustible individuals rather than as repressed placeholders in a collective order. An influential nineteenth-century belief held there to be a natural convergence, albeit a long-term one, between these two goods. Now we struggle to hold on to the more limited and skeptical faith that the quests for these two goods do not, as a conservative fatalism would have it, contradict each other. The democratic project, freed from both dogmatic optimism and dogmatic pessimism, is the effort to identify the practical arrangements lying in the zone of potential overlap between the conditions of material progress and the conditions of individual emancipation. The hope of finding such a zone of overlap is reasonable because both practical progress and the freeing of the individual depend upon the acceleration of collective learning through practical experimentalism. Both require that we subject social practices to experimental tinkering, and advance toward those practices that encourage us to tinker all the more.

One of the enemies of democratic experimentalism is institutional fetishism: the belief that abstract institutional conceptions, like political democracy, the market economy, and a free civil society, have a single natural and necessary institutional expression. Institutional fetishism is a pervasive type of superstition in contemporary culture. It penetrates each of the disciplines mentioned earlier, and it informs the language and debates of ordinary politics. The old-fashioned idea of enlightenment would today best be applied to efforts to dispel the institutional fetishism vitiating orthodox doctrines in each of the social disciplines. Dispelling it would be the full-time job of a generation of social critics and social scientists.

Today, the cause of democratic experimentalism throughout the world has a specific focus. The commanding issue before us is how and in what direction to renew the repertory of varied but analogous institutional arrangements that the advanced industrial democracies have come to share since the time of the last great war. The old conflict between statism and privatism, command and market, is dying. It is in the process of being replaced by a new conflict among alternative institutionalized versions of political and economic pluralism. The premise of this emerging dispute is that representative democracies, market economies, and free civil societies can assume legal–institutional forms very different from those that have come to prevail in the rich industrial democracies. According to this belief, the existing variations among the governmental and economic institutions of these democracies represent a subset of a much broader range of unrealized institutional possibilities.

Institutional divergence in the forms of democracies, markets, and civil societies may be the wholly intentional result of conscious deliberate invention. More often, however, it is the half-chosen byproduct of institutional recombinations and variations undertaken under pressure of economic ambition and political rivalry. The most successful countries, in economic development as well as national self-assertion, have often been the most insistent pillagers of practices and arrangements from all over the world. This involuntary institutional experimentalism has recently been most evident in formerly or still communist countries reconstructing their economies as well as in the forward tier of the developing world. We see its signs, for example, when the practical economic and political requirements of mass privatization lead Eastern European governments to experiment with widespread distribution of equity stakes in industry and with the pooling of these shares by investment funds charged with exercising responsibility for oversight of the firms in which the fragmented owners hold equity; or when, as in present-day China, workers, managers, and local governments hold joint residual rights of ownership in "township–village enterprises"; or when, as in Brazil today, labor law combines the contractualist principle of freedom of the union from governmental tutelage with the corporatist principle of automatic and comprehensive unionization of the entire laborforce.

Among the great spiritual enemies of the experimentalist impulse in the remaking of institutions is the pervasive superstition of institutional fetishism: the unwarranted and inhibiting identification of abstract institutional conceptions like representative democracy and the market economy with a particular, contingent set of institutional arrangements. This fetishistic attitude toward the institutional arrangements of society receives encouragement from many of the dominant discursive practices of the social sciences, with their characteristic inability to imagine structural discontinuity and reinvention. The same attitude finds support as well in the working assumptions of much normative political philosophy, with its misguided separation of prescriptive principle from institutional design. The disappointments and disillusionments of twentieth-century history, culminating in the collapse of communism – the most dramatic instance of willed institutional innovation in this century – seem to confirm the perception of historical constraint inspiring and expressing the fetishistic habit.

The convergence thesis

Institutional fetishism today gains a pseudoscientific respectability through a largely implicit but nevertheless persuasively influential idea: the notion of a convergence toward a single set of best available practices throughout the world. According to this idea the institutional evolution of the modern world is best understood as an approach, by trial and error, toward the only political and economic institutions that have proved capable of reconciling economic prosperity with a decent regard to political freedom and social security. Variations in the institutional arrangements of successful contemporary societies are real but secondary; if anything, they tend to become narrower as the relentless lessons of experience leave ever less room for the reconstructive imagination.

The many-sided influence exercised by this subterranean thesis is all the more remarkable because the thesis represents a striking reversal – a reactionary interlude – in what has been the main direction of social and historical thought since the late nineteenth century: the escape from functionalist and evolutionary determinism in social and historical explanation and the growing appreciation of the ways in which the practical institutions and the enacted beliefs of a people join to shape a distinct form of life. There are two basic objections to the reactionary thesis of convergence. The first objection is that, as we have learned from the explanatory failures of theories like Marxism, we always have alternative institutional means to the realization of practical objectives; functional requirements underdetermine institutional responses. The rightwing Hegelianism of the convergence thesis conceals a stark downgrading of historical contingency and human freedom. The second objection is that, as Adam Smith and Karl Marx both understood, in choosing one set of economic institutions over another, we also choose a certain way of living and of connecting with other people. We cannot separate the practical and the spiritual shape of our civilization.

The intellectually regressive thesis of convergence toward the best available practices worldwide reinforces the authority of the political project that exercises greatest influence in the world today, especially in the developing world: the project of neoliberalism, sometimes also called the Washington consensus. It is this distinctive project rather than the abstract idea of convergence that stands today as the most formidable obstacle to democratic experimentalism. Neoliberalism is the program of macroeconomic stabilization without damage to the internal and external creditors of the state; of liberalization, understood both more narrowly as acceptance of foreign competition and integration into the world trading system and more generally as the reproduction of traditional Western contract and property law; of privatization, meaning the withdrawal of the state from production and its devotion, instead, to social responsibilities; and of the development of social safety-nets designed to compensate, retrospectively, for the unequalizing and destabilizing effects of market activity. This program has twin counterparts in the rich industrial democracies: one, overtly intolerant of governmental activism in the economy and hostile to worker and welfare rights; the other, a chastened, liberalized version of social democracy that is fast becoming the new center of gravity of Western politics. The distinguishing attributes of this chastened social democracy are: first, its continuing commitment to the welfare state and to investment in people, as both an end in itself and a condition of economic success; second, a desire to rid the regulated market economy of statist, corporatist, and oligopolistic constraints upon economic flexibility and innovation, especially in the transition to a postfordist style of industrial organization, accompanied by sympathy toward bottom-up association and participation by people in local government and social organization; and, third, an unabashed institutional conservatism, expressed in skepticism about large projects of institutional reconstruction and in the acceptance of the current legal forms of market economies, representative democracies, and free civil societies.

The outer limit of the reconstructive reach of this program is the idea of a partnership between governments and firms bringing into question neither the legal character of the property regime nor the legal structure of the state and of its relation to civil society. The program of chastened social democracy must be accomplished within the limits of a particular style of property and politics. The property regime makes access to resources depend upon the decisions of managers and financiers overseeing stocks of private wealth, much of it inherited or given as anticipated inheritance. The practical capacity to achieve economies of scale, the legal rights of free accumulation and transmission of personal wealth, and the organizational habits of managerial discipline exercised in the name of property come to seem natural and inseparable companions. The political regime of de-energized politics favors low levels of popular engagement, and surrenders to technical expertise what it robs from active popular self-government, dissolving political choice into a series of loosely linked and narrowly focused policy debates.

The practical men and women who run the rich industrial democracies believe that it would be impractical to energize politics through an intensification of popular political action focused upon a choice among well-defined programs of structural change. The paradoxical result of their antipragmatic pragmatism is nevertheless to deny collective problems their collective solutions. Politics degenerates into a series of narrow factional deals among unevenly organized groups. Each group finds itself trapped in its present understanding of its interests and identity. As a result, the derision of structural change becomes a self-fulfilling prophecy.

THE PRACTICAL PROMISE OF DEMOCRATIC EXPERIMENTALISM: FROM THE EXISTING POLICY DEBATE TO THE MISSING PROGRAMMATIC CONVERSATION

The shape and limits of a policy debate

The cost of this inhibition to institutional experimentalism must be measured in both tangible burdens and intangible defeats: in suffering and impoverishment as well as in the failure to breathe new life into the democratic project by reinventing its practical forms. Consider, for example, the most typical of present-day policy discussions in Europe and North America: the debate about the relation among wage levels, job security, and national competitiveness. In carrying this typical debate from its familiar starting points to unexplored territory, my aim is to show how we may move, step by step, from the present political conversations of the rich industrial democracies to a realm of institutional experiments that these conversations suppress. You might begin almost anywhere else – with the problems of racial strife, or entrenched poverty, or deindustrialization and urban decay, or fiscal crisis of the welfare state – and advance in a similar direction.

The discussion about wage levels, job security, and national competitiveness characteristically begins with the observation that workers in most European countries, especially those traditionally supportive of a corporatist political economy, enjoy relatively more security and higher wages than in the United States. American workers, by contrast, have sustained a substantially higher average level of employment throughout the ups and downs of the business cycle. To moderate the perverse trade-off between greater unemployment (as in Europe) and more severe wage repression or job insecurity (as in the United States), while keeping the national economy competitive, labor markets – so the argument goes – must be made more flexible. The economic and educational resources people need in order to reskill in an innovative and unstable economy are generic, many-sided, and transferable. A major task of the partnership between governments and firms is to combat rigid forms of job tenure and to limit the vested rights of relatively privileged and organized segments of the laborforce. Governments can then commit themselves to organizing a national system for the continuous reskilling of labor and for education throughout a working lifetime.

Innovation in the institutional forms of the market economy

This conclusion typifies the outer limit of the practical progressive position in the present-day politics of the industrial democracies. Its deficiencies are already becoming familiar. To remedy them requires a more far-reaching level of institutional innovation than the practical progressives seem ready to countenance or even to consider. Educational investment proves insufficient unless firms restructure in ways that make them capable of putting reskilled labor to effective use. Moreover, if entrepreneurship in the development of postfordist, high-skill-oriented firms is to flourish in sufficient numbers, and if economic opportunity is to be more thoroughly democratized, there must be more routes of access to productive resources than the established form of the market economy affords. Firms must have access to capital, technology, and technical assistance, if only on temporary and conditional terms. They must be able to seek those resources from organizations free from the constraints of short-term profit-making. Large, fordist-style businesses must not be advantaged in the competition with such enterprises by the ability to protect themselves against instability in the markets in which they operate through devices such as the internal generation of investment funds and the division of their workforce into long-term and temporary workers. Smaller firms must be able to combine the advantages of flexibility and of scale by joining, with public support, in networks of cooperative competition. Governmental help for this and other aspects of industrial reconstruction may in turn work through the agency of social funds and support centers enjoying considerable autonomy. Such entities, intermediate between the state and the firm, might experiment with alternative forms of decentralized capital allocation, while continuing to face the discipline of competition and financial responsibility.

Such overlapping institutional innovations cannot fully develop without, in turn, transgressing and transforming the traditional system of property rights. The unified property right, vesting concentrated power in the owner or his agent, would gradually give way to a system of fragmentary, conditional, and temporary property rights, granting residual rights of control and claims to returns from productive assets to a range of different types of stakeholders including social funds, local governments, small-time entrepreneurs, and workers.

A property regime resulting from such a sequence of cumulative change is not recognizable as either socialism or capitalism because it fails to conform to the legal logic of a unified property right held by the individual owner or by the state. In fact, one of its merits would be to enable different systems of contract and property – that is to say, different sets of legal devices for the decentralized allocation of economic power and access – to coexist within the same economy. Their practical consequences might then be experimentally assessed.

Such a regime of disassembled and recombined property rights creates a framework within which social assessment of the structure and consequences of economic activity – a major aim of the old socialist program – can be reconciled with an even greater decentralization of economic opportunity and initiative than the conventional property-rights system permits. The result is to moderate the tension between the practical requirement of economies of scale and the commitment to competition, although at the cost of limiting, in time and scope, the power the traditional owner enjoys. Most significantly, such a direction of reform lays a more promising basis than does the inherited system of property rights for the solution of the problem lying at the heart of economic growth in particular and of practical progress in general.

Practical progress depends upon both innovation and cooperation. Although successful innovation may itself require teamwork, it invariably threatens to overturn the habits and expectations upon which established practices have come to rely. The central problem of institutional design for growth is to develop the arrangements most likely to invite and withstand recurrent innovation because they mix cooperation with competition, recognize the interests of all involved in the joint effort, and ensure fundamental individual security in the midst of change. By this most important – and most practical – standard the conventional property regime is simply too crude. Its historical justification lies in a bygone age when savings over current consumption – what Marxists called surplus extraction – overshadowed cooperation and innovation as a constraint upon growth.

The class structure of the industrial democracies

So far I have considered how we would need to reshape firms and the relations among firms, workers, and governments for investment in people to achieve its desired results. From another direction we might begin to press against the limits of the established institutional settlement by asking how governments could acquire the resources needed to make such social investments on a massive scale and in a manner counteracting inherited advantages of economic and educational opportunity. The relentless disintegration of Marxism and of other forms of leftist theory tempt some people to forget that we all continue to live in class societies in which stark disparities of inherited privilege shape people's life chances. Marxism may be dead, but class is doing as well as ever.

In the United States, for example, econometric studies calculate that over half of the assets held by people under the age of fifty can be imputed to anticipated inheritance through gifts *inter vivos*. When we add the disparity of educational opportunity, the combined effect becomes overwhelming. The United States, where most people when questioned describe themselves as "middle class," has, like other contemporary democracies, a relatively simple and straightforward class structure, composed of four main classes: a professional–business class, a class of small-scale, independent businesspeople, a working class with a whitecollar and a bluecollar segment, and an underclass. Historical studies reveal that the only massive and persistent form of social mobility in America since the late nineteenth century has been the movement from the bluecollar to the whitecollar segment of the working class: the children of industrial workers and farmhands became clerical workers almost as propertyless and just as powerless as their parents.

The tenacity of the class structure bears on my argument about the institutional deepening of the conventional policy conversation in several ways. The commitment to flexibility, innovation, and access in a vibrant, democratized market economy cannot be reconciled with the unforgiving assignment of individuals to a predetermined class fate. Nor, considering the matter from the standpoint of the fiscal basis of public policy, could we ever hope to generate adequate funding for investment in people without rearranging law so that a public right of inheritance from society came to supplant a private right of inheritance from the family. More generally, the stubbornness of class hierarchies sheds a disturbing retrospective light upon the economic and political institutions that continue to sustain them and to bear their imprint. Institutional conservatism begins to look bad if its effect is acquiescence in arrangements that constrain democratic experimentalism by reproducing class privilege.

Social-endowment accounts settled by society upon each individual should therefore progressively replace private inheritance. Some portion of these accounts would represent unconditional claims upon the state for the satisfaction of minimal and universal needs. Another portion would be suited to individual circumstance. Yet another portion might be granted as reward for demonstrated promise or achievement. Some part might consist in the provision of services by a unified public apparatus on the traditional model of the welfare state. Another part might result in points to be spent by the individual, on his own discretion or with the approval of trustees, among competitive service providers. The chief object of such accounts would be education, directed to the acquisition of practical and conceptual capacities and continuing throughout a lifetime. The school would assume its central mission in a democratic society of rescuing the child and the adult from his family, his class, his country, his historical period, and even his own character, and giving him access to alien experience.

The core justification of such accounts is the reason for fundamental rights themselves under a regime of democratic experimentalism. If we are effectively to broaden the agenda of short-term politics, favoring repeated innovation in the small and structural change in the large, we must withdraw some matters from this agenda. People must be and feel secure in a haven of vitally protected interests lest their insecurity tempt them to abandon their newfound freedom. They must also be equipped with the economic and cultural instruments of individual and collective self-determination. The relation of fundamental rights and social endowments to the quickened experimentalism they make possible is like the relation of a parent's love to a child's willingness to make and to remake himself by risking moral adventure.

Such a direction of change, however, can fulfill the promise of liberalism and social democracy only by repudiating their received institutional forms. Thus, replacement of private inheritance by social endowment implies a mechanism of accumulation, savings, and investment different from the one that has prevailed under the traditional property regime. It, too, invites us to develop, through the fragmentation and recombination of property rights, new and varied means for the decentralized and competitive allocation of capital.

Innovation in the institutional forms of political democracy

The preceding discussion has focused upon changes in economic institutions. However, we can neither achieve nor maintain such changes without also innovating in the institutional forms of democracy and of civil society. A democratized market economy cannot be inaugurated, nor can its institutions retain their integrity, unless the constitutional structure of government comes to favor rather than to inhibit the repeated practice of radical reform; the legal framework of party politics sustains a high level of popular political engagement; and civil society gains a public-law structure encouraging its self-organization with a richer repertory than private contract and corporate law afford.

The long-triumphant version of democratic politics in the West has two main components: a preference for styles of constitutional organization making reform depend upon consensus, and a way of organizing politics favoring the political quiescence of the people, interrupted, rarely and unpredictably, by interludes of social crisis and collective enthusiasm. The constitutionalism of deliberate deadlock, slowing down the transformative uses of governmental power, finds its most straightforward expression in the checks-and-balances machinery of American-style presidentialism. It is, however, no less clearly expressed by forms of parliamentary government that concentrate political action in a class of professional politicians championing unevenly organized and powerful interests against a background of popular political demobilization. Practices and arrangements hostile to popular political mobilization succeeded, in the development of modern politics, the qualifications to the suffrage and the recourse to many intermediate levels of popular representation, devices intended by the proto-democratic liberalism of the early nineteenth century to dampen popular frenzy and to make property safe. The mobilization-hostile arrangements that replaced these proto-democratic devices ensured that, contrary to the expectations of radicals and conservatives alike, universal suffrage would prove consistent with class hierarchy. Such arrangements continue to shape a style of political history in which bursts of anti-institutional populist reform come and go, leaving the basic forms of the state and economy relatively unchanged, or changing them only under pressure of extreme crisis.

The direction of change in economic institutions sketched earlier cannot long be reconciled with these inherited inhibitions to democracy. Although we can begin to introduce such economic reforms within the limits of the not-too-democratic democracy we have inherited, we cannot complete or preserve the reforms within these limits. The reforms require a permanent vigilance over the social consequences of economic activity and the emergence of new and unforeseen varieties of privilege and rigidity. Moreover, the reconstruction of these received political institutions should be a focus of concern in its own right, extending the program of democratic experimentalism to the reorganization of government and of the electoral contest over governmental power. Instead of beginning with economic reforms and being led by them to the need for supportive political reforms, we might just as well, within the discontinuous logic of uneven development, move in the opposite direction. The choice of sequence is circumstantial.

A constitutionalism favorable to the engagement of the universal electorate in the rapid resolution of impasse among branches of government should take the place of a constitutionalism friendly to the slowing down of politics. Among the devices of such an alternative constitutionalism can be the combination of personal plebiscitarian and parliamentary forms of power, the resort to plebiscites and referenda, and the facility to call anticipated elections at the initiative of any branch of government. A legal structure of electoral politics favorable to a persistent heightening of the level of popular political mobilization can take the place of one that turns electoral politics into an occasional and minor interruption of practical affairs. Among its instruments may be rules of mandatory voting, free access for a broad range of political parties and social movements to the means of mass communication, the public financing of political campaigns, and the strengthening of political parties.

Innovation in the institutional forms of civil society

The counterpart to this energizing and quickening of politics is the organization of civil society. A disorganized or unevenly organized society cannot reinvent itself. Its discussion of alternative futures would come lifelessly from books rather than vigorously from the localized experiments and debates of real movements and associations.

To abandon the organizational requirements of civil society to the traditional instruments of private law is to acquiesce in starkly uneven organization. The facilitative devices of contract and private law will be used by those who, in a sense, are already organized. The organized can find in their legally sanctioned association reinforcement for their pre-existing advantage.

When the laborforce of a society remains hierarchically segmented, for example, traditional unionization, in the form of a contractualist labor-law regime, will most likely come to life in the hands of the relatively privileged workers who hold stable jobs in capital-intensive industry. Once unionized, these workers will discover that they share common interests with their employers against the disorganized majority. They may develop cooperative practices with the bosses at the workplace that will seem to render unionization superfluous. Partial unionization will in the end have proved a transition to a stage when relatively privileged workers no longer want unions, and relatively unprivileged workers never establish them. The problem in this admonitory story is not the triumph of cooperative cooption over adversary militancy but the long shadow that background inequality casts upon the traditional private-law devices for the organization of civil society.

To redress this problem civil society may acquire elements of a public-law structure. Such a structure may be organized on the basis of neighborhood, job, or shared concern and responsibility. It may create norms and networks of group life outside the state, parallel to the state, and entirely free of governmental tutelage or influence. Different groups and movements may compete for position in these multiple orderings of civil society just as political parties compete for place in government. Thus, we would at last have succeeded in giving practical and progressive content to one of the ambitions of interwar European legal thought – the ambition of developing a social law distinct from both the law of the state and the law of private initiative. In such a law the empowering practice of voluntary association would find a congenial home.

THE IMAGINATION OF ALTERNATIVES: SOCIAL-THEORETICAL ASSUMPTIONS OF DEMOCRATIC EXPERIMENTALISM

First and second natures in social life

These examples of democratic experimentalism suggest how, from the starting points of conventional debates of policy and routine conflicts of interest, we may be driven to successive levels of institutional reimagination and reconstruction. The driving force may be frustration at the inability to satisfy tangible interests within the limits imposed by established arrangements. Or it may be impatience at the contrast between democratic ideals and practical realities. Whatever its source and whoever its agent, it forces us, at each step along the way, to reshape our interests and to reinterpret our ideals. The internal relation between thinking about interests and ideals and thinking about institutions or practices is not just a method of inquiry or a strategy of discourse; it is a defining attribute of transformation in history.

To move in a certain direction of institutional change is implicitly to prefer some varieties of individual and social experience to others. It is a virtue of a set of institutions – and one with which a democrat and an experimentalist must be especially concerned – to be relatively catholic in its openness to diversity of experience. No institutional order, however, can be neutral among forms of life; it tilts the scales in one direction or another. The false goal of neutrality gets in the way of the real aim of experimental diversity by being harnessed to the fetishistic veneration of what should be seen as fallible and transitory arrangements.

If politics is fate, it wins its fateful power by imposing upon society a second nature of entrenched institutions and enacted beliefs whose origins in conflict and contingency we then forget. The cognitive work of social thought and the practical work of democratic experimentalism have joined in modern history to push this fatalism back. Their joint endeavor is now in trouble. We find ourselves bereft of the intellectual instruments with which to understand and to reimagine the formative institutional and imaginative structures of our societies. So too we have reached a moment in the history of practical politics when the democratic project has bogged down into institutional compromises that betray professed social ideals and frustrate recognized group interests. As a result of this double interlude in the work of enlightenment and emancipation, we may risk forgetting the secondness of our second nature. Thus, for example, the low levels of political engagement in the United States may be attributed to intractable, prepolitical features of American culture rather than to politically chosen arrangements, reinforced by the collective habits to which they give rise.

The answers given to a thousand loosely connected questions about practical arrangements give a society its shape. There are reasons why these questions are answered, at a certain place and time, in one way rather than another. They are not, however, the kinds of reasons that consist in the revelation of the single, necessary legal–institutional form of democracies, markets, and free civil societies, or in the discovery of the only plausible institutional vehicles for professed social ideals or recognized group interests. They explain the localized triumph of some solutions over others without denying the freedom – or the need – for later reimagination and rearrangement. They reaffirm the secondness and therefore the revisability of our second nature.

Routine and revolution

Some may object that structural change is a byproduct of forces that we cannot hope to tame or direct: quasi-revolutionary periods of mobilization and strife caused by unforeseen and unwanted crisis. From this idea there arises the view that legal–institutional change in particular and social change in general take place in exceptional moments of frenzied, crisis-driven renovation. The best that an institutional imagination, in legal thought or political economy, can hope for is to systematize and complete, during the generations following the magical moment, the creative but chaotic work of that moment. Thus, the last such period was the social-democratic reconstruction – known in the United States as the New Deal – undertaken during and after the years of world depression and world war.

This view, however, suffers from several connected flaws, each of which betrays the contaminating influence of institutional fetishism upon the would-be votaries of democratic thought. First, the relation between crisis and reconstruction changes in history. As some forms of organization and discourse can be designed to inhibit challenge and change and require to be broken before they can be bent, others can invite their own piecemeal revision. A democratic experimentalist will not stand waiting for the next magical moment. Rather than have us be crowned by history, he will insist that we crown ourselves.

Second, the reconstructive experience is not an impenetrable oracular episode. Ideas inform it and shape its legacy. Unless we struggle for alternative ideas about the practical institutional forms for the realization of our interests and ideals we shall find ourselves bound to the ideas that happen to lie at hand at the moment of transformative opportunity.

Third, the supposedly routinized sequel to the charismatic and revolutionary intermezzo is never as routinized as it looks. The issues that were apparently settled in the foundational period constantly open up again; if ever there were an incomplete contract, it is the contract that the victors make with the vanquished when they establish a new institutional settlement. For example, it is impossible to say whether affirmative action oriented to race and gender categories rather than to actual disadvantage, negotiation of trade agreements with other countries ensuring the transnational mobility of capital while strengthening the national imprisonment of labor, or the delegation of public welfare responsibilities to private providers – all characteristic obsessions of contemporary American public policy and legal debate – represent fulfillments or betrayals of the New Deal settlement. The invocation of the original compact in such contexts is pointless and unavailing.

Real interests and structural change

According to another objection, the focus upon sustained and cumulative institutional tinkering in the service of democratic experimentalism amounts to the imposition of a rationalistic blueprint upon a humanity that is always otherwise engaged. When it is not occupied with the day-to-day struggle over survival, consumption, and preferment, it is absorbed in the clash of group and national identities. This line of argument, however, misunderstands the subtle and paradoxical relation between the politics of group identities and the failures of democratic experimentalism.

We can best explore this relation in the setting of nationalism itself. The distinctive trait of contemporary forms of national self-assertion by contrast to the consciousness of collective distinction in earlier historical periods is that they express a will to difference in the face of the waning of actual difference more often than they represent the self-confident attachment to a unique way of life. As one people comes to resemble its neighbor in actual custom and belief, it hates its neighbor all the more – for being the same rather than for being different. It hates in itself the experience of collective impotence in the production of a distinct civilization. The relentless rivalry of economies and of cultures produces a worldwide churning and recombination of institutionalized practices and enacted beliefs: anything tried out in one place might, at any moment, be transplanted to another. The most successful societies are the best pillagers and recombiners.

The result is that collective identities are emptied out and made abstract. Precisely because these collective identities signal the will to difference more than actual difference, they are not, like real sets of customs and customary beliefs, porous, negotiable, and revisable. They become, instead, the objects of an intransigent faith. Although this inversion of identity and difference may be more clearly manifest in nationalism, it also applies to the politics of group recognition within nations – the politics combining claims to practical social advancement with claims to voice and respect for the culture of the disadvantaged group. The intensity of this politics of groupism is often proportional to the elusiveness of the cultural differences that it is meant to serve.

The cure to the rage of the impotent will to collective difference is, paradoxically, the strengthening of the collective capacity to produce actual difference. A distinct form of life must in the end take institutionalized form. If it fails to live in practice, it will die in imagination. Conversely, the character of political, economic, and social institutions will favor or

disfavor the institutional expression of collective originality. The capacity
for such expression depends upon the repeated practice of structural
reform. The resulting experience of collective capability stands a better
chance of sustaining magnanimity and tolerance than the frustrated and
disoriented will to difference. Moreover, the customs and beliefs it produces can accommodate compromise and influence precisely because
those beliefs and customs are real. For all these reasons the politics of
national and group identities is not an alternative or an antidote to the
work of democratic experimentalism. It shows by its misdirection why
that work is important.

THE DISCIPLINARY TOOLS OF DEMOCRATIC EXPERIMENTALISM

The twin disciplines of the institutional imagination

The progress of democratic instrumentalism requires practices of institutional imagination. Two twin disciplines should inform such practices:
political economy and legal analysis as parallel practices of institutional
imagination. Neither of these disciplines exists other than in fragmentary
and inchoate form. The conceptual materials with which to develop them
nevertheless lie at hand. Moreover, their development responds to intellectual perplexities and opportunities internal to the present situations of
economic and legal theory. There may be recurrent although not insuperable conflict between the goods of material progress and of individual
emancipation. However, there is no conflict between service to democratic
experimentalism and insight into law and economy. Institutional fetishism
is as dangerous to the insight as it is to the experimentalism.

These parallel practices of institutional imagination stand the best
chance of flourishing in a climate in which social concern and relentless
inquiry are viewed as natural allies, and in which thinkers try to walk the
narrow path between surrender to the ruling intellectual orthodoxies and
refuge in a haven of unchallenged, self-congratulating heresy. Not since
the intellectual practice of the philosophical radicals of the early nineteenth century have we seen such habits of mind regularly joined in the
study and criticism of society. In field after field the central place has
come to be occupied by a passive-submissive doctrine. Under the nearly
transparent disguise of a pseudoscientific apparatus, this doctrine implies
the naturalness, necessity, and rationality of the social arrangements that

have come to prevail in the history of the industrial democracies. At the same time, the idea of a counterscience, playing by different rules and engaged in a different conversation, on the model of nineteenth-century Marxism and Hegelianism, should no longer be credible. There is in the end only one world of conversation, just as there is in the end only one world of institutional experiment. We must somehow struggle to uphold a culture of criticism that engages with these dominant orthodoxies while refusing to let them shape the agenda of inquiry and debate.

The twin disciplines of institutional thinking should move in an intellectual space shaped by the minimalist standards of insight described in the opening pages of this book. They must identify the shaping influence of fundamental institutions and beliefs while also acknowledging the replaceable and ramshackle, although often resilient character of these formative contexts. They must also recognize the internal relation between thinking about interests or ideals and thinking about institutions or practices, and turn it into an intellectual and political opportunity.

The nonexistence of institutional economics

This book proposes a way to place legal analysis in the service of democratic experimentalism. To that end, it explores in detail the character and limits of a form of legal analysis that has become increasingly influential throughout the world. An understanding of this style of legal doctrine will provide us with the instruments with which to change it, turning legal thought into a marriage between social realism and social prophecy. The book then concludes by suggesting how we can use this changed practice of legal analysis to imagine our alternative futures, thus keeping the promise made in these initial pages. Before turning to this task, consider the predicament of what should be the other great discipline of the institutional imagination: political economy.

No truly institutional economics exists. Nineteenth-century German and early twentieth-century American institutionalism in economics vanished without producing an intellectual practice capable of mounting a serious challenge to general-equilibrium analysis. The economic development theory of the 1950s and 1960s, which struggled in the direction of a structural understanding of economic change, never resolved the ambiguity of its self-presentation as either a subordinate branch of mainstream economics or a critical alternative to it. All these aborted beginnings of an institutional economics drew much of their energy from their programmatic direction: the will to resist, in one way or another, the conventional institutional definition of the market economy. The lesson of their failure is that a programmatic intention comes to nothing in social and historical study unless it can draw upon both a powerful vision and a reproducible method: a vision of how things are and might be, a method for understanding the actual in the light of the possible.

The consequence of this failure has been the trivialization or mystification of institutions by the ascendant forms of economic analysis. Three ways of disposing of the problem of institutions have been paramount.

Pure economic theory has simply affected a posture of causal and normative agnosticism about economic institutions, waiting for institutional assumptions to be stipulated from outside, by some alternative practice of description or explanation before the analytic apparatus can be brought to bear on the understanding of economic behavior in a particular setting. The Coasean idea that maximizing behavior treats institutional arrangements like any other part of its factual background – to be reckoned with and bargained around, save for the egregious and elastic category of transaction costs – has appeared to validate this relegation of the institutional to the shadowy world of the stipulated boundary conditions and the empirical variables of market activity.

The more ideologically reactionary and aggressive forms of political economy have identified a particular system of market institutions and of private law as the natural and necessary form of the market economy and, by extension, as the indispensable support of the market economy, the pure framework of coordination among market agents. Students of the history of legal thought will recognize in this idea a throwback to the characteristic conception of nineteenth-century legal science: that a free society has a definite, predetermined legal–institutional form, which analysis reveals and observation confirms. That the history of modern legal thought has been in large part the history of the subversion and self-subversion of this idea makes it all the more surprising that the idea should continue to live in economics. But live it does, to the point of penetrating the most influential contemporary accounts of the institutional history of the market economy. These accounts represent the movement of economic history as a convergence, through discovery, trial, and error, toward the institutional practices and legal rules that are indeed required by a market economy. The property regime is the quintessence of this evolutionary achievement. Political interventions into this institutional order deserve skeptical resistance because they are likely to be costly, self-defeating, and subversive of freedom. The point is to forget that the distinctive institutional and social character of every such order is itself the singular and surprising product of practical and ideological conflict.

The most insidious way of suppressing the significance of institutions is the one we find entrenched in the theoretical practice of the American disciples of Keynes (who rendered his doctrine politically palatable by emptying it of most of its political content) and in the standard public-policy application of economic analysis. Here the technique is to search for lawlike correlations among large-scale economic aggregates like the levels of savings, employment, and investment, to acknowledge in principle that the stability of these correlations depends upon a host of detailed background institutional conditions, and then to disregard this admission in the actual practice of economic analysis and policy argument.

So long as politics stays away from institutional experiment and structural change, the denial of the concession in the practice gains a semblance of plausibility. The correlations among the aggregate economic phenomena retain the lawlike appearance they never deserved. The institutional arrangements begin to look like the natural form of a modern regulated market economy.

The forms of avoidance and superstition I have just enumerated are no occasional sideshow in the history of recent economic theory. They are very close to being the heart of the thing itself. Attachment to them wins honor and glory.

A truly institutional economics would not be a study of economic behavior and of stable relations among economic aggregates against a stipulated and unexamined institutional background, nor would it be the Owl of Minerva flapping its wings over the triumphal historical march of the one true market economy toward world diffusion and dominance. It would take as its subject the study of economic institutions themselves, of their causes and consequences, of why they are as they are but might be different, of the hidden variety of their existing forms, and of the transformative opportunities these existing variations supply and conceal. Such an institutional economics requires a far more intimate and continuous relation among formal analysis, empirical description, and causal conjecture than the dominant analytic practices of economic theory have allowed. They would increase the explanatory reach of economic theory but only by robbing it of some of its formal self-sufficiency. For they would be part of a weakening of the distinct methodological identities of the different disciplines that deal with the structure of society. The closest partner of such an economics would be an institutionally oriented method of legal analysis, a practice of legal analysis as institutional imagination.

THE ARRESTED DEVELOPMENT OF LEGAL THOUGHT

The genius of contemporary law

To grasp the potential of legal analysis to become a master tool of institutional imagination in a democratic society we must begin by understanding what is most distinctive about law and legal thought in the contemporary industrial democracies. In this effort no contrast is more revealing than the comparison of the substantive law and legal methods of today with the project of nineteenth-century legal science and the law of nineteenth-century commercial economies.

Consider how the law and legal thought of today may look to a future student who tries to identify its deepest and most original character within the larger sequence of legal history. Suppose that we use in this endeavor less the search for recurrent doctrinal categories and distinctions Holmes pursued in *The Common Law* than the reciprocal reading of vision and detail Jhering offered in *The Spirit of Roman Law*. The latter method rather than the former respects the place of law between imagination and power, and connects the self-understanding of legal thought to the central tradition of modern social theory founded by Montesquieu. Viewed in this light the overriding theme of contemporary law and legal thought, and the one defining its genius, is the commitment to shape a free political and economic order by combining rights of choice with rules designed to ensure the effective enjoyment of these rights.

Little by little, and in country after country of the rich Western world and of its poorer emulators, a legal consciousness has penetrated and transformed substantive law, affirming the empirical and defeasible character of individual and collective self-determination: its dependence upon practical conditions of enjoyment, which may fail.

This conception stands out by contrast to the single most influential idea in the law and legal thought of the nineteenth century, an idea developed as much in the case-oriented discourse of American and English jurists, or the aphoristic and conclusory utterances of French lawyers, as in the relentless category-grinding of the German pandectists. According to this earlier idea a certain system of rules and rights defines a free political and economic order. We uphold the order by clinging to the predetermined system of rules and rights and by preventing its perversion through politics, especially the politics of privilege and redistribution.

A consequence of this animating idea of contemporary law has been the reorganization of one branch of law and legal doctrine after another as a binary system of rights of choice and of arrangements withdrawn from the scope of choice the better to make the exercise of choice real and effective. The governing aim of this dialectical organization is to prevent the system of rules and rights from becoming or remaining a sham, concealing subjugation under the appearance of coordination.

Sometimes this binary reshaping takes place by marshalling countervailing rules and doctrines within a single branch of law, as when the doctrine of economic duress and of unequal bargaining power complements and qualifies the core rules of contract formation and enforceability, or freedom to choose the terms in a labor contract is restricted by selective direct legal regulation of the employment relation. At other times the dual structure works by assigning the choice-restricting and freedom-sustaining arrangements to a distinct branch of law, as when collective-bargaining law attempts to correct the inability of individual contract to compensate for the power disparities of the employment relation. At yet other times the dual structure has taken the form of a coexistence of two legal regimes for the governance of overlapping social problems. Thus, fault-based liability may be strengthened rather than undermined by the refusal to extend it to the compensation for the actualization of the risks inherent in a line of business and by the development of insurance systems disregarding fault-oriented standards of compensation.

The binary structure that has reorganized private law in every industrial democracy recurs, on a larger scale, in the relation of governmental regulation to private law as a whole. The entitlements afforded by the welfare state, and the enjoyment by workers of prerogatives relatively secure against labor-market instability and the business cycle, have been understood and developed by twentieth-century lawyers as devices for guaranteeing the effective enjoyment of the public-law and private-law rights of self-determination. If the market economy, representative democracy, and free civil society have certain inherited and necessary forms, these forms must nevertheless be refined and completed so that they may provide the reality as well as the appearance of free choice and coordination to every rights-bearing individual.

The supreme achievement of this sustained exercise in correction is to make the individual effectively able to develop and deploy a broad range of capacities. He can then form and execute his life projects, including those most important ones that he may need to imagine and advance through free association with other people. Class hierarchies may never-theless have persisted with barely diminished force. The majority of the people may be an angry and marginalized although fragmented mass of individuals, who feel powerless at their jobs and hopeless about their national politics, while seeking solace and escape in private pleasure, domestic joys, and nostalgic traditionalism. According to this mode of thought, however, these burdens of history and imperfection merely show that we must patiently continue the work of securing the effective enjoy-ment of rights.

The theme of the dialectic between the realm of free economic and political choice and the realm of that which is withdrawn from choice for the sake of choice is all the more remarkable because it fails to track any specific ideological position within the debates of modern politics and modern political thought. It merely excludes positions that from the van-tage point of those who inhabit this imaginative world may seem extremist. It excludes the old nineteenth-century idea that a particular scheme of private and public rights will automatically secure economic and political freedom if only it can be protected against redistributive interventionism. It also repels the radically reconstructive idea that no real and widely shared experience of individual and collective self-determi-nation will be possible unless we revolutionize the present institutional system by substituting, for example, "socialism" for "capitalism." Yet while the spirit of contemporary law may seem to antagonize only unbelievable or insupportable alternatives, it generates, in detail, endless practical and argumentative work for the analyst and the reformer. Thus, it resembles, in the generality of its scope and the fecundity of its effects, the bold conception that preceded it in the history of law and legal thought: the project of a legal science that would reveal the in-built legal and insti-tutional content of a free society and police its boundaries against invasion by politics.

The limit of contemporary legal thought

There is nevertheless a riddle in the career of this idea. Until we solve this riddle, we cannot correctly understand the genius – and the self-imposed poverty – of contemporary legal thought, nor can we fully appreciate the extent to which the development of law remains bound up with the fate of democratic experimentalism. When we begin to explore ways of ensuring the practical conditions for the effective enjoyment of rights, we discover at every turn that there are alternative plausible ways of defining these conditions, and then of satisfying them once they have been defined. For every right of individual or collective choice, there are different plausible conceptions of its conditions of effective realization in society as now organized. For every such conception, there are different plausible strategies to fulfill the specified conditions.

Some of these conceptions and strategies imply keeping present institutional arrangements while controlling their consequences: by counteracting, characteristically, through tax-and-transfer or through preferment for disadvantaged groups, their distributive consequences. Other conceptions and strategies, however, imply a piecemeal but cumulative change of these institutional arrangements. These structure-defying and structure-transforming solutions may in turn go in alternative directions. They may mark the initial moves in different trajectories of structural change.

Thus, the reach toward a recognition of the empirical and defeasible character of the rights of choice should be simply the first step in a two-step movement. The second step, following closely upon the first, would be the legal imagination and construction of alternative pluralisms: the exploration, in programmatic argument or in experimental reform, of one or another sequence of institutional change. Each sequence would redefine the rights, and the interests and ideals they serve, in the course of realizing them more effectively. I have already given an extended example of what such reforms and arguments might look like when I suggested, earlier in this book, how we may move from a familiar, structure-preserving policy debate to one challenging and changing the institutional and imaginative presuppositions of the debate. However, contemporary legal theory and doctrine, and substantive law itself, almost never take this second step. Theirs is a striking instance of arrested development.

The failure to turn legal analysis into institutional imagination – the major consequence of the arrested development of legal thought – has special meaning and poignancy in the United States. For surely one of the flaws in American civilization has been the effort to bar the institutional structure of the country against effective challenge; to see America's "scheme of ordered liberty" as a definitive escape from the old history of classes and ideologies; to refuse to recognize that the spiritual and political ideals of a civilization remain fastened to the special practices and institutions representing them in fact. Experimentalism has been the most defensible part of American exceptionalism; yet only under the pressure of extreme crisis have Americans brought the experimentalist impulse to bear upon their institutions. Those American thinkers have been the greatest who, like Jefferson and Dewey, tried to convince their contemporaries to trade in some bad American exceptionalism for some good American experimentalism. Those periods of American history have been the most significant when interests became entangled in ideals because both ideals and interests collided with institutional arrangements.

COMPLEX ENFORCEMENT AT THE
THRESHOLD OF STRUCTURAL CHANGE

Structural but episodic intervention

What force arrests the development of legal thought in the move from the discovery of the institutional indeterminacy of free economies, societies, and polities to the exploration of their diversity of possible institutional forms? We can shed an oblique but revealing light on this riddle by reconsidering it from the perspective of what has come to be known in American law as the problem of complex enforcement and structural injunctions.* Although the procedural device has developed more fully in the United States than anywhere else, the opportunity it exploits in the relation of law to society is fast becoming universal. The new mode of procedural intervention seems like a natural extension and instrument of the central idea of contemporary law. Nevertheless, the incongruities of its theory and practice make the arrested development of this idea all the more startling.

Alongside the traditional style of adjudication, with its emphasis upon the structure-preserving assignment of rights among individual litigants, there has emerged a different adjudicative practice, with agents, methods, and goals different from those of the traditional style. The agents of this alternative practice are collective rather than individual, although they may be represented by individual litigants. The class-action lawsuit is the most straightforward tool of this redefinition of agents.

The aim of the intervention is to reshape an organization or a localized area of social practice frustrating the effective enjoyment of rights. The characteristic circumstance of frustration is one in which the organization or the practice under scrutiny has seen the rise of disadvantage and

---

* See Lewis Sargentich, "Complex Enforcement," 1978 (unpublished, on file in Harvard Law Library).

marginalization that their victims are powerless to escape. Subjugation, localized and therefore remediable, is the paradigmatic evil addressed by the reconstructive intervention.

The method is the effort to advance more deeply into the causal background of social life than traditional adjudication would countenance, reshaping the arrangements found to be most immediately and powerfully responsible for the questioned evil. Thus, the remedy may require a court to intervene in a school, a prison, a school system, or a voting district, and to reform and administer the organization over a period of time. Complex enforcement will demand a more intimate and sustained combination of prescriptive argument and causal inquiry than has been characteristic of lawyers' reasoning.

The basic problem in the theory and practice of the structural injunctions is the difficulty of making sense of their limits. Once we begin to penetrate the causal background of contested practices and powers, why should we stop so close to the surface? The evils of unequal education for different races, for example, may soon lead an American structural reformer in one direction to question the legitimacy of local financial responsibility for public schools and in another direction to challenge the institutional arrangements, such as subcontracting and temporary hiring, that help reproduce an underclass by segmenting the laborforce. The more circumscribed corrective intervention is likely to prove ineffective. If causal efficacy is the standard of remedial success, one foray into the structural background of rights-frustration should lead to another. Once we start to tinker with relatively peripheral organizations such as prisons and asylums and to reshape them in the image of ideals imputed to substantive law, why should we not keep going until we reach firms and bureaucracies, families and local governments? As we deepened the reach and extended the scope of intervention, the reconstructive activities of complex enforcement would become ever more ambitious, exercising greater powers, employing bigger staffs, and consuming richer resources.

The missing agent

None of this, of course, will happen. It will not happen because no society, not even the United States, will allow a vanguard of lawyers and judges to reconstruct its institutions little by little under the transparent disguise of interpreting the law. The mass of working people may be asleep. The educated and propertied classes are not. They will not allow their fate to be determined by a closed cadre of priestly reformers lacking in self-restraint. They will put these reformers in their place, substituting for them successors who no longer need to be put in their place.

The deepening of the reach and the broadening of the scope of complex enforcement would soon outrun the political legitimacy of the judiciary and exhaust its practical and cognitive resources. Moreover, in the name of the mandate to intervene the better to secure the effective enjoyment of rights, judges would usurp an increasing portion of the real power of popular self-government.

So what should the judges do, and what do they do in fact? They have sometimes seemed to want to do as much as they could get away with: better some penetration of the structural background to subjugation than none; better marginal social organizations than no organizations at all. The difficulty arises from the disproportion between the reconstructive mission and its institutional agent. Complex enforcement is both structural and episodic. The work of structural and episodic intervention seems required if we are to ensure the effective enjoyment of rights and execute the mandate of substantive law. It is a necessary procedural complement, not a casual afterthought, to the genius of contemporary law. But who should execute such structural and episodic work in contemporary democratic government?

No branch of present-day presidential or parliamentary regimes seems well equipped, by reason of political legitimacy or practical capability, to do it. The majority-based government of the parliamentary system, or the executive branch of the presidential regime, cannot reinterpret rights and reshape rights-based arrangements in particular corners of social life without danger to the freedom of citizens. Moreover, they would soon find themselves distracted and demoralized by countless forms of petty anxiety and resistance. The administrative agencies or civil service might have more detachment and expertise but correspondingly less authority in the choice of a reconstructive direction or in the exercise of a power free to forge singular solutions to localized problems. Legislatures and parliaments would become both despotic and ineffective if they were to deal, in an individualized and episodic manner, with structural problems and institutional rearrangements. The judiciary lacks both the practical capability and the political legitimacy to restructure, and to manage during restructuring, the deserving objects of complex enforcement. Its unsuitability to the task will be all the more manifest if the frustration of rights enjoyment by intractable disadvantage turns out to be a common incident of social life, and if the cure demands an increasingly invasive reach into the background of practices and institutions.

The truth is that no part of present-day government is well suited, by virtue of practical capacity or political intervention, to undertake the job of structural and episodic reconstruction. The mission lacks – as every novel and serious mission in the world does – its proper agent. The best response, then, is to forge the new agent: another branch of government, another power in the state, designed, elected, and funded with the express charge of carrying out this distinctive, rights-ensuring work. Such a move, however, would demand the very openness to institutional experimentalism in which contemporary law and contemporary democracies have proved so markedly deficient. It would require us, as lawyers and as citizens, to complete the move from the accomplished first step of insistence upon the effectiveness of the enjoyment of rights to the missing second step of institutional reimagination and reconstruction.

In the absence of such an extension of the cast of available agents, any of the existing, somewhat unsuitable agents might accept or refuse the work, and then, having accepted it, push it as far as it wanted or could. In the United States, the judiciary, especially the federal judiciary, has been this incongruous, sometime, and half-hearted agent. In other countries it could be any other power in the state. From this marriage of the indispensable work to the unsuitable agent there arises the implicit theory of the structural injunctions in American law. This theory requires us to split the difference between two persuasive and incompatible propositions: the maxim that we must carry out the mandate of substantive law whether or not we have available the right agents and instruments, and the contrasting maxim that the implementation of law must take place under the discipline of institutional propriety and capability.

Thus the problem of complex enforcement sheds a double light upon the arrested development of contemporary legal thought. It shows how fidelity to law and to its imputed ideals may drive, unwittingly and on a small scale, into the institutional experiments that we have refused straightforwardly to imagine and to achieve. It also demonstrates how our failure to take the second step disorients and inhibits our small-time reconstructive work. This chapter in the history of contemporary law wonderfully illustrates the combination of self-concealment and self-disclosure in a ruling vision.

THE SPELL OF RATIONALIZING LEGAL ANALYSIS

Legal thought and social democracy

Why have law and legal doctrine failed to make the move from their characteristic focus upon the effective enjoyment of rights to the recognition and development of transformative institutional opportunity? Why have they worked in the belief that individual and collective self-determination depend upon empirical and defeasible conditions without turning more wholeheartedly to the legal analysis and construction of the contrasting practices and institutions capable of fulfilling these conditions? Why, therefore, have they not gone on to identify in these small and fragmentary alternatives the possible beginnings of larger alternatives: different institutional pathways for the redefinition and transformation of representative democracy, market economy, and free civil society? Why, in other words, have they failed to extend their rejection of the nineteenth-century idea that free polities and economies have a predetermined legal form, constitutive of freedom itself, into a more thoroughgoing rebellion against institutional fetishism?

The most important reasons for the arrested development of legal thought lie in the history of modern politics. Nevertheless, the simple attribution of the limits of contemporary legal thought to the constraints upon the political transformation of social arrangements is insufficient as explanation on several grounds.

The same period that saw the development of legal thought arrested also witnessed a connected series of radical reforms in the institutional and ideological context of political and economic life: the reforms labeled in Europe as social democracy and described in the United States as the New Deal. These changes had one of their points of focus and support in Keynesianism: a connected series of institutional and ideological innovations, freeing national governments from sound-finance doctrine and thus diminishing the dependence of public policy upon the level of business confidence. These were radical reforms because we cannot understand the force and shape of the major political, economic, and discursive routines of the contemporary industrial democracies – such as the political–business cycle – except by reference to them. They helped set the boundary conditions within which individuals and organized groups would, in the succeeding period, understand and defend their interests.

It is nevertheless true that, like any institutional settlement, the social-democratic compromise implied renunciation of a broader realm of conflict and controversy. National governments won the power and the authority to manage the economy countercyclically, to compensate for the unequalizing effects of economic growth through tax-and-transfer, and to take those investment initiatives that seemed necessary to satisfy the requirements for the profitability of private firms. In return, however, they had to abandon the threat radically to reorganize the system of production and exchange and thereby to reshape the primary distribution of wealth and income in society.

The refusal of legal analysis to move from the concern with rights enjoyment to the pursuit of institutional change may seem merely the legal counterpart to the foreclosure of broader conflict by the social-democratic settlement. The role of the practical legal reformer would be to continue and to complete the unfinished work of the social-democratic reformation. The task of the legal thinker would be to develop a theory of law that, freer of the nineteenth-century devotion to a predetermined private-law system, would do justice to social-democratic commitments. From this angle the reluctance to pass from the theme of effective rights enjoyment to the practice of institutional criticism appears to be a consequence of the renunciation of broader institutional experimentalism. Such a renunciation represented an essential term of the social-democratic compromise. Not until that compromise gets challenged and changed could we expect legal analysis to continue on the trajectory I earlier traced. As it has been challenged if at all mainly from the right, so the argument would conclude, there is little reason to expect such a forward impulse.

The trouble with this account of the sources of institutional conservatism in the practice of legal analysis is that it relies upon too static and one-sided a picture of institutional settlements and of their relation to legal thought. For one thing, there is no watertight division between the reconstructive moment of crisis and energy and the supposedly barren sequel. Not only have problems and alternatives touching on the design of institutions continued to appear, but it is also often hard to say which of the solutions considered is more faithful to the earlier, foundational compromise. For another thing, institutional change is not just a cause of reimagination; it is also a consequence. If we have indeed renounced a functionalist and evolutionary determinism in our understanding of institutional history, we must grant to our practices of social imagination such as legal analysis some power of productive apostasy and practical presentiment. Finally, the exculpatory picture fails to acknowledge the self-subversive and self-transformative capacities of a tradition of discursive practice such as that of legal analysis. The history of legal thought over the last hundred years provides – I shall soon argue – a striking example of these capacities. Why have they fallen into disuse?

The method of policy and principle

The failure to move from the moment of attention to rights enjoyment to the moment of institutional reimagination is more than the silent echo in law of political quiescence in society. It reveals the influence of a now canonical practice of legal analysis: one that enjoys increasing influence throughout the world but that has until now found its most elaborate development in American legal doctrine and theory. I shall call it rationalizing legal analysis, giving, for the purpose, specific content to the term "rationalizing." It is a style of legal discourse distinct both from the nineteenth-century rationalism and from the looser and more context-oriented analogical reasoning that continues to dominate, in the United States as elsewhere, much of the practical reasoning of lawyers and judges.

There is no such thing as "legal reasoning": a permanent part of an imaginary organon of forms of inquiry and discourse, with a persistent core of scope and method. All we have are historically located arrangements and historically located conversations. It makes no sense to ask "What is legal analysis?" as if discourse (by lawyers) about law had a permanent essence. In dealing with such a discourse, what we can reasonably ask is "In what form have we received it, and what should we turn it into?" In this book I argue that we now can and should turn it into a sustained conversation about our arrangements.

Rationalizing legal analysis is a way of representing extended pieces of law as expressions, albeit flawed expressions, of connected sets of policies and principles. It is a self-consciously purposive mode of discourse, recognizing that imputed purpose shapes the interpretive development of law. Its primary distinction, however, is to see policies of collective welfare and principles of moral and political right as the proper content of these guiding purposes. The generalizing and idealizing discourse of policy and principle interprets law by making sense of it as a purposive social enterprise that reaches toward comprehensive schemes of welfare and right. Through rational reconstruction, entering cumulatively and deeply into the content of law, we come to understand pieces of law as fragments of an intelligible plan of social life.

Within such a practice analogical reasoning is defined as the confused, first step up the ladder of rational reconstruction. The often implicit purposive judgements guiding the analogist point upward, for their authority and consistency, to more comprehensive ideas of policy and principle. The repeated practice of policy-oriented and principle-based analysis should, so the most ambitious and influential views of the practice teach, lead to ever higher standards of generality, coherence, and clarity in the rational representation of law.

The ideal conceptions representing law as an imperfect approximation to an intelligible and defensible plan are thought to be partly already there in the law. The analysts must not be thought to make them up. They are not, however, present in a single, unambiguous form, nor do they fully penetrate the legal material. Thus, legal analysis has two jobs: to recognize the ideal element embedded in law, and then to improve the law and its received understanding. Improvement happens by developing the underlying conceptions of principle and policy and by rejecting, from time to time and bit by bit, the pieces of received understanding and precedent that fail to fit the preferred conceptions of policy and principle. Too much pretense of discovering the ideal conceptions ready-made and fully potent within existing law, and the legal analyst becomes a mystifier and an apologist. Too much constructive improvement of the law as received understanding represents it to be, and he turns into a usurper of democratic power. In fact, because the apologetic mystification may be so insecurely grounded in the actual materials of law, both these countervailing perversions of rational reconstruction are likely to end in an unjustified confiscation of lawmaking power by the analyst.

In what vocabulary should we think of policy and principle or to what conceptions should we resort in trying to connect policies and principles to one another, and in preferring some to others? The major schools of legal theory in the age of rationalizing legal analysis can most usefully be understood as the contrasting operational ideologies of this analytic practice. Each school proposes a different way of grounding, refining, and reforming the practice. Thus, for example, one school may look to goals of allocational or dynamic economic efficiency while another may start from a view of the proper roles and responsibilities of the different institutions within a legal system. Nevertheless, the same argumentative structure recurs in all these theories: the purposive ideal conceptions of policy and principle, whatever their substance, are partly already there in the law, waiting to be made explicit, and they are partly the result of the improving work undertaken by the properly informed and motivated analyst.

The diffusion of rationalizing legal analysis

The practice of legal analysis theorized in this manner now enjoys immense and increasing influence. It may dominate only a minor part of the practical discourse of lawyers and lower-court judges, preoccupied with preventing conflict, controlling violence, and negotiating compromise. It nevertheless is coming to occupy the central imaginative space in the way in which the judicial, legal-professional, and legal-academic elites talk about law and develop its practical, applied understanding. At a minimum, it preempts an alternative imagination of law from holding this space and exercising this influence.

Given its historical specificity, this style of legal discourse spreads unevenly throughout the world, and takes on in different places characteristics shaped by an earlier history of methods and ideas. It has received its most lavish elaboration in the contemporary United States, for reasons later to be explored, but its worldwide influence grows steadily. In this respect it is an event characteristic of an historical situation in which humanity finds itself united by a chain of analogies, in experiences, problems, and solutions, and anxious reformers of society and culture pillage and recombine practices and institutions from all over the world. It is in this way rather than by the cruel devices through which capital becomes hypermobile while labor remains imprisoned in the nation-state – or in blocs of homogeneous nation-states – that mankind is becoming truly one. Countries in which a more analogy-bound practice of legal reasoning continues to enjoy greater respect (for in all countries such a practice enjoys actual influence), or in which the project of nineteenth-century legal science clings to a life-in-death, soon become theaters for the conflict between the old doctrinalism and the new style of rational reconstruction in law.

A familiar difference of emphasis illustrates how, as it spreads through the world, the method adapts to the idiosyncratic compulsions born of the many histories it intersects. In the United States the continuing duality of common law and statutory law has repeatedly suggested the idea that the retrospective, reconstructive, and dynamic interpretation of law under the guidance of connected policy and principle has a broader and more persistent role to play in judge-made law than in the judicial construction of statutes. Only slowly have lawyers knocked these barriers down, claiming in statutory construction the same freedom to keep on reinterpreting and reconstructing that they attribute to the internal development of the common law.

In civil-law countries the path-dependent history of attitudes toward rational reconstruction in law followed a different course. The project of nineteenth-century legal science, which found its most systematic expression in the work of the German pandectists, was understood by its votaries to be the rescue and refinement of the old Roman–Christian common law of Europe. A struggle developed between two attitudes toward codification – codification as the taming of the power of the jurists by democracy and codification as the convenient summation of the jurists' doctrines. Where the first attitude prevailed, as in postrevolutionary France, there was a concerted attempt to uphold literalism in the interpretation of law. This literalism outlived its political roots and helped preempt pandectism, as it helps restrain today the full-fledged inauguration of rationalizing legal analysis. But where, in the late democratizing countries of most of Europe, private and academic jurists retained their law-shaping authority throughout the era of great codifications in the late nineteenth and the early twentieth centuries, codes were imagined by the jurists as the compressed expression of their science. Democratic institutions, where they existed, confirmed and corrected doctrines that predated them. In such a climate the road to rational reconstruction in legal analysis was open. No association between codification and literalism took hold. A long history prepared the reception of today's rationalizing legal analysis.

The antiexperimentalist influence of rationalizing legal analysis

As it spreads through the world, rationalizing legal analysis helps arrest the development of the dialectic between the rights of choice and the arrangements that make individual and collective self-determination effective – a dialectic that is the very genius of contemporary law. The most important way in which it does so is by acquiescing in institutional fetishism. It represents the legally defined practices and institutions of society as an approximation to an intelligible and justified scheme of social life. It portrays the established forms of representative democracy, the regulated market economy, and civil society as flawed but real images of a free society – a society whose arrangements result from individual and collective self-determination. If these forms are never the only possible ones, at least they are, according to this point of view, the ones that history has validated – a history marked by both the intractability of social conflicts and the scarcity of workable arrangements.

Rationalizing legal analysis works by putting a good face – indeed the best possible face – on as much of law as it can, and therefore also on the institutional arrangements that take in law their detailed and distinctive form. It must restrict anomaly, for what cannot be reconciled with the schemes of policy and principle must eventually be rejected as mistaken. For the jurist to reject too much of the received understanding of law as mistaken, expanding the revisionary power of legal analysis, would be to upset the delicate balance between the claim to discover principles and policies already there and the willingness to impose them upon imperfect legal materials. It would be to conspire in the runaway usurpation of democratic power. Thus, deviations and contradictions become intellectual and political threats rather than intellectual and political opportunities, materials for alternative constructions.

A simple parable helps bring out the significance of these constraints for the suppression of the institutional imagination in legal thought and shows how contrasting practices of legal analysis may become self-fulfilling prophecies. Suppose two societies in one of which the institutional arrangements are perceived to be slightly more open to challenge and revision than in the other. In the marginally more open society the jurists say: "Let us emphasize the diversity and the distinctiveness of the present arrangements, their accidental origins and surprising variations, the better to criticize and change them, pillaging arrangements devised for other purposes and recombining them in novel ways." The practice of such a style of legal analysis over time will result in institutions that invite practical experimentalism, including experimentalism about the institutions themselves. Imagine, by contrast, a society in which the institutions seem marginally less open to revision. The jurists may say: "Let us make the best out of the situation by putting the best plausible face upon these arrangements, emphasizing their proximity to a rational and infinitely renewable plan. In the name of this rational reconstruction we may hope to make things better, especially for those who most need help: the people likely to be the victims of the social forces most directly in control of lawmaking." The sustained practice of this method will, however, help close down our opportunities for institutional experimentalism. It will do so both by turning away from actual experiments and by denying us a way of thinking and talking, collectively, about our institutional fate in the powerful and irreplaceable detail of law. Such is the world rationalizing legal analysis has helped make.

THE COMPLEX STRUCTURE OF LEGAL CONSCIOUSNESS

The moment of nineteenth-century legal science

No style of discourse, however powerful its influence, occupies the whole of a legal culture or penetrates all of a legal mind. Even in those places where it is most articulate and effective rationalizing legal analysis gains its characteristic position from its coexistence with different ideas of law. Before turning to the roots and limits of the policy-oriented and principle-based mode of legal reasoning, consider the ordinary shape of this coexistence today. I take my examples from the legal culture that has pushed furthest beyond the limits of nineteenth-century legal science – that of the United States – and I tell the story in the form of a simplified sequence. Three moments of legal consciousness, each uniting a vision of law with a method of legal analysis, have followed one another in time. The later, however, do not fully displace the earlier. They become super-imposed upon the preceding ones. This superimposition produces the complex coexistence of distinct ideas of law and practices of analysis marking the legal culture in which, increasingly, we have come to move.

The first moment in this sequence is the moment of nineteenth-century legal science. The animating idea is the effort to make patent the hidden legal content of a free political and economic order. This content consists in a system of property and contract rights and in a system of public-law arrangements and entitlements safeguarding the private order. Hard law is the distributively neutral law of coordination defined by this inbuilt legal content of the type of a free society. It must be distinguished from bad, soft, political law: the product of the hijacking of governmental power by groups who use lawmaking power to distribute rights and resources to themselves.

The methodological instrument for this substantive vision of law is the repertory of techniques we now know derisively as formalism and con-ceptualism. We should not characterize them as a crude deductivist prejudice about language and interpretation, for they make sense in the context of the idea of a predetermined legal content to a free order. Thus, conceptualism explores the packages of rule and doctrine inherent in the organizing categories of the rights system – categories like property itself – while formalism infers lower-order propositions from higher-order ones. Discursive practices designed to police the boundaries between dis-tributively neutral, good law and redistributive, bad law complement these

basic methods. The primary such policing practice is constructive interpretation, redescribing and reforming bad law, whenever persuasively
possible, as good law. The back-up policing practice is constitutional in-
validation, striking down those instances of redistribution through law
that cannot be preempted through improving interpretation. By deploying
all these methods legal science carries out its fundamental mission of
representing in a system of legal rules and ideas, and thereby securing
against perversion, the scheme of political and economic freedom. Its
scientific task matches its political responsibilities.

This approach to law suffocated social conflict. All the active interests
and ideologies that wanted more from the promises of modernity, and
refused to see in the institutions of their society a scheme of neutral coordination, waged war against it. The project of legal science, however, was
not merely attacked from without. Like every powerful imaginative practice, it undermined itself. Its votaries discovered that at every turn in the
march from relatively greater abstraction to relatively greater concrete-
ness in the definitions of rules and concepts there was more than one
plausible turn to take. Thus, a method designed to vindicate conceptual
unity and institutional necessity revealed nevertheless unimagined diversity and opportunity in established law.

The single most important instance of this insight into unwanted indeterminacy was the discovery of irremediable conflict among property
rights. The doctrine of *sic utere* was one of many announcing the hope that
under a private-property regime each rightholder could enjoy absolute
discretion within the citadel of the right. So long as he did not invade any-
one else's zone of right and property he could enjoy the privileges of his
whims. He could treat property as an alternative not only to personal
dependence but also to social interdependence. Practical lawyers, however, discovered that the conflict among rights, reasonably and
conventionally exercised, was both pervasive and unavoidable. The law in
practice turned out to be rife with *damnum absque iniuria* – instances of
damage one rightholder could, with immunity or without liability, do to
another – and with competitive injury – the infliction of economic harm
resulting from the ordinary practices of economic competition.

Every initiative in the deployment of rights proved to have what the
economists later called "externalities." To prohibit the initiatives or to
make the rightholder pay for all of them ("internalizing the externalities")
would be to inhibit productive action and to eviscerate the force of the
rights. But to allow the rights-invading use of rights and to pick and
choose in the imposition of liability for the prejudicial consequences was

to recognize the poverty of the pure logic of rights. There was no way to resolve the conflicts, or to make the selections, by probing more deeply into the system of categories and doctrines. It was necessary to take a stand and to justify it by reference to judgements of purpose, whether avowedly factional or allegedly impersonal. Doctrines of competitive injury and of *damnum absque iniuria* revealed the ineradicable contest among property rights, however such rights might be defined, in the law of a market economy. They marked horizontal conflicts among owners, and required policy compromises to resolve them.

Legal thought took much longer to recognize a second, vertical style of conflict: a series of unavoidable and interlocking choices about the conditions on which economic agents could run risks without incurring immediate economic death. The red line of failure and liability at which economic agents must cease to function, going bankrupt or paying for the consequences of the harms they inflict upon others, has no fixed and natural place in the legal logic of a market economy. The jurists and the legislator had to confront a connected set of dilemmas: immediate bankruptcy for failed firms or the chance for a second life through reorganization under the control of present management (the Chapter 11 of American bankruptcy law); unlimited or limited liability in combined economic activity; the governmental monopoly of money-making or its independent creation by banks, and, with the choice of the public monopoly of money and the emergence of a central banking system, insured or uninsured bank deposits.

The structure of these dilemmas was always the same. The impulse to contain moral hazard and to make people responsible for the uncompensated consequences of their activities had to be balanced against the need to encourage risk-taking behavior in production and in finance. There was never a way to distinguish beforehand, and in general, rule-bound terms, the good risk-bearing activities from the bad ones. Indeed, the impossibility of making such a distinction has been one of the reasons to prefer a market economy in the first place. Similarly, the existence of a class of people happy to pay a premium for the privilege of running a risk has been said to be the historical justification of "capitalism," if by capitalism we understand not just the abstract conception of a market economy but a particular version of that economy rewarding personal success with personal wealth.

The red line was not only movable, it had to be moved all the time, and no particular way of demarcating it seemed wholly satisfactory. Once again, the choices had to be made by purposive judgements of policy that the jurists were powerless to infer from the supposed legal logic of the economic order. We still struggle to understand that assumptions about the possible institutional forms of the market economy – assumptions worked out in the detailed language of law – shape what we imagine the possible solutions to both the horizontal and the vertical conflicts among property rights to be.

It is one thing to recognize that horizontal and vertical conflicts among property rights are pervasive; that we cannot infer the solutions to them from the abstract conception of a market economy and of its legal logic; and that such localized solutions as we may adopt must rely upon fragmentary and contested compromises among policies or interests. It is another thing to identify in some of these solutions the germs of a market economy and of a system of private law distinct from the ones established in the contemporary industrial democracies.

For example, Chapter 11-style corporate reorganization in American bankruptcy law provides an alternative to the death of a firm in the red: the management of the firm may be given a chance to borrow and to reform while the firm holds its creditors at bay. (Similar provisions exist in the bankruptcy laws of all the industrial democracies.) There are analogies to Chapter 11 in many fields of law, all the way from the intervention of the IMF and of consortia of governments to rescue countries undergoing liquidity crises to the public supervision of regional economic reconstruction when major parts of industry risk going broke. (Think of the selective turnaround decisions undertaken by the *Treuhandgesellschaft* in the reconstruction and privatization of East German industry.)

Suppose that we lack reliable, *ex ante* economic standards by which to identify the deserving beneficiaries of selective turnaround. Suppose, further, that the success of selective turnaround – the wisdom of the initial decisions and the support for their continuing execution in firms and communities – depends, as so many economic initiatives do, upon several interlocking forms of cooperation: between firms and local governments, between local governments and community organizations, between investors and workers, between insiders (jobholders in the rescued enterprises) and outsiders (workers in established firms and job seekers). Under these assumptions, selective turnaround may demand a comprehensive and complex legal structure of cooperation among interests.

Such a structure may include transactions that amount to continuing discussions; reciprocal reliance and adjustment that stop short of becoming articulated contracts; property rights that violate the traditional property-right logic of the brightline demarcation of zones of entitlement;

and supervisory or coordinating associations that stand midway between governments and firms. To develop such suggestions would be to reinvent the legal form of the market economy. To begin reinventing the legal form of the market economy would be to bring pressure to bear against the inherited legal forms of representative democracy and of free civil society.

There is a difference between recognizing that conflicts among property rights must be resolved by flawed, rough-and-ready compromises, and seeing in some of these compromises the possible starting points of a cumulative institutional transformation. It is, however, no more than a difference in how far we keep moving away from the original idea of a market economy with an inbuilt and determinate legal logic. Nonetheless, although legal thought has decisively done the first of these two jobs, it has just as unequivocally failed to accomplish, or even to imagine, the second.

The self-subversive work of legal thought, illustrated by the progressive discovery of the horizontal and vertical conflicts among property rights, has had two remarkable features. The first is that it has gone so far. The second is that it has nevertheless stopped where it has.

Under these restraints, legal analysis has slowly developed its insight into the political constitution and the institutional contingency of the market economy. The whole movement of legal doctrine and legal theory for the last hundred and fifty years has been a struggle to develop this insight and to understand its implications. The struggle, however, was waged by, as well as against, legal science; legal science waged war against itself.

Contemporary jurists mistakenly believe themselves to be free of the taint of this vision of law. Thus, American legal theory regularly congratulates itself on its rejection of "Lochnerism": the fetishistic acceptance and constitutional entrenchment of a particular private-rights system against all efforts to redistribute rights and resources and to regulate economic activity. In fact, however, Lochnerism has survived as an undercurrent of later moments of legal consciousness. In this latent position it has turned out to be all the more recalcitrant to criticism. To be sure, it has enjoyed its most vigorous afterlife in economics rather than in legal thought: all but the most austere and self-denying versions of economic analysis continue to rely upon the idea of a natural legal–institutional form of the market economy, open to only minor variations.

This belated and unconfessed Lochnerism also continues to leave its mark upon law. It does so, sometimes, in the form of organizing conceptions such as the state-action doctrine in American law and the functional equivalents to that doctrine in other legal systems. State-action doctrine assumes the validity of a distinction between social arrangements that are politically constituted and social arrangements that are somehow just prepolitically there. Yet that distinction rather than one of its now derided byproducts – the special authority of private-law rules and concepts to mark neutral baselines against which to judge governmental activism – was precisely the central axiom of Lochnerism. Sometimes we can identify the influence of this vision of law in a set of attitudes eluding precise doctrinal manifestation, such as the willingness to accept the greater stability and rationality of the central rules of private law. This view contrasts private law to the circumstantial and controversial efforts of the regulatory and redistributive state as if the rules of property and exchange were any less artificial than the provisions for tax-and-transfer. However, the single most important demonstration of the continuing power of the project of legal science is rationalizing legal analysis, the style of discourse that displaced nineteenth-century legal science while remaining dependent upon many of its assumptions and devoted to many of its ambitions.

The moment of rationalizing legal analysis

The second moment in contemporary legal consciousness is the moment of rationalizing legal analysis itself: the policy-oriented and principle-based style of legal analysis that, recognizing the reliance of legal analysis upon the ascription of purpose, gave to the guiding purposes the content of general conceptions of collective welfare or political right. This idealizing and generalizing discourse about law in the language of connected principle and policy ideas was not, however, the sole successor to the earlier project of legal science. At least two different vocabularies for thinking and talking about law have flourished in the aftermath of that project: the view of law as the outcome of a series of compromises in a well-ordered conflict of organized interests – the conception sometimes labelled "interest-group pluralism" – and the idea of law as the flawed but tentative embodiment of impersonal ideals of welfare and right. I shall soon have more to say about the paradoxical and disconcerting transactions between these two vocabularies: the one leading to an understanding of law as a series of regulated contracts among interest groups; the other producing a view of law as a partial expression of general and idealized purpose. The latter approach rather than the former has achieved canonical status in professional and academic legal culture. It is, in any event, the one closest in spirit and consequence to the legal science it displaced. The coexistence of these two vocabularies serves to introduce the central organizing distinction of the new style of legal analysis.

Rationalizing legal analysis puts the contrast between law as impersonal policy and principle and law as factional self-dealing by powerful interest groups in place of the more ambitious and inflexible contrast between law as a distributively neutral framework of coordination among free and equal individuals and law as an illicit, redistributive intervention by the government in this framework. Correctly understood, the parallel between these two pairs of distinctions should be too close for comfort. What is gone is the idea of a fixed system of private and public rights implicit in the very definition of a free political and economic order. Rationalizing legal analysis has rejected, together with that idea, its chief corollary: the claim of the private-law system of property and contract to provide a distributively neutral standard against which to judge the legitimacy of governmental "intervention." It has nevertheless rescued from the ruin of that claim the commitment to represent law as the search for a public interest capable of description in the language of policy and principle and resolutely contrasted to factional self-promotion through lawmaking.

No component of public interest seems more important than the commitment to assure people of the practical conditions effectively to enjoy the rights of free citizens, free economic agents, and free individuals. The regulatory and redistributive activity of the state gains legitimacy, and demonstrates its connection with the public interest, by having as its mission the satisfaction of the requirements for the effective enjoyment of rights.

The self-conscious task of this representation of law was to imagine as law the regulatory and redistributive activity of an activist government. This is the work in which rationalizing legal analysis has been most successful. The larger task was to reimagine from the perspective of social democracy the working methods of legal reasoning and the entire body of law and legal institutions including traditional private law. In this larger work the success of rationalizing legal analysis, and of its supporting cast of theories of law, has been far less certain. Indeed, the incompleteness of the larger mission has given contemporary jurists an excuse to disclaim broader intellectual or transformative ambitions; there is so much work left to do. Spellbound by the Atlas complex it has willed upon itself, legal thought halts in its journey away from the nineteenth-century project of legal science.

Later sections explore the motivations and the limitations of this now dominant way of thinking and talking about law. Once again, the combination of real social conflicts and irrepressible intellectual self-subversion has begun to expose its frailties. The endless strife over group benefits and burdens, social incorporation and exclusion, in the era of regulatory and redistributive government undermines the authority of the idea that any particular pattern of regulation and redistribution could be held up as the authoritative correction to the preexisting social order: the one that would make real the promises of liberal democracy. More troubling yet is the discovery that the most important sources of frustration of the effective enjoyment of rights may lie in practices and institutions that the policy tools of an institutionally conservative social democracy are unable to reach and that the lawyer's discourse of policy and principle is powerless to represent.

As a strategy for limiting inequality, tax-and-transfer has ordinarily had disappointing results. In few countries has it produced more than marginal increases in equality of wealth and income, and it has had an even more modest effect upon the distribution of economic power. Every major effort at redistribution through tax-and-transfer produces economic stress and crisis either directly through disinvestment and capital flight or indirectly through its corrosive effects upon public finance. This practical disappointment finds expression in a mode of discourse contrasting equity and efficiency as goals locked in a tense and often inverse relation. The alternative would be a reorganization of the system for production and exchange, and of the relations between public power and private initiative, influencing the primary distribution of wealth and income, while affirming and extending the scope of market activity. Such an alternative, however, depends on institutional experiments, including experiments in the property regime, that the social-democratic compromise seems to have foreclosed.

As the limits of the social-democratic compromise become manifest, rationalizing legal analysis finds itself pulled between two forces. On the one hand, it clings to the attempt to put the best face on the established institutional settlement, treating it not as a transitory and accidental set of compromises but as a lasting and rational framework, to be perfected rather than challenged or changed. On the other hand, however, to take seriously the view of law as an embodiment of social ideals, describable in the language of policy and principle, is to admit that these ideals may come into conflict with actual practices and organizations. Complex enforcement is the single most striking expression of this countervailing impulse in legal doctrine. Up until now, a division of domains has concealed this conflict of directions. The immunization of institutional arrangements against close scrutiny has prevailed in the vision of substantive law. The selective probing of institutions has remained largely confined to development of procedural remedies such as those of complex enforcement. The consequence of this procedural innovation, we have seen, is to use the available roles and agents of the legal process incongruously: judges undertake complex enforcement because they want to, because the mandate of substantive law seems to require that someone undertake it, and because all other branches of government seem just as unsuited to the task as the judiciary is. Lacking the resources of authority, expertise, and funds with which to do the job, they do it haltingly and at the margins, until they run out of power and out of will. Thus, by the self-subversive logic of evolution in legal ideas, we derationalize procedure the better to vindicate the rationalization of substantive law. At the next turn of our thinking, we might well ask why we should not derationalize substantive law the better to affirm our interests and ideals.

There are several equivalent ways in which to describe the core of weakness and self-subversion in rationalizing legal analysis; later sections approach this task from a number of directions. On one description the focus of perplexity in rationalizing legal analysis is the difficulty of sustaining the organizing distinction between factional interest and impersonal policy or principle. Every particular definition of the public interest, in the idealized language of policy and principle, will seem either too indeterminate to guide judgement toward particular outcomes or too difficult to disentangle from controversial beliefs, connected, in turn, to factional interests.

The most revealing and disconcerting aspect of this discursive practice, however, becomes apparent when we focus on the relation between legal ideals and social facts. Consider, as an example, the typical form of a law-review article by an American legal academic at the close of the twentieth century. Such an article typically presents an extended part of legal rule and doctrine as the expression of a connected set of policies and principles. It criticizes part of that received body of rule and doctrine as inadequate to the achievement of the ascribed ideal purposes. It concludes with a proposal for law reform resulting in a more defensible and comprehensive equilibrium between the detailed legal material and the ideal conceptions intended to make sense of that material. But why should the reform stop at one point rather than another? Why should it not advance more deeply into the stuff of social arrangements, reconstructing them for the sake of the ideal conceptions, and then, later on, redefining the ideal conceptions in the light of the actual or imagined rearrangements? An implicit judgement of practical political feasibility controls the answer to this question. Given that most of the institutional background must, as a practical matter, be held constant at any given time, proposals for institutional tinkering should remain modest and marginal. Moreover, given that the author is speaking in the impersonal voice of the quasi-judge or the quasi-bureaucrat, the reform proposals should never seem too sectarian. Thus, the practice of rationalizing legal analysis comes to be shaped by implicit constraints that the analytic practice itself leaves largely unchallenged and unexplored. From this conformity to shadowy and unjustified constraints arises the sense of relative arbitrariness, of confusion between normative justification and practical strategy, that, increasingly, becomes part of the actual experience of doing legal analysis.

The example of the law-review article may seem limited in its significance to the situation of a jurist who, without administrative or adjudicative responsibilities, but with a desire to remain connected to the worlds of practical administration and adjudication, offers proposals to reform law. Yet the earlier example of the complex injunctions suggests that the problem reappears in many of the roles in which we practice legal analysis. The judge must revise received legal understandings, from time to time, but if he revises too many of them, or revises a few of them too radically, and if in so doing he challenges and changes some part of the institutional order defined in law, he transgresses the boundaries of the role assigned to him by rationalizing legal analysis. What keeps him within these boundaries? The happy assurance that most of the received body of law and legal understanding at any given time can in fact be represented as the expression of connected policies and principles? If so, how could such a harmony between the prospective history of law as a history of conflicts among groups, interests, and visions and the retrospective rationalization of law as an intelligible scheme of policy and principle ever occur? Or is the restraint of revisionary power by the judge something that comes from an independent set of standards about what judges may appropriately do? If so, from where do these standards come? Whatever their content and origin, how can they escape imposing a severe and wandering constraint upon our capacity to reimagine and to reconstruct law as the expression of policy and principle?

The moment of the tactical reinterpretation of legal doctrine

Such varieties of bafflement have today become an integral part of the experience of doing policy-oriented and principle-based legal analysis. Together with the destabilizing forces that come from outside – from the real politics of an activist, regulatory, and redistributive government – they have given rise to a third moment in the evolution of modern legal consciousness, superimposed upon the two earlier moments, of nineteenth-century legal science and rationalizing legal analysis. This third moment is the redefinition of the principle-based and policy-oriented style of legal discourse as a tactic deployed in the service of a distinctive family of political projects.

I shall label this family of political projects conservative reformism: the pursuit of programmatic goals, such as more economic competition or greater equality of practical opportunity and cultural voice, within the limits imposed by the established institutional order. A specially influential version of conservative reformism in the development of the tactical moment in contemporary legal consciousness has been what I shall label progressive pessimistic reformism.

Two beliefs and a commitment define progressive pessimistic reformism. The first belief is what makes it a species of conservative reformism: no institutional change is in the cards. Moreover, even if such a change were possible and desirable, we, the jurists, cannot be its legitimate and effective agents. The second belief is what makes it pessimistic: in the politics of lawmaking, the self-serving majority will regularly dump on marginalized and powerless groups. Even if we could ensure cumulative change in the formative arrangements and enacted beliefs of society, it would likely make things even more dangerous for the most vulnerable groups. Their protective rights might be swept away in the enthusiasm of a reconstructive period. The tax-and-transfer schemes of an institutionally conservative social democracy and the retrospective improvement of law by rationalizing legal analysis offer the weak their best hope. Indeed, seen in this revealing light, social democracy and rationalizing legal analysis are the twin instruments of the same political project. By putting the best face on the law, by representing it as impersonal policy and principle rather than as the triumph of powerful and partial coalitions of interests, the lawyer can make things better for the people who need help most. In the name of the idealizing interpretation of law, he can redistribute rights and resources to the repeated victims of the lawmaking coalitions. The progressive commitment is, therefore, the determination so to use rationalizing legal analysis.

From such a vantage point the canonical style of legal doctrine may be a lie, but it is a noble and a necessary lie. It gives insurance against the worst as well as the promise of modest but real improvement in the condition of those who, without its help, would stand to lose most.

The analytic practice accompanying this vision of law hardly differs from the recourse to ideal purposes in rationalizing legal analysis. It *is* rationalizing legal analysis with an ironic proviso: that although the assumptions of the method may not be literally believable they serve a vital goal. The subtlety in this conversion of vision into vocabulary and of vocabulary into strategy is that the strategic imperative requires the agent to continue speaking the vocabulary of the vision in which he has ceased to believe. In so doing, he fails fully to grasp the hidden restraints implicit in his supposedly strategic language. Rationalizing legal analysis, it turns out, is not equally well suited for all varieties of politics. It suits an institutionally conservative politics: one that renounces persistent and cumulative tinkering with the institutional structure and seeks, instead, to redistribute rights and resources within that structure.

When the major problems of society begin to require, for their solution, experimentalism about practical arrangements, this defect proves fatal. The tactic avenges itself against the tactician.

The present form of legal consciousness is not one of these moments of legal thought or another. It is, rather, the combination of all three. All three ways of thinking coexist not only in the same legal and political culture but often in the same individual minds. The result is a discursive community bound together, as discursive communities so often are, according to the principle enunciated by the narrator in Proust's novel: we are friends with those whose ideas are at the same level of confusion as our own.

INTEREST-GROUP PLURALISM AND RATIONALIZING LEGAL ANALYSIS

Two incompatible vocabularies about law

Before looking more deeply into the roots and limits of rationalizing legal analysis consider how the rationalizing vocabulary of policy and principle relates to its major rival and complement in contemporary legal and political culture: the vocabulary of interests and interest groups. We can infer that the language of policy and principle is not the self-evident medium in which to represent law from the present use of at least one alternative language. The assumptions of these two vocabularies of law talk are incompatible. The boundaries of their legitimate application are controversial in theory and movable in fact. It matters whether we use one or the other and where we use it.

Strangely, however, the two approaches to law coexist more or less peacefully in contemporary legal and political culture. Both approaches, otherwise so different in message and consequence, converge in the dissociation of legal analysis from institutional imagination. This convergence makes their peaceful coexistence possible.

Interest-group pluralism, as we may call it, represents law as the product of bargaining and conflict among organized interest groups. In a democracy the primary but far from the sole locus of this lawmaking activity is legislation, with its background in electoral party politics. In more muted form, the same group rivalry and compromise may also take place through the selection and activities of courts and administrative agencies. According to interest-group pluralism, each fragment of law represents a trophy or a truce in an ongoing conflict among interest groups. The legal outcomes of this conflict remain legitimate so long as the conduct of the conflict continues to satisfy two requirements. The first requirement is that the contending groups play by the groundrules established in law, especially the law defining the arrangements of constitutional democracy and electoral politics. The second requirement is that no groups be significantly underorganized or underrepresented. If any group is underorganized the long-term solution is to organize and represent it, assuring voice to the voiceless. The short-term solution is to afford it special protection or compensation.

Under this alternative vocabulary we should interpret law by identifying the bargain each piece of law inscribes. An understanding of the balance of forces that produced the law, of the aims of the preponderant forces, and of the concessions they may have made to secure their objectives, may all help. Rather than retrospective and rationalistic reconstruction in the language of idealized policy and principle we have the attempt to understand law as the episodic expression of practical compromise in the presence of real conflict: conflict of ideal visions as well as of material interests.

Interest-group pluralism, so described, is not a sociology of lawmaking. It is, like rationalizing legal analysis itself, a prescriptive discourse, providing an account of how law becomes legitimate and of how it should be represented. It is not about something different from rationalizing legal analysis; it is about the same thing. It is not a heresy; it is one of the two conventional discourses about law in the present. How, then, can these two seemingly incompatible vocabularies coexist?

Ordinarily, they coexist by being made to apply in different domains. The language of interests and interest groups has traditionally been reserved for the domain of legislation and electoral politics. The language of policy and purpose has been deployed in the domain of the professional interpretation of law, especially in the setting of adjudication but also by any analyst or administrator who takes the perspective of a judge. Thus, the traditional way of managing the duality of languages about law is to switch from one to the other according to the context in which the discourse takes place.

The movable boundary between the vocabularies

But why, you may well ask, should the boundary between these approaches to law be drawn in one place rather than another? Why not, for example, project the words and methods of interest-group pluralism into the adjudicative setting, using it as a way of deciding cases as well as a way to describe lawmaking? Consider three objections to such a projection.

A first objection is that the compromise, and the underlying balance of forces, may be too vague. It may be hard to tell, for example, just how much the producers and distributors of whole milk triumphed over consumers in the making of laws and administrative regulations restricting the distribution, or the price, of powdered-milk substitutes for whole milk. It may be hard to tell how much labor unions had to concede to industrialists in order to secure the passage of legislation limiting or slowing the closure of manufacturing plants in the face of foreign competition. It may, indeed, be hard to identify the exact bargain or weigh the effective power of the moving interests. But the question remains: Compared to what? However vague the play of conflict and compromise, and the identities of winners and losers, they have roots in a tangible social reality. By contrast, the idealized purposes and policies of rationalizing legal analysis lack a secure position in the real life of society. They may be invoked in electoral and legislative debates. For the most part, however, they have a floating and many-sided character until captured, refined, and developed by the systematic discourse of the legal analyst.

A second objection is that the contrast between the two approaches is itself misguided. Policy and principle play a formative role in the party-political and legislative conflict over lawmaking. Visions help shape interests. Politicians struggle over rival conceptions of the common good. The rationalizing legal analyst merely seizes upon this society-regarding element in the materials of law and does his job by purifying and developing it, separating it from the dross of self-dealing with which it may be entangled. This objection, however, mistakes the force of the contrast between the two approaches to law. We need not understand interest-group pluralism as a doctrine affirming and accepting the ascendancy of material interests over ideological opinions. Its point is, rather, to assert the centrality and the legitimacy of conflict, over spiritual as well as material interests, or rather over what results from the combination of the two, and then to suggest how law in a democracy can be understood as the regulation of conflict by groundrules and as the moderation of conflict by compromise.

The resulting view sees each piece of law as a little bit of this and a little bit of that. We need not discern in law an inchoate and developing rational scheme in order to recognize its legitimacy and to read its meaning. We can acknowledge conflict and compromise among ideological claims as well as among crude grabs for money and privilege. Rationalizing legal analysis rebels against this surrender to the disorder of conflict and compromise. It looks, retrospectively, at each extended piece of law as a possible fragment in a comprehensive and rational ordering of social life. Here is a real distinction, in spirit as well as in words.

When we put aside these two objections, each tainted by misunderstanding, to the projection of the interest-group approach into the adjudicative setting, we come to a third, more subtle objection. By insisting upon the interpretation of law as the embodiment of policy and purpose in the adjudicative setting, we impose a vital constraint upon the selfish pursuit of group interests in the politics of lawmaking. The political agents of a coalition of powerful interests will know that once the laws they make pass into the hands of the judges and the jurists, those laws will be read as efforts to advance a public interest. Constructive interpretation will seek, whenever possible, to rescue law from factional selfishness. When the rescue is too difficult and the selfishness too egregious, judicial review, in a constitutional democracy, may strike down the laws it has been unable to reconstruct.

Thus, to succeed in their aims, the driving interests will have to make concessions, giving their legal projects the semblance of conformity to public interest and describing them in a language making this conformity plausible. At a minimum, the appeal to ideal purposes in rationalizing legal analysis would play the role in which Marxist theory casts ideology. Ideology legitimates dominant interests by universalizing them, presenting them as instruments of a broader collective good. The legitimating universalization cannot work unless it gains a measure of real force, moderating the self-regard of the dominant interests.

The trouble with this pragmatic justification of the surprising switchover from one vocabulary about law to another is that it relies upon a factual assumption that may often prove false. Rent-seeking and sectarian conduct, under the cover of devotion to the public interest, may be all the more dangerous and successful when they are allowed to survive under disguise. You have only to examine the records of legislative and electoral debates to see how elastic and ambiguous the language of public interest can be. Sometimes, group selfishness may be tamed by being made to speak the magnanimous rhetoric of social concern. If hypocrisy is the tribute that vice renders virtue, this rhetoric may be usable as the device of a minimalist but realistic political morality. Just as often, however, self-dealing through law may be more effectively controlled by being recognized for what it is.

This is no mere dispute in speculative political theory. It has practical implications for legal reasoning. Law viewed as a contract among interest groups may be interpreted restrictively. Law seen as an embodiment of impersonal principle and policy may be taken as the starting point of expansive analogies. When law is represented in the interest vocabulary, procedural standing may remain on a short leash. When it is discussed in the policy and principle vocabulary, the willingness to expand standing and to multiply remedies may follow in the wake of constructive interpretation and expansive analogy.

Even those who are hostile to the criticism of established institutions and ideals and remain inside the imaginative world of present-day legal and political culture will have trouble making the case to draw the frontier for the application of these two conventional legal vocabularies at the boundary between legislation and adjudication. A recent development in American legal thought confirms the point. Twenty years ago a group of rightwing American legal scholars, trained in mainstream economics, began to question the parallelism between the two approaches and the two institutional settings. They drew a distinction between two types of law: rent-seeking law and general-interest law. (In principle, a similar distinction could be made within judge-made law, although the opportunity for rent-seeking might be greater in legislation.) They proposed in effect that legal interpretation, including judicial interpretation, adopt the carry-out-the-contract method for the first type, and the purposive policy method for the second. They offered lists of practical telltale signs by which to distinguish the two variants of law: how much particularistic detail a statutory scheme includes; how richly the legislative record abounds in the overt expression of group interests and compromises; and, above all, how readily we can find in the statute indicia of rent-seeking, such as bars to market entry. They argued that the advantage of recognizing rent-seeking legislation for what it was lay in the hope of putting it under quarantine, preventing its analogical extension, and containing its procedural advancement. Some of these scholars later became influential judges, and, as judges, began to practice what they had preached. They have in effect internalized within adjudication a distinction that had previously been thought to track the boundary between legislation and adjudication.

Disturbing implications

We can draw two conclusions from these arguments and events. The first conclusion is that both rationalizing legal analysis and interest-group pluralism can coexist despite their diversity of description and direction because they share a decisive negative attribute. This attribute is the aversion to institutional tinkering, the capacity to dissociate the representation of law from the imagination – and the probing – of its structural background. For interest-group pluralism, law is group conflict and compromise against an institutional background that can be left unchallenged and even unseen. The arrangements for representative democracy and the market economy are the uncontroversial residues of past conflicts and compromises. Implicitly, however, interest-group pluralism must advance a stronger claim on behalf of the institutional arrangements: that, through trial and error, they approach the character of a perpetual-motion choice machine. They supply a framework unbiased among interests and therefore equally open to all compromises. The counterpart to this view in political economy is the type of institutional history and institutional analysis ("new institutionalism") that tries to explain the genesis and diffusion of economic institutional arrangements by simple extension from the same style of rationality marking economic decisions within a settled economic system. Thus, for example, the institutions of the modern European market economy would be the (necessary) rational response to the problems and opportunities produced by factors such as the population growth and technological development. If the framework itself were defective and self-reproducing, if it were only one of many possible forms of democracy and of the market, and if each of these forms had different consequences for the bargains groups could strike, interest-group pluralism would be a radically incomplete practice. It would need to be supplemented by some other way of representing and making law, which might wholly alter its meaning.

Rationalizing legal analysis results in a similar practice and depends upon similar presuppositions. Its discourse of policy and principle remains focused upon the redistribution of rights and resources within the present institutional order. Its method of improvement through constructive interpretation requires us to put the best face on the law and therefore on the practices and institutions defined in law. Consider, for example, the attitude toward constitutional interpretation in American constitutional doctrine, which offers an extreme case of rationalizing legal analysis. There is no room in that attitude for the possibility that the type of democracy the country needs is one that the arrangements of the American constitution cannot accommodate without comprehensive revision. If a certain type of democracy is the best, it must be possible to find it in the constitution. If it cannot, by hook or by crook, be found in the constitution, it must not be as good as it looks. The pressure on reconstructive rationalization resulting from the cult of the constitution may be an extreme instance of the containment of institutional criticism and tinkering, but it is merely the extreme instance of something pervasive in the beliefs and methods of the now dominant style of legal doctrine.

The second conclusion to draw from the comparison of the two conventional approaches to law is even more straightforward. If there are two vocabularies for representing law, and if their boundaries of application are both controversial and movable, why should there not be five vocabularies, or one vocabulary different from these? To study the coexistence of these two languages about law in the present legal and political culture is to gain an unsettling sense of their contingency.

I now propose to make good on this sense of contingency by exploring four complementary perspectives upon the motives and the limits of rationalizing legal analysis. Each of these perspectives represents both a partial account of the animating mission of rationalizing legal analysis and a view of its frailties. By connecting the criticism of this discourse to an understanding of its work from its own viewpoint we can hope to gain access to its internal imaginative world. If our defects are God's fifth column within the human heart, the flaws in a discursive practice generate its energy of self-subversion. We should study rationalizing legal analysis in depth because it is becoming the most influential style of legal discourse throughout the world. We should also study it because it can supply, through its self-subversion, the means with which to turn legal thought into an instrument of institutional imagination.

THE FOURFOLD ROOT OF RATIONALIZING LEGAL ANALYSIS: THE PREJUDICE AGAINST ANALOGY

An entrenched prejudice

The simplest way to define the point of rationalizing legal analysis is to say that it represents a way to think clearly and connectedly about law. On this view, if you reflect long and hard enough about law you will end up with something like this principle-based and policy-oriented style of purposive legal reasoning. On this account of the aims of legal doctrine, the chief enemy is the surrender of legal analysis to unreflective analogy. Much of lawyers' reasonings in many legal traditions gives a central role to analogical comparison and distinction, clinging to the ground of usage and precedent and refusing to climb up the ladder of abstraction, generalization, and system. The decline of the project of nineteenth-century legal science may leave a vacuum that undisciplined analogy can once again occupy. It cannot, however, occupy that space for long – so the argument goes – if we are to be clear-sighted in our thinking about law.

If we persist in a practice of analogical judgement we discover that the drawing of analogical comparisons and distinctions relies, at least implicitly, upon judgements of purpose connected to significant human interests. As the factual situations multiply on one side, the effort to articulate and connect these purposes advances on the other side. Under the double pressure of experience and analysis, a loose, unshaped mass of analogies begins to take form. The invoked purposes move toward greater generality of definition. They begin, little by little, to resemble the policy and principle-laden purposes of rationalizing legal doctrine. Through this reciprocal clarification of relevant context and guiding purpose, the law, in Lord Mansfield's phrase, works itself pure: it approaches its desired form as an intelligible and defensible scheme of human association. An unreconstructed practice of analogical judgement turns out, in retrospect, to be the first, confused step toward reasoning from policy and principle. It stands to rationalizing legal analysis as crawling stands to walking.

The criticism of this antianalogical prejudice can best begin with an effort to characterize the family of analogical modes of practical reasoning, for it is a family of loosely related ways of making and justifying practical decisions. Three minimalist attributes mark the space of analogy.

Attributes of analogy

The first attribute is the recurrent dialectic between ascription of purpose and classification of circumstance. We compare or distinguish fact situations for the purpose of applying certain rules, and we reformulate the rules in relation to the fact situations they would govern, according to a view of the purposes these reclassifications and reformulations will advance. There is no sensible way of comparing or distinguishing situations to the end of rule governance apart from purposive judgements. An analogical comparison is not inherently in the facts; it is a way of grouping facts that helps us advance certain interests. The point is hardly that we can pretend things are any way we like. It is rather that we cannot marry rule to circumstance effectively unless we are willing to bring both the definition of appropriate circumstance and the definition of relevant rule under the light of an understanding of the interests served by our rule-applying endeavor and by the particular rules to be applied. Whether a tricycle counts as a vehicle under the rule prohibiting vehicles in the park, and whether therefore tricycles should be analogized to automobiles, depends on whether we think the rule is meant to avoid danger, noise, or some other, tricycle-including objective.

In the passage back and forth among guiding purpose, relevant rule, and typical fact situation, formal, even syllogistic deductive inference may play a role. It may play a role encoded within the more inclusive dialectic of analogy. However, the minor premise of the syllogism – tricycles are (or are not) vehicles – is the whole work of analogy. The prehistory of the syllogism is the history that matters.

The second attribute of the family of practical reasoning through analogy is that the guiding interests or purposes on which the analogist draws are open-ended. They do not make up a closed list, nor are they hierarchically ordered in a system of higher- and lower-order propositions, the former trumping the latter. They reflect the variety, renewal, and disorder of real human concerns. Analogical reasoning is not just some purist practice imposed upon these concerns from the vantage point of higher insight or authority; it is an integral part of their ordinary articulation in everyday life. Today tricycles may not count as prohibited vehicles because they are neither noisy nor dangerous to able adults, but tomorrow people may be concerned with toddlers in the park, a practice may develop of allowing them to roam around, and they may be frightened if not endangered by tricycles. Either sympathies or practices may change. Most often, they may change together.

This same example suggests that the list of relevant purposes and interests remains open in another way. The distribution of energy and authority among the familiar interests at play in a set of analogical comparisons and distinctions may be changing all the time. If marriage is a long conversation, then so is the larger marriage of a discursive community. What at one moment provides the focus of anxiety may, at another, seem a distant threat. The impossibility of ordering the analogy-relevant purposes hierarchically is a consequence of the refusal to subordinate social experience to schematic containment.

The third attribute of the family of analogical judgements is an extension of the second. Analogical reasoning is noncumulative: its repeated practice over time does not turn it, little by little, into a system of hierarchically ordered, more abstract and more concrete propositions, because the guiding interests or purposes themselves do not move toward a system of axioms and inferences. As convergence and simplification take hold in some fields, divergence and complexity increase in others. There may be progress in the use of analogy. Its form, however, is subtle: expansion of the scope of problems over which the analogical judgements range, richness in the articulation of guiding aims, and refinement in the connection of animating purpose to recurrent circumstance. A developed practice of analogical judgement is one resembling a more self-conscious and bounded version of many of our ordinary methods of moral and political judgement: bounded by the starting point in legal materials, and made self-conscious by the determination to articulate the aims of an endeavor that is both collective and coercive.

The groundlessness of the prejudice against analogy

A false idea about discursive practices underlies the antianalogical prejudice. To view analogy as an inchoate form of abstract and axiom-bound reasoning is to acquiesce in an imperialism of practices. It is to treat the standards of justification in rationalizing legal analysis or in its equivalents as if they carried a presumption of rational authority. But why should we accept such a presumption? The family of prudential and analogical practices is more widespread in historical experience and more entrenched in human concerns than is any more abstract or deductive mode of moral, political, and legal reasoning. Even in the world history of legal doctrine, analogical and glossatorial forms of reasoning have exercised far more influence, over more sustained periods, than the principle-seeking abstractions of systematic or rationalistic jurists. Often, the party of analogy has had a self-confident sense of its superiority in the encounter with the party of rationalization. Thus, for example, the late defenders of Roman republican jurisprudence looked down on legal rationalization as the corruption of a higher and more subtle craft by the double force of Greek rationalism and bureaucratic domination. American legal realists and post-realists repeated this move when they romanticized the common law as the product of an experimental and context-bound reasoning that made legal abstraction look obtuse. The superstitious conceptual imperialism of the rationalizers has met its match in the countersuperstition of an ineffable legal art. All too often this language of artistic and practical prudence has been made to immunize legal thought against social criticism.

The incongruity of the scorn for analogy becomes more evident when we remember that an analogical style of thinking has served as the vehicle for the single most influential conception in the history of ideas about spirit and personality in the West: the understanding, in the monotheistic Semitic religions of Judaism, Christianity, and Islam, of the relation between God and humankind by analogy to the relations among people. The narrative of revelation deepens the narrative of personal encounter, and affirms the revolutionary transvaluation by which the personal comes to be valued more highly than the impersonal as a source of insight and authority. Analogical reasoning and knowledge of people are constant companions: the interpretation of self-experience and the interpretation of other people's experience provide each other with the analogies that rescue us, if only a little bit, from both solipsism and self-obscurity. The suppression of analogical judgement in legal thought would, if it could be accomplished, result in a radical dehumanization of the law: one method for people, and another for rules.

We should rid ourselves of both the superstition of conceptual imperialism and the countersuperstition of legal art. Practices are practices. They serve multiple, half-articulate purposes, as they also shape the aims we can pursue and the possibilities we can entertain. They lack permanent essences. We have become accustomed to the idea that the methods of natural science vary, slowly and obliquely, with the content of our scientific explanations. The same applies to legal reasoning: thus, I have already given the example of how the style of rationalization in present-day legal thought differs from the methods of nineteenth-century legal science, and of how this methodological shift is bound up with a change in the substantive vision of law.

Our practices of discourse can be changed, sometimes deliberately but always slowly. The reason why it is hard for us to change our practices is that, to a large extent, we are the sum of practices of discourse and action. The reason why we can change our practices nevertheless is that they never exhaustively define us: we enjoy a residue of productive and creative capacity that they fail to use up or to tame. The goals we pursue through them are never our only possible aims.

If we are to credit the presumption of higher authority for the rational reconstruction of law, by the method of principle and policy or by any other, we cannot base this presumption upon the need to think clearly and connectedly about law. We must claim a more selective and a more social value for the rationalizing practice. The value most often invoked to this end is the commitment to sustain the rule of law and a regime of rights.

THE FOURFOLD ROOT OF RATIONALIZING LEGAL ANALYSIS: UPHOLDING A REGIME OF RIGHTS

The rule of law and the regime of rights

The most commonly stated justification of rationalizing legal analysis is belief that the integrity of a regime of rights or of the rule of law requires something like that approach to law. On this view the principle-based and policy-oriented style of legal doctrine is the indispensable antidote to arbitrariness in legal reasoning. It enables people to stay secure in their entitlements while restraining power under law. Within broad limits people can understand what the law means and how it will be enforced. Citizens can participate in the same process of public justification that the judges themselves must use. More importantly, the character of the reasons for decision given in rationalizing legal argument enjoys a power of significant generalization and selection.

A context-bound analogical method supposedly lacks these powers: if the list of relevant purposes is open, and if the method of reasoning is non-cumulative, the basis for criticizing any particular analogical comparison or distinction will always remain weak. Consequently, the analogist will be able to get away with almost anything he wants. If he appears to be constrained, the constraint will come less from the analogical method itself than from a background of densely shared custom and culture. However, a major reason for valuing the regime of rights and the rule of law in the first place is to relieve diversity of some of its terrors. If we were in the situation of the stereotyped tribe, bound together by richly defined and shared vision and value, we would hardly need – or want – the rule of law. The rule of law belongs to an historical circumstance deficient in the constraints that would make the practice of analogy predictable.

If analogy fails to constrain arbitrariness, so, on the other hand, does the willingness to treat legal reasoning as a proxy for the ongoing ideological conflict in society. If legal analysis were merely the continuation of politics by other means, the settlement of rights in any particular case would remain subordinate to the ideological commitments of whomever held the power to decide. Democracy would go down together with rights: no matter what laws the representatives of the people chose to establish, the legal analysts would be able to remake them at will under the pretense of reinterpreting them. Thus, rationalizing legal analysis – so its defenders claim – holds the vital position between the depressive mindlessness of law as analogy and the manic irresponsibility of law as ideology.

What exactly is the regime of rights, or its reverse side, the rule of law? The rule of law exists when powerholders remain bound by general rules, even if these are rules established by the powerholders themselves. For them to be bound means, in part, that the rules must be interpreted, applied, and enforced in ways that can be publicly understood. The reasons for decision must not turn on case-by-case judgements of strategic interests bearing no general and reasonable relation to the rules. The consequences of an interpretation may be relevant to its persuasiveness, but only so long as they draw weight and meaning from impersonal goals of welfare or right.

When the rule of law prevails, people enjoy security in a regime of rights. They know that established law and legal doctrine will shape their entitlements, and that the interpretive development of legal rules and doctrines over time will be shaped by the common understanding of words as well as by impersonal concerns, reasonably attributed to the law, that all can grasp. Consequently, the rule of law and the regime of rights can exist even in the absence of democracy. A certain kind of unliberal democracy – democracy as majoritarian government – can exist without the regime of rights.

Rationalizing legal analysis and the regime of rights

The rule of law and the regime of rights, so the argument goes, require rationalizing legal analysis, or something very much like it, as the public method for the understanding of law and for its development through justified application. In this practice of "reasoned elaboration" of law as a purposive enterprise, the concern with generality of understanding and application is paramount. We must respect the distinction between lawmaking and law application. We must balance deference to past precedent against the need to leave the law, after a decision, in an organized state: one allowing judges, other officials, lawyers, and ordinary people alike to understand and to obey the law, and every extended part of it, as a reasonable plan rather than as a formless collection of accidents and deals. In such a plan, differences of treatment relate to governing purposes, described as policy and principle.

In assessing the claim of rationalizing legal analysis to represent the indispensable antidote to arbitrariness in law, we must ask comparative questions. Every practice of legal analysis, short of an extreme and impractical deductivism, recognizes some leeway of judgement as necessary to its work. Every practice of legal analysis, short of an extreme and impractical intuitionism, generates opportunities for discretionary judgement that it resists seizing, for fear that to seize them would be to claim and to impose illegitimate and unsustainable power. Rationalizing legal analysis, it turns out, generates forms of arbitrariness that are at least as troubling, intellectually and politically, as those of its familiar rivals. Its claim to be required by the rule of law or the regime of rights is, therefore, untenable.

The two genealogies of law

Begin with the contrast, implied by the rationalist reconstruction of law and its method of reasoned elaboration, between the prospective and the retrospective genealogies of the legal order. Prospectively, the law is the product of real collective conflict, carried on over a long time, among many different wills and imaginations, interests and visions. When the rule of law is established in the form of democracy, this pluralism gains explicit and affirmative value: to make possible the collective choice of social arrangements in the presence of deeply rooted pluralism and to organize the conflict so as to invigorate the pluralism rather than suppressing it is one way to define the point of democracy. If democracy were simply an attempt to discover and approximate a justified scheme of life, ordinarily best known to experts and philosophers, or if its conflicts of interest and vision were shallow or unworthy, the proper role of democratic institutions in a democratic society would be marginal and the scope of democratic choice narrow.

The shaping force of the plurality of interests and visions, wills and imaginations, in the prospective genealogy of law is not confined to democratic societies. It holds, in historical fact if not in official doctrine, for almost any real social situation. It fails to hold only in two limiting – and largely mythical – circumstances.

In one such circumstance lawmaking power is concentrated in a single mind, or in a tightly knit group of like-minded rulers. It is not enough, however, for these individual or collective dictators to wield all power; it is necessary that they somehow manage to keep this power over time, preventing their successors from abridging it. Then, even more miraculously, they must render society pliant to their wishes and prevent it from changing their laws in the course of applying them. To execute such a design they need intermediaries – slave masters and sentinels. Such underlings, however, threaten to have aims of their own.

The other limiting case is that of the fictional tribal society in which consensus of value and understanding smothers conflict of will and imagination. In such a circumstance, however, custom takes the place of state-created law; the same activities serve to make, reproduce, and apply law.

Law produced through the prospective genealogy of irremediable conflict will be messy, and all the more messy in a democracy valuing and institutionalizing pluralism. It will be rich in compromises embodying different balances among contrasting interests and visions. Warring solutions to similar problems will coexist. Their boundaries of application will continue uncertain. Interests and ideals favored in some domains will be discounted in others for no better reason than the sequence in which certain decisive conflicts took place and the relative influence enjoyed by contending parties of opinion at each time. Intellectual fashions will join with preponderant interests to produce results that neither interests nor fashions alone would have allowed us to predict. Defeated or rejected solutions will remain, incongruously, in corners of the law as vestiges of past approaches and prophecies of possible alternatives. Multiple exceptions will eviscerate solutions thought to be dominant. The potential of such exceptions to become alternative general solutions will nevertheless lie dormant. What to some seems the sleep of reason will be hailed by others as the genius of compromise and the triumph of experience.

Law as represented from the retrospective standpoint of rationalizing legal analysis, however, must show another face. Large chunks of law, with their integral gloss of received legal understanding, must be redescribed and reconstructed as gropings toward a plan. Moreover, it must be a plan yielding to statement in the generalizing and relatively abstract language of principle and policy. The abstraction-resistant logic of a Burkean traditionalist – or, for that matter, of the classical Roman jurists – will not be good enough. Such a plan is one that a single mind – a single will and a single imagination – might have conceived.

Revisionary power

According to the tenets of this dominant jurisprudence, legal analysis must enjoy a measure of revisionary power. The legal analyst must be free to reject some of the received legal understandings as mistaken as he refines and develops the interpretive scheme of policy and principle. Revisionary power is not merely a requirement of practical efficacy, exercised to adapt received law to changing circumstance. It is also an imperative of rational persuasion.

Every law student has had the experience of a suspect ease at performing retrospective rationalization: given, for example, a small number of seemingly inconsistent decisions and a call to reconcile them, there is almost always some more or less plausible set of purposes, arguments, and distinctions that can lend a semblance of ordered reason to the material. Some such efforts may be more convincing than others: there is a sliding scale of plausibility and persuasion. On this scale, however, we find no clear markers distinguishing the legitimate and the exorbitant instances of retrospective justification.

If legal analysis were to make sense of all the received legal understandings, it would make sense of none of them. Revisionary power is a condition of persuasive authority as well as of practical adaptability.

From connected policies and principles to theory-like conceptions

Given a stipulated measure of revisionary power, how do we know which received legal understandings in a certain part of law to reject as mistaken? We must see which of these understandings fail to fit the developing scheme of policy and principle. These purposes and policies amount, in turn, to fragments of a more comprehensive prescriptive conception of whole areas of law and social practice. Such conceptions must have a theory-like character.

To be sure, for all but the academic jurists, the transformation of connected sets of policies and principles into fully articulated prescriptive conceptions may be left unrealized, as an ideal limit or a regulatory ideal, rather than an actual achievement, of discourse. Although the transformation may be left unrealized, it must nevertheless be presupposed. If connected policies and principles were not fragments of more comprehensive, theory-like conceptions, they would be little more than glorified grounds for analogical comparison and distinction. The same arguments applying against the disorder of analogy would apply against them. If principles and policies fail to be anchored below in context-bound analogies, they must be fastened, above, to prescriptive theories. This fastening highlights further the contrast between the prospective and the retrospective genealogies of law: between law as the product of relatively disordered conflict and law as the expression of relatively ordered theory.

Insight into the role of theory-like conceptions as ideal limits of policy and principle arguments enables us to sharpen the contrast between the two genealogies of law. Rationalizing legal analysis and its supporting theories represent extended areas of law and legal doctrine as moving toward the conceptual order of comprehensive prescriptive theories. These may be theories of the market, or of representative democracy, or of reciprocal responsibilities owed individuals in everyday life, or of the family and the development of personality within it. The voice of reason must speak, although belatedly, in history, redescribing and reorienting the historical mess.

Too much revisionary power is just as incompatible with the self-appointed mission of professional legal reasoning as too little. Its consequence would be to undermine altogether the difference between interpreting law and applying it. Under cover of interpreting the law, the legal analysts would become its real authors, usurping the powers of the democratic branches of government and upsetting security in the enjoyment of rights. It is not clear what the suitable measure of revisionary power in rationalizing legal analysis is, nor even where we should look for the ideas and standards that would guide us in setting such a measure. I shall soon return to this problem. For the moment it is enough to appreciate that the integrity of rationalizing legal analysis requires that severe constraints apply to the exercise of its revisionary power.

The ineradicable divergence between the two genealogies of law

For such constraints to be workable, the prospective and the retrospective genealogies of law must intersect to a large degree – to what degree exactly depends upon our view of the suitable measure of revisionary power. Law prospectively made as the product of conflicting wills and imaginations, interests and ideals, must resemble law retrospectively represented as the expression of connected policies and principles. The legal analysts must bridge the gap, whatever it is, by exercising the revisionary power of legal analysis. An unacknowledged and covert exercise of this power is an even more troubling source of arbitrary and unjustified power than a candid recognition of it. If, however, the gap between the prospective and the retrospective genealogies of law becomes too great, the pressure will be overwhelming to conceal some of the revisionary exercise, presenting as faithful interpretation what is in fact reconstructive improvement.

On what assumptions could the prospective and retrospective genealogies substantially coincide in their results? We must suppose that the lawmaking forces are not as distinct and opposed as they think they are. They act as agents of hidden assumptions – a latent shared consciousness or ideology – or of dimly understood practical imperatives – such as the institutionally determinate imperatives of efficiency and growth. It is not enough for these hidden, shaping constraints to apply statically, at slices of historical time. They must provide an evolutionary logic, moving law over time in the direction of a plan that we can, after the fact, redescribe in the language of developing and consistent ideal conceptions. From the dark battlefield, where ignorant armies clash, comes the rational plan. We can recognize its shape only after the half-conscious builders have already put its elements in place. The intersection of the prospective and the retrospective genealogies of law depends upon the belief in an immanent evolutionary rationality, practical or moral, commanding the development of law and dwarfing the apparent antagonism of the lawmakers. Legal analysis may fill in the holes, and refine the rough edges, in the legitimate fulfillment of its responsibility for improvement. To a large extent, however, it plays the role of the Hegelian Owl of Minerva, spreading its wings at the fall of dusk and revealing to power its hitherto unrecognized reason.

The contrast between the prospective and the retrospective genealogies of law applies less clearly to judge-made law like the

Anglo-American common law. Notice, however, why. The power to declare law must be concentrated in a relatively insulated and continuous elite. This elite may believe its task to be that of working out over time the requirements of implicit norms of human coordination or social hierarchy, norms only marginally influenced by conscious choice. The presupposition of an immanent evolutionary logic continues to hold in such a view. We reconcile the prospective and the retrospective genealogies of law by circumscribing the scope of conflict and choice about the terms of social life. To the extent we see judges and judicial decisions, in a system of judge-made law, as agents of contentious, factional interests and visions, the problem of the two genealogies reappears.

The contrast between the retrospective and the prospective genealogies of law has left its mark in the two conventional vocabularies of law talk: the interest-group language of law as deals and the idealizing language of law as policy and principle. Neither vocabulary is an accurate description of the law-related practices in which it is chiefly deployed. Their uneasy coexistence nevertheless provides an oblique testimonial to the problem of the double genealogy of law.

There are two distinct problems with the assumptions that would entitle us to hope for a substantial overlap between the two genealogies. First, these assumptions have become literally unbelievable in the light of the development of contemporary social and historical thought. Second, were they true, they would have the effect of weakening the significance of democracy, drastically limiting the range of social affairs we can bring under democratic control. Consider each of these objections in turn.

We hardly need take a very controversial stand in the disputes of contemporary social theory to recognize that the related ideas of a short list of possible institutional systems and of a predetermined evolutionary sequence of stages of institutional development have both taken a beating. Historical learning and practical experience have joined to undermine them. It is true that the combination of functional explanation with assumptions about the existence of indivisible institutional systems or stages has survived in certain variants of economics and of economically oriented institutional history. The overall direction of social and historical studies for over a century can nevertheless be described as a halting march away from this once dominant species of determinism. Its residues survive in our vocabulary – in our use of terms such as capitalism or in our contrast between revolutionary and reformist politics – even as we try to extirpate it from our active beliefs.

We may continue to believe that functional advantages – comparative success, for example, in favoring technological dynamism or resource and manpower mobilization – may help account for the relative success of certain arrangements. However, the functional advantages do not select out from a closed list or a unilinear sequence of institutional orders. They work with the institutional and ideological materials that lie at hand, and that happen to have been generated by many loosely linked sequences of practical and imaginative conflict.

Moreover, a preexisting structure of influence and advantage always tilts the scales of institutional choice: the functional advantage is usually balanced against the pressure to minimize the trauma to the established structure of privilege. Thus, for example, instead of seeing the system of private law fashioned in eighteenth- and nineteenth-century Europe as the discovery of the natural legal structure of market society, we have begun to see it, more realistically, as a compromise. It reconciled the prerogatives of the social classes formed in the decaying hollow of the European *Ständestaat* with the practical advantages offered by the decentralization of economic opportunities and the generalization of economic rights. If the compromise was ramshackle and movable in the large, it was also ramshackle and movable in each of its parts.

I have already suggested how nineteenth-century legal science, having set out to vindicate the idea of a rational system of rights, contributed, through its self-subversive power, to the overthrow of this conception. If contemporary social and historical studies have failed to reject evolutionary and functionalist determinism even more decisively, the reason may lie in the unfounded though understandable fear that too thoroughgoing a rejection of the determinist creed will abandon us to causal agnosticism.

It is true that the combination of functional explanation with assumptions about the identity, indivisibility, and sequence of institutional systems, and with beliefs about the lawlike forces governing their evolution, hardly exhausts the possible ways of justifying the idea of a rational scheme revealed through the historical development of law. It has nevertheless been the most sophisticated and influential brand of legal–institutional determinism so far. The objections against it apply to all styles of explanation that discount the path dependency of social change, the looseness of the relations among the many sequences bound up in any real history, the destabilizing influence of breakthroughs and failures of imagination, and the tendency of our ideas about social and historical reality and possibility to become self-fulfilling prophecies.

Moreover, an evolutionary logic capable of reconciling the prospective and the retrospective genealogies of law needs to do more than explain convergence toward an institutional system with a logic of its own. It needs to account for convergence toward a justified order: one that it would be both futile and wrong to resist. This is a standard that even the functionalist and evolutionary determinism of yesterday's social theories have trouble meeting. It requires confidence in the self-executing convergence of might and right. It relies upon a rightwing Hegelianism. Rightwing Hegelianism is, in effect, the secret philosophy of history of the rationalizing legal analyst. However, it cannot stand the light of day; its influence depends upon its largely unconscious character.

Suppose, however, that some such account of the overlap between the retrospective and the prospective genealogies of law did hold good. The consequences would be embarrassing to the claims of democracy. Collective self-government, with guarantees of pluralism and dissent and safeguards against public and private oppression, would remain possible. Nevertheless, the range of social life open to collective – or individual – self-determination would greatly narrow. Democracy must mean, among other things, the power to choose the terms of social life, not to have them imposed, without our knowledge or consent, through the hidden influence of determining forces. If democracy restricts the scope of collective self-determination through majority rule and party government, it does so in the name of respect for individual self-determination as well as out of a desire to uphold the conditions for rotation in government. A hidden rational plan, retrospectively manifest in the development of law, empties both individual and collective self-determination of much of their power. It turns them into the unconscious instruments for affirming a higher, providential necessity. Organized collective conflict and controversy may seem less important than expertise in understanding, as a lawyer, an economist, or a philosopher, the dictates of this rational destiny. Democracy, however, opposes destiny, whether the destiny is rational or not.

The two dirty little secrets of contemporary jurisprudence – jurisprudence in the age of rationalizing legal analysis – are its reliance upon a rightwing Hegelian view of social and legal history and its discomfort with democracy: the worship of historical triumph and the fear of popular action. The rightwing Hegelianism finds expression in a daily practice emphasizing the cunning of history in developing rational order – advances toward allocational efficiency, or clarifications of institutional responsibility, or principles of moral and political right – out of the unpromising stuff of historical conflict and compromise. The discomfort with democracy shows up in every area of contemporary legal culture: in the ceaseless identification of restraints upon majority rule, rather than of restraints upon the power of dominant minorities, as the overriding responsibility of judges and jurists; in the consequent hypertrophy of countermajoritarian practices and arrangements; in the opposition to all institutional reforms, particularly those designed to heighten the level of popular political enagagement, as threats to a regime of rights; in the equation of the rights of property with the rights of dissent; in the effort to obtain from judges, under the cover of improving interpretation, the advances popular politics fail to deliver; in the abandonment of institutional reconstruction to rare and magical moments of national refoundation; in the single-minded focus upon the higher judges and their selection as the most important part of democratic politics; in an ideal of deliberative democracy as most acceptable when closest in style to a polite conversation among gentlemen in an eighteenth-century drawing room; and, occasionally, in the explicit treatment of party government as a subsidiary, last-ditch source of legal evolution, to be tolerated when none of the more refined modes of legal resolution applies. Fear and loathing of the people always threaten to become the ruling passions of this legal culture. Far from being confined to conservative variants of contemporary legal doctrine, these passions have left their mark upon centrist and progressive legal thought.

Consider, for example, the single most characteristic and influential piece of American legal thought in the second half of the twentieth century: the Hart and Sacks legal process materials, only recently published in book form. This work attempted to absorb some of the legal realist critique of traditional doctrinal methods and to accommodate the variety of forms of lawmaking that proliferated in the aftermath of the New Deal while vindicating the method of purposive policy-oriented and principle-based analysis as the lawyer's master tool. It fell squarely within what I earlier described as the second, rationalizing moment of contemporary legal consciousness. In the legal process materials, however, lawmaking by democratic legislatures appears as a last-ditch way to make law, when all else fails. We find ourselves suddenly and incongruously thrown back to the world of late medieval legal theory in which the prince's *gubernaculum* – now exercised by the democratic branches of government – represents an episodic, corrective intervention in a seamless web of coordination, patiently reproduced by the *jurisdictio* of all the case-deciding agencies of government and society.

This marginalization of what we expect, in a democratic society, to be the chief source of law makes the work of rationalizing reconstruction more plausible. If we can quarantine the political branches and leave the case-by-case development of law in the hands of experts committed to a method of reasoned elaboration, we can expect the law over time to "work itself pure." The restraints upon democracy open the space in which the self-fulfilling prophecies of rightwing Hegelianism can come to pass. A law that is constantly worked over by the votaries of policy and principle may eventually look as if it were the expression of the theory-like prescriptive conceptions toward which policy and principle arguments must move.

The provisional conclusion of the argument carried up to this point is that we lack a credible and legitimate bridge between the prospective and the retrospective genealogies of law. Some have hoped to supply the missing link by resorting to a special set of legitimating and restraining ideas about the exercise of revisionary power in legal analysis. The law as seen by judges, or by legal analysts standing in the imaginative position of judges, ought, on this view, to look different from how it may look to a citizen, an historian, or a social scientist. A modest measure of revisionary power is all professional legal analysis can properly enjoy. A self-restrained exercise of this power will suffice to close the gap between law as politics and law as reason.

Revisionary power reconsidered

Return now to the question left open earlier. To what ideas can we safely appeal in the effort to determine the proper measure of revisionary power in legal analysis? Consider the leading candidates. We may say that professional tradition within a legal culture determines the suitable level of revisionary power. Supposing we could agree to grant the jurists this implied authority over the reconstructive reach of their own discourse, we would still find that the factual assumption of the proposal fails. There usually exists no consensus among the jurists, much less within the larger society, about the level of revisionary power suitable to legal analysis. Everyone has heard of the American debates about judicial activism and judicial self-restraint, the vocabulary in which Americans have most often dealt with the problem of revisionary power. A similar debate, cast in a different vocabulary, has existed in every major legal tradition – common-law and civilian, secular and religious law. A chain of analogous concerns extends from the discussion of judicial activism in the United States to the ancient disputes about the creative power of the *istihsan* and *istislah* in the Islamic shari'a. Controversy over the extent of revisionary power is pervasive and irrepressible because it raises, in the form of a question about method, the most conflictual of queries: Who can do what to whom?

A second proposal for the source of a revision-making standard is the appeal to a prescriptive theory of the proper responsibilities of a judge in particular or of a professional legal analyst in general. If the regime of rights is established within a political democracy, such a doctrine would be a variant of democratic theory. To serve the purpose, however, it must not merely be someone's controversial theory. It must be the account of the responsibilities of the different agents of a legal system that makes the best sense of the institutional traditions, arrangements, and ideals of the polity – best sense meaning both the most sense and the most defensible sense. It must, in other words, have the same relation to these institutional rules that connected policies and principles, and the ideal conceptions they become, have to established law and to received legal understandings generally.

Now, however, we find ourselves back with the problem of the two genealogies and of the unbridgeable gap between them. The role-shaping arrangements of a particular legal system are as much products of contending wills and imaginations, of clashing ideas and interests, as any other part of the law. What seems established at any given time is the outcome of many loosely linked sequences of conflict and controversy, and of the more or less lopsided compromises that contained them for a while. The assumptions on which such compromises could converge toward a theory-like conception are neither credible nor legitimate. If we could believe them, we would find their implications for democracy disconcerting.

When we put aside the consensual and the theoretical solutions to the problem of setting the standard of revisionary power in legal analysis, we may come to a third, agnostic position. From this position we refuse to sit in judgement on a collective discursive practice such as legal analysis. We hold that such practices are deeper than our theories and richer than our agreements. We say that the appropriate level of revisionary power in legal reasoning is just the one that legal reasoning possesses. We must then keep our fingers crossed that the amount of revision required for a good-faith exercise of the method of purposive policy and principle will remain modest, modest enough to maintain the distinctions between legislation and adjudication as well as between the open conflict of interests and ideologies in party politics and the reasoned development of judge-made law.

What entitles us to keep our fingers crossed in this expectation? We need to find the entitlement in beliefs that would explain how the prospective and the retrospective genealogies of law might turn out substantially to coincide. The gap between the two genealogies may remain so wide that any actual extent to which legal analysis rejects received legal understandings as mistaken may be too little to rescue the law from its analogical and political disorder, yet too much to preserve the difference between law and politics. Thus, the discussion of revisionary power in legal doctrine ends up restating, rather than relieving, the problem of divergence between law as prospectively made and law as retrospectively represented and reconstructed.

The argumentative structure of contemporary legal theory

The recurrent argumentative structure of contemporary mainstream schools of legal thought now becomes more intelligible. Remember that each of these schools recognizes the need to ground the discussion of policy and principle in a set of theory-like prescriptive conceptions. Each refuses to treat the guiding purposes invoked in legal reasoning as merely magnified reasons to make or to reject analogical comparisons. Each gives priority to the vocabulary suited to its preferred conceptions: doctrines of moral and political right, goals of allocational efficiency, or standards for keeping each agency of the legal process to its own business. Each school acknowledges that the legal analyst must put some of the ideational material of policy and principle into the law in the legitimate exercise of his improving work while discovering some of the material already there, waiting to be made patent, in the established law. Each walks the line between an unbelievable idealization of the law, which might give cover to the usurpation of power by lawyers, and the outright usurpation of power that would result from the hypertrophy of the lawyers' responsibility to improve law through the revisionary rejection of some received legal understandings as mistaken. For each, the problem of the intersection between the prospective and the retrospective genealogies of law remains crucial: there must be a large degree of intersection for the restraints upon the improvement and the idealization of law to be simultaneously feasible.

None of these schools of legal thought, however, offers a persuasive or even articulate reason to suppose that such a large-scale intersection exists. None shows how it could exist, if it did, without making trouble for the claims of democracy. Each is, therefore, permeated by the spirit of rightwing Hegelianism, implying an immanent and authoritative rationality in the development of law. Each has a hard time reconciling itself to the idea that democratic politics might be the primary, rather than a subsidiary or ultimate, source of law.

The idea that legal history is punctuated by interludes of collective enthusiasm and institutional innovation – such as the post-Civil War Reconstruction and the New Deal in the United States – moderates this discomfort with democratic politics without removing it. In this view, normal legal analysis remains remote, in its methods and attitudes, from the creative moments that give it its cues. Nevertheless, this two-track approach to legal history absorbs more democracy than do the conventional schools of legal thought precisely because it concedes less to rightwing Hegelianism. The moments of collective refoundation interrupt, unpredictably, the evolutionary progress of law, introducing untried ideas and highlighting suppressed anxieties.

Arbitrariness in the antidote to arbitrariness

We now have the means to identify and explain the overlapping and complementary forms of arbitrariness characteristic of rationalizing legal analysis. There is the arbitrariness that consists in choosing one vocabulary of policy and principle rather than another and one family of theory-like prescriptive conceptions instead of its rivals. If the identity of functional advantages and teleological forces in history is irremediably controversial, its controversial character becomes troubling when the choice of teleologies turns into a reason to wield coercive state power in one way rather than another.

There is the arbitrariness that comes from stretching the ordered rationality of established law and legal understanding: the trouble is that it can be stretched, more or less plausibly, in too many different ways, depending upon the preferred vocabulary for talking about policy and principle. To every increment of stretching there corresponds some unacknowledged and unaccountable exercise of power.

There is the arbitrariness that results from doing the work of overt improvement more or less resolutely – that is to say, with more or less revisionary power. Not only do we lack an agreed-upon definition of the appropriate measure of revisionary power; we also lack a body of ideas to which we can justifiably turn in the search for such a standard.

There is the arbitrariness produced by the impulse to play fast and loose with whatever theory-like conceptions of connected policy and principle we happen to prefer, tinkering with the conceptions in ad hoc ways the better to limit their overt conflict with established law and legal understanding.

Is the cumulative effect of these related forms of arbitrariness greater or smaller than the homely uncertainties of context-bound and open-ended analogical reasoning? We lack the metric with which to make this comparison. What we can say with assurance, however, is that the element of misunderstood and undisciplined discretion in rationalizing legal analysis is both less transparent and more ambitious than its counterparts in the disorder of casuistry.

It is less transparent because it depends in each instance upon the speculative use of speculative conceptions, in a context of practical decision in which the pressure is heavy to understate controversy. The pressure is heavy because the whole point of the exercise is to sustain the view of legal analysis as a practice of highly bounded and guided rational deliberation. The analogist wears his uncertainties on his sleeve, exhibiting them as part of his business. The rationalizing legal analyst must deny his brands of arbitrariness because each of them brings him face to face with the demoralizing problem of the two genealogies and of the gap between them.

If the arbitrariness of the method of principle and policy is less transparent than its equivalents in analogical reasoning, it is also more ambitious. More than providing just another description of law, it proposes another way to make law better. Moreover, it wins some of its territory from the retreat of popular democracy.

The interpretation and defense of rationalizing legal analysis as a requirement of the rule of law or of a regime of rights therefore fail. The canonical style of legal doctrine cannot be understood as the inevitable consequence of the need to think clearly and connectedly about law. Nor can we explain and justify it as the antidote to arbitrariness that secures the rule of law and a regime of rights. It needs a more focused purpose.

THE FOURFOLD ROOT OF RATIONALIZING LEGAL ANALYSIS: PESSIMISTIC PROGRESSIVE REFORMISM

Conservative reformism

Conservative reformism is the family of political projects to which rationalizing legal analysis has been harnessed and from which it has received much of its energy and its meaning. When we can no longer make sense of the generalizing and idealizing method of legal thought as a requirement of the rule of law, we can still make sense of it as the indispensable tool of a certain way of diminishing the evils of society by improving the effects of the law. The distinctive characteristic of conservative reformism is the combination of commitment to programmatic aims with institutional conservatism.

The programmatic aims in conservative reformism are the familiar ideological commitments defining the major positions in contemporary political and legal debates. They may be cast in the vocabulary of the political parties, and of the latent parties of opinion: economic competition and individual initiative, broader and more equal distribution of the benefits of economic growth and of opportunities for political and cultural voice, greater social solidarity and development of associational life. Alternatively, they may appear in the language of the social policies and ideals lawyers impute to bodies of law: standards of antisubjugation and antidiscrimination, for example, in contexts in which legislation shapes the distribution of governmental benefits, or presumptions of fiduciary responsibility in situations in which managerial self-interest conflicts with responsibility to absent principals and stakeholders. There are no hard and fast distinctions between the expression of these ideal commitments in party politics and in law, and the distinctions among the ideals themselves remain elusive and evanescent. All come from the world of ideas about the democratic project. All, therefore, bear upon the area of overlap between the conditions of material progress and the conditions of individual emancipation.

In the discourse of conservative reformism, these ideals, and the ways in which we relate them to group interests, are to be defined and executed within the framework of the established institutions, especially the inherited institutional forms of representative democracy, the market economy, and a free civil society. There may be occasional and localized institutional adjustments, but they will be treated as adaptations to changed circumstance, or as returns to the canonical form of the regulated market economy, rather than as the possible beginnings of one or another route of cumulative structural change. The distinction between refining the institutional order and changing it may seem relative, and indeed it is. The argument of this section, however, supports the thesis that it matters whether the main focus of imaginative and practical energy lies in the effort to make the best out of the established institutional order or in the attempt to generalize and extend an experimentalist tinkering with this structure. It matters to the future of democracy and therefore to hopes for freedom and prosperity.

All versions of conservative reformism -- the standard type of a programmatic position in contemporary politics – suffer from a characteristic internal instability. The two sides of each position – the defining ideal commitments and the institutional conservatism – fight against each other. When we hold fast to the established institutional structure we discover that we give up much of our professed ideal. If, for example, our program is one of extending economic competition and decentralization, but the established property regime prevents further breakup of aggregations of economic power without great losses in economic efficiency, we may resign ourselves to the decentralization possible under the present system, singling out for punishment only the most egregious instances of monopoly power. So we must look elsewhere, to the increase of output, for example, in the hope that its benefits may "trickle down" to the working majority of the country.

Conversely, we may radicalize our defining commitment and transgress, for its sake, the boundaries of the established institutional settlement. In my example, transgression means looking for successive alterations of the property regime that would make higher levels of economic decentralization possible, without sacrificing scale or efficiency. The method is to allow property claims that are fragmented in some respects to be pooled or combined in other respects. Having radicalized our commitments by tinkering with their habitual institutional forms, we soon find that the actual or imagined institutional change prompts us to redefine our commitments.

Our conception of economic democracy and of its relation to political democracy changes. The familiar contrasts between right and left start to shift under our feet, for what had seemed to be a conservative program – the program of free markets and passive government – now turns out to be a radical program, requiring the dissociation of property rights. The dismemberment of traditional property rights and the vesting of their component powers in different rightholders may in turn facilitate and demand practices of cooperative competition among firms and decentralized partnerships between firms and governments.

The standard situation in contemporary political and legal debates is that the choice between retrenchment and radicalization is never explicitly made. However, the avoidance of the choice through the unresolved conflict between ideal commitments and institutional assumptions is hardly neutral between these two options; it amounts to a *de facto* retrenchment of the ideal commitments under the disguise of their rhetorical reiteration. In the following discussion of rationalizing legal analysis as reformist politics, there will be many occasions to see how the problem of internal instability comes to occupy a central place in lawyers' work and how its characteristic nonresolution produces an effective retrenchment of the ideals attributed, as policy and principle, to law.

Pessimistic progressive reformism

The social-democratic compromise and the practice of rational reconstruction in legal analysis are the two most important examples of conservative reformism, uniting in themselves the ideal commitments and the institutional conservatism of contemporary politics. They connect by theme as well as by assumptions: much of the most ambitious political and intellectual work of rationalizing legal analysis has consisted in developing the categories and doctrines that reconcile the regulatory and redistributive law of the social-democratic compromise with the preexisting corpus of legal doctrine. This deep connection helps explain the extraordinary authority of the brand of conservative reformism we might label pessimistic progressive reformism.

Pessimistic progressive reformism is the commitment to treat the weakest and poorest groups in society – those most likely to have lost out in the political struggles over lawmaking – as the primary beneficiaries of the rational and retrospective reconstruction of law. By representing law as the expression of connected policy and principle, regarding impersonal conceptions of the common good or of political right, the jurist gains the power to tame the strong and to protect the weak. He can redistribute rights and resources, marginally but significantly, to those who stand in greatest need of them. He can do so in part by finding the rudiments of the improved understanding of law in the established legal materials and in part by exercising his proper role of correction and completion of the law.

What saves this view of the mission of the jurists from some of its paternalist and sectarian character (making the weak the lawyers' wards) is an idea that, although rarely articulated, exercises enormous influence over the self-image and the program of legal thought. There is an important sense in which the average citizen of a rich industrial democracy – not just the member of "discrete and insular minorities" – feels himself to be an angry outsider, angry at his rulers or his bosses or both and powerless to change the constraints upon his situation. Students of popular consciousness and political culture have observed that the belief that the state and big business are run as a racket to the benefit of predatory elites is widespread. This belief may sometimes take a surprising turn when it combines with the idea that these elites secure social peace by distributing benefits to an underclass or to social marginals and misfits while sacrificing the interests of the broad mass of working people.

In such a setting the legal work of pessimistic progressive reformism takes on a charged and focused meaning. It may count as an example – indeed the prime example – of the implicit partnership between the elites and the marginalized at the cost of the ordinary working people. However, it may also serve as an instrument with which to lighten the influence of self-serving elites upon the substance and the administration of law. To this extent, the ward of the jurist becomes everyman. The condition for this role reversal, however, is that the pretenses of popular democracy fail to hold true. As a result, everyman becomes the vulnerable outsider on which the real makers of law are forever likely to dump. The practitioner of rationalizing legal analysis is to be his friend.

Rationalizing legal analysis as aversive social therapy

The central theme in the argument of this section is the way in which rationalizing legal analysis, at its intellectually and politically most ambitious, becomes an aversive therapy for the ills of industrial democracies, striving to moderate disadvantage and exclusion, yet prevented by its method and vision from identifying or addressing the sources of these evils in the arrangements of society. It makes sense to understand the jurisprudence of policy and principle as the instrument of a certain style of reformism. However, study of the connections between the legal and the political parts of this project helps undermine faith in both. A nonaversive therapy, it turns out, could not be rationalizing legal analysis, nor could it have judges as its chief agents. It would have to be legal analysis recast as institutional imagination. Its primary interlocutor would be the democratic citizenry at large. Its chief ambition would be to inform the conversation in the democracy about the collective present and the alternative collective futures, deepening the sense of reality by broadening the sense of possibility.

The country in which the legal work of pessimistic progressive reformism has advanced furthest is the United States. The sanctity attaching to the American constitution and, by extension from it, to other parts of the institutional order, the antiprogrammatic and antimobilizational quality of much of ordinary American political discourse, the famous habit of recasting political issues as judicial ones, and the position of lawyers as self-confident coordinators of the political and economic elites rather than as a distinct and subordinate caste within the elites have all joined to make the translation of conservative reformism into legal discourse seem especially plausible. In moments when progressive lawyers have despaired of the possibilities of popular politics or feared its dangers, and found the doors of the political branches of government closed, they have been especially tempted to see in politics through judges the providential surrogate for politics through politics. They have then been regularly disappointed. Just as regularly they have failed to draw from their disappointment the right lessons.

The example of substantive equal protection: rational disharmonies

In the history of recent American law and legal thought the most spectacular example of progressive pessimistic reformism has been the development of the doctrine of substantive equal protection in constitutional law as well as the related body of rules, doctrines, categories, and ideals in the law of antidiscrimination. An exploration of the limits of this legal endeavor – its limits as social imagination and, above all, as social reform – sheds light not only upon pessimistic progressive reformism but also upon the larger family of political projects to which it belongs. If only we press far enough in this direction, we come to the threshold of legal analysis as institutional imagination. The criticism itself forges many of the instruments that a practice of legal reasoning more loyal to both experimentalism and democracy requires.

After a brief reference to the disharmonies of equal-protection doctrine I go on to discuss the grounds for skepticism about the power of that doctrine, and of doctrines like it, to help the people who would most stand in need of its help. I broaden the discussion by showing how, in two contrasting political economies, rationalizing legal analysis as social reform is driven by its vision and its method to pursue aims only obliquely related to the real sources of collective anxiety and group disadvantage. Then I deepen the discussion by exploring the connections between the practical infirmities and the imaginative deficiencies of this legal discourse. The reasons why it works so selectively, and sometimes so perversely, as social reform connect closely to the reasons for the myopia of its insight into social reality and social possibility.

The equal-protection clause of the constitution of the United States has become the favored vessel of ambitious reformist rationalization of the law, just as in the period of the Lochner-style decisions the due process clause of the constitution had served the same purpose. By the close of the twentieth century, however, the range and the variety of work that equal-protection doctrine was made to do had strained the conceptual consistency of the doctrine beyond repair. The result was a characteristic conflict between the pressure to make feasible compromises, or to have legal doctrine echo the political compromises that had been made, and the countervailing impulse to tell a general story about the law that would work as political theory.

What is the story about the shape of equal-protection doctrine that tracks the actual doctrinal distinctions as they stood at the close of the twentieth century while remaining in communion with a theory-like account of motivating ideals and of the relation of these ideals to social practices? For the sake of exemplary simplification, focus upon one half of substantive equal-protection doctrine, the system of suspect classifications, heightening scrutiny of the differential treatment of people by law. Race was the clear instance of a suspect classification, triggering the highest degree of scrutiny. Gender and age had been added, triggering a lower, "intermediate" level of scrutiny. Physical impairment and sexual orientation had come most recently onto the list. Their status remained uncertain. Put to one side the other, complementary half of the doctrine, the effort to evaluate the differential treatment by reference to the relatively fundamental character of the private interests it violates and the relatively compelling character of the governmental goals it serves. Because so much conflict over the content of law takes the form of a struggle over the distinction in the treatment of people, equal-protection doctrine occupies a special place in the system of legal ideas. It is not merely another topic within the law; it is also, by synecdoche, the problem of law itself, just as property is not simply another right but the exemplary instance of rights.

To appreciate the explosive potential of the doctrine of substantive equal protection, and the perplexing character of the constraints imposed upon its expansion, imagine its application to the vital citizen-forming and hierarchy-generating subject of education. The separation between private and public schools in the United States is part of a system enabling the professional–business class in much of the country to opt out of the public-school system, and send their children to favored private schools. The shrinking of the parochial-school system that has accompanied, in the United States, the decline of the Catholic working class has accentuated the contrast between the elite private schools and the public schools. The association of democracy in public education with local control has further aggravated the problem of educational hierarchy: first, by making schools dependent upon local finance and, second, by strengthening the hold of families and communities over the schools in their midst. The first mission of the school in a democracy is to rescue the child from his family, his class, his country, and his historical period, equipping him with the means to think for himself, by broadening his access to alien experience. The future citizen must be a little prophet. The hereditary transmission of educational opportunity converges with the hereditary transmission of economic advantage to produce a class society. Class society conspires with community and family control to stunt and silence the little prophet.

Suppose you concluded that to undermine this hierarchy and break this conspiracy we need to prohibit the private schools altogether in those parts of the country where they are important. (For the public schools to change in other, more numerous parts of the country, social desegregation, by movement among neighborhoods, would have to develop on the model of racial desegregation. Although radical in reach, such a reform represents less of an imaginative stretch than the disbanding of private schools.) The professional–business class must be required to place its children in the public schools, and indeed in public schools subject to a program of social desegregation. The consequence would be twofold: they, the most influential element in the republic, would gain a vital interest in the improvement of the public schools, and their presence would help raise expectations in the classroom.

Although the consequences of such a change would be far-reaching, and would now in the United States seem unthinkable, the argument in its favor can readily be constructed by analogy to the single most famous instance of intended social reform through law in the history of twentieth-century America: the campaign for the racial desegregation of schools from the Brown decision onward. The attack on social apartheid would follow the attack on racial apartheid. The claim of "separate but equal," repudiated in one domain, would now be rejected in the neighboring domain. The movement from race to class in the list would occur in the area most tangibly connected with the social and cultural requirements of democracy.

Along the way, we would need to reinterpret state-action doctrine – the most notable residue of the nineteenth-century idea of a natural, prepolitical system of rights – as well as the right of free expression under the

First Amendment to the constitution. Of all "private" activities, schooling, the subject of legal obligations imposed upon parents, might most readily be understood to be "affected by a public function." Overcoming the First-Amendment obstacle would, in turn, demand an enrichment of our understanding of the content and conditions of free cultural life in a democracy. Just as we may come to demand that government fragment and redistribute access to the means of mass communication out of the characteristically modern ambition to make the exercise of the right of free expression real, so too we may come to see in the extirpation of social apartheid in education a necessary instrument of inclusive cultural emancipation and effectively informed citizenship.

These doctrinal obstacles, although formidable, are no more daunting than countless similar objections the law confronted and rejected in the course of bringing substantive equal-protection doctrine to its present state. The real constraints come from the balance of political forces and ideological conceptions. Simple national comparison suggests that this system of influences is more local and revisable than it may at first appear to be. For at the very time when prohibition of private schools seemed inconceivable in the United States, it was under active debate in the United Kingdom. The distance between the unthinkable and the familiar may be short in the history of politics and of law.

The point is simple. If problems like racial and social apartheid are to be imagined and solved in the form of legal doctrines, such as substantive equal protection, it is important to probe the hidden relations between different forms of legal imagination and different practices of social reform. Having set the stage for such an inquiry, rationalizing legal analysis turns off the lights.

Consider the most promising candidates for the role of an account of equal protection that makes sense as both detailed doctrine and coherent theory. The simplest and most comprehensive account defines the subject matter of the suspect classifications as those state-supported social disadvantages from which people find themselves unable to escape by the forms of economic and political initiative readily available to them. Equal protection would, on this view, be the chief of many instruments in contemporary law ensuring the conditions for the effective enjoyment of rights: of many rights, not just a particular right. It would generalize the most distinctive concern of contemporary law by overturning those obstacles to self-advancement through work, enterprise, and education in which the government is complicit. It would be a doctrine of antisubjugation, addressing not just the practical tools for the effective exercise of particular entitlements but the basic conditions for the use of the central nexus of political and economic capacities, vital to effective political and economic action.

Attractive as it may be, as a theory connecting equal protection with the genius of contemporary law, this account fails in each of its two major component parts. The restriction according to which the disadvantage must be state-supported – the threshold of state action – represents the most striking residue in present-day legal thought of an otherwise repudiated, earlier vision of law and society. It supposes that we can meaningfully distinguish between disadvantages that are created by politics and others that are just there as the result of a prepolitical evolution of natural social forces. Our inability so to divide the social world has in fact been one of the chief lessons taught by legal analysis over the past hundred years. Politics, including the politics of state power, influences, directly or indirectly, all social arrangements. The distinguishing premise of the state-action doctrine would be more believable if it were true that a free economy naturally expresses itself in a certain system of contract and property. Thus, although politics might be responsible for maintaining the free-market system, it could not be held responsible for the distinct legal–institutional form of that system. However, this belief is false.

The convergence of close comparative study with programmatic argument, against the background of antinecessitarian ideas in social and historical study, awakens us to an appreciation of the different legal–institutional forms that market economies do take or have taken. It invites interest in the much broader range of possible variations that these actual variations suggest. The refusal to use the existing private-law rules and arrangements as a neutral baseline by which to judge the legitimacy of governmental regulation and redistribution began, long ago, to penetrate law and legal thought. As a result, the conflict between accepting the assumptions of state-action doctrine and rejecting them has become a conflict within the law, not just between the law and social theory.

The second half of the proposed theory of substantive equal protection – the identification of the rights-defeating disadvantages that people find themselves powerless to escape – fails because it is both overinclusive and underinclusive of the distinctions established in doctrine. It is overinclusive because there are circumstances of fateful disadvantage about which equal protection remains silent. The most important of these is membership in a lower class, particularly but not exclusively an underclass of unemployed and unstably employed unskilled workers. Historical and contemporary evidence suggest the overwhelming influence of the hereditary transmission of economic and educational advantage. The same evidence emphasizes that sustained, large-scale intergenerational mobility has in the country of this example – the United States – taken place only between the bluecollar and the whitecollar segments of the working class. The children of bluecollar workers have become whitecollar workers, with a similar level of propertylessness and powerlessness. Only very occasionally, however, at the state level and in relation to the direct distribution of certain governmental benefits and burdens, has equal-protection doctrine ever recognized class or poverty as a suspect classification.

Even while being overinclusive, this theoretical proposal is also underinclusive when compared to the social differences recognized in the accepted list of suspect classifications. As the causal criticism of equal protection will soon suggest, the black or the woman who belongs to the professional–business class may capture a disproportionate share of the practical benefits of this constitutional doctrine and of the related law of antidiscrimination. Yet, as individuals, they may often be very far from the circumstance of inescapable disadvantage. They may in fact sometimes succeed in using the protections of the doctrine both to advantage themselves in the competition with white male rivals and, more ominously, to distance themselves from the oppressed and marginalized blacks and women for whom they stand, in the charmed light of the law, as virtual representatives.

Consider now a second proposal to connect the actual distinctions of substantive equal-protection doctrine with a coherent political conception. The selective criterion for suspect classification is governmental complicity in denials of opportunity to people based upon prejudice. Prejudice, in this proposal, is aversion to certain physically inscribed characteristics of people, or unwarranted belief about the negative consequences of such characteristics for the capacities of individuals. Race, gender, age, and physical handicap would all fall comfortably within the scope of the criterion. Class position would be excluded, as indeed it is by established doctrine.

A threshold objection to this approach is that, like the more ambitious alternative I have just criticized, it relies upon the restrictive and untenable criterion of governmental complicity. In addition, it gives to physically based disabilities a privilege relying for its authority upon mistaken beliefs about the social order. According to one such belief, prejudice about membership in physically characterized groups presents a unique danger to a free society, particularly when prejudice finds reinforcement in law. It is as if the institutional structure of society, established and perfected by law, presented no insuperable obstacle to the effective enjoyment of rights except when perverted in its working by spiritual vices: irrational animosity and blind superstition. Once you become persuaded that disadvantage and marginalization have roots in practices and institutions; that free economies, societies, and polities can take very different institutional forms; and that these forms differ widely in the extent they generate or correct disadvantage, the privilege accorded by this approach to birth and superstition becomes far less convincing.

One of the many consequences of this emphasis is to give the disadvantaged and the disappointed an irresistible reason to redescribe as genetic fate forms of life that may have substantial elements of choice. Consider, for example, the politics of homosexuality as it has developed in the United States. To bring homosexuality under the umbrella of equal-protection doctrine there is pressure to support the view that people inherit sexual orientation. Although inheritance may indeed turn out to play a major role in sexual orientation, it seems just as likely that, like so much else in our moral experience, it will be found to be the joint outcome of inherited predispositions, social influences, and cumulative choices. A conception of its dignity would be better suited by its representation as a chosen destiny rather than a blind fate. Yet such a representation, however realistic and dignified, would fall outside the scope of established equal-protection doctrine.

Suppose we stipulated that the empirical assumptions justifying the privilege granted to prejudice about ascriptive groups were justified. There would still be a problem of unjustified selectivity in the list of suspect classifications. The fat, the ugly, and the stupid (as measured by IQ tests) may all compete for inclusion under the benefits of substantive equal protection, citing the mounting evidence about the detrimental consequences of their conditions, the irrelevance of their infirmities to their denied economic or educational opportunities, and direct or oblique governmental complicity in the maintenance of prejudicial admissions or employment practices. To the objection that they form no distinct group, the answer can be that these groups are just as distinct as "the handicapped" or "gays." The simple truth is that these categories fail to come under the aegis of substantive equal protection not because their inclusion would be illogical but because they map no living movements and organized conflicts in the politics and culture of the country.

This observation suggests a third, more realistic and less inflated account of the point of substantive equal protection, tracking more closely the origins and evolution of the doctrine. According to this third view, sub-stantive equal protection, and the related body of antidiscrimination law, should first be understood as a response to the extraordinary problems created by the aftermath of slavery, Civil War, and Reconstruction. This was not merely a species within a well-defined genus of problems. It was a threat to the unity and the continuity of the republic, to social peace as well as to social justice. As a politics of groupism, combining demands for social advancement with demands for cultural recognition, has advanced in the United States, first other cultural–racial minorities and then other non-racially based groups have won places as suspect classifications. Not the logic of natural kinds but the history of insurgencies of American civil society governs this progression.

Nothing is wrong with this third approach to substantive equal protec-tion except that it disappoints the demand for theory-like prescriptive conceptions in rationalizing legal analysis. So why not suppress the demand rather than suppressing the approach? The focus upon singular historical crisis and upon the rise of civil society accounts for the compo-sition of the list of suspect classifications. It does so while remaining loyal to the aspirations and anxieties, the conflicts and controversies, out of which Americans make this list.

Such an account need not be merely an explanation; it holds normative force to the same extent that the historical romance of a real national democracy carries authority. Nevertheless, it makes no rational excuses for the content of the list of suspect classifications at any given time, no excuse other than the path-dependent character of historical change. The length of this list depends upon the power and influence of the forces wanting to make the list longer. Moreover, this deflationary approach refuses to present this historical experience as the manifestation of a dis-crete and coherent theory-like conception, such as the commitment to prohibit governmental complicity in all collective disadvantages from which people are unable to escape by the readily available means of edu-cational advancement, economic initiative, and political action. For these reasons, it leaves undone the work that the method of policy and principle requires of legal reasoning. It is too realistic to be rationalistic, and refuses to discern the workings of reason in history.

The rational disharmony revealed by the criticism of these different candidate interpretations of equal-protection doctrine is typical of the rational disharmony in rationalizing legal analysis itself. It exemplifies the same disorder we discovered when we earlier tested the claim of this canonical method of legal analysis to represent a requirement of the rule of law or of a regime of rights. At this turn in the argument, the rediscovery of rational disharmony serves the purpose of triggering skepticism about the practical benefits of the doctrine – and of doctrines like it – to those who most need its help. I now explore and develop the grounds for such causal skepticism.

For this purpose we need not take the doctrine at its word, crediting its own account of the evils it seeks to redress and the class of beneficiaries it wants to assist. Its word, after all, is unclear, and, to the extent that it is clear, rests upon doubtful factual assumptions. Instead, we can accept the third of the three approaches to substantive equal protection – the most historical and deflationary – as the most telling. Armed with this understanding we can ask to what extent these most spectacular examples of pessimistic progressive reformism in law serve the vague but powerful aims of equal opportunity and equal voice, of protection and incorporation of the marginalized and the downtrodden. These aims hold the central place in the agenda of progressive reform, pessimistic or not.

The example of substantive equal protection: failures of efficacy

A causal criticism of substantive equal protection as pessimistic progressive reformism can begin with the familiar conjecture that the doctrine helps least the members of the targeted groups who stand in greatest need of its help. The least needy capture, according to this hypothesis, a disproportional part of the benefits. Thus, a black or a woman who is a member of the professional–business class is more likely to gain the advantages than a black or a woman who belongs to the working class. Successive degrees of meritocratic promotion in a career, and the decisive influence exercised by the initial admission to central educational or productive institutions, are characteristically more salient in the experience of the professional–business class than in that of the working class. The specialization of experience reinforces the superior ability of the professional–business class to mobilize both legal and rhetorical resources in the defense of its interests.

It is even more likely that the doctrine will benefit members of the working class, both bluecollar and whitecollar, more than members of the underclass, especially when the working class is unionized or otherwise organized. The disorganized underclass, unstably employed in unskilled, dead-end, and temporary jobs, is least able to enlist the legal and rhetorical strategies of antidiscrimination in its own defense.

Moreover, it is close to being entirely off the charts: without either voice or place, exposed to the extremes of physical and economic insecurity, denied stability at work, sustenance in the family, and safety at home, it remains largely beyond such help as may come in the form of vetoes to racial and gender discrimination.

A second step in the development of the complaint comes when we move beyond the discovery of the disproportion between need and help to probe the dynamic effects of this disproportion upon the combined realities of race, gender, and class. Substantive equal protection and the related law of antidiscrimination become expressions and instruments of the politics of groupism. A combination of characteristics defines the special quality of these politics. First, the demand for the economic protection and advancement of disadvantaged groups combines with a demand for recognition and therefore also for political and cultural voice. Second, the politics of groupism work on a certain vision of the relations between the working-class majority of the country and the oppressed minorities. The majority may be economically and educationally stratified, and remain vulnerable to economic risk and instability. However, it suffers no deeply entrenched disabilities imposed by forms of prejudice and exploitation in which government has a hand. By contrast, women and minorities suffer from the combined state-supported or state-tolerated disabilities of economic oppression and cultural voicelessness.

Third, the focus falls upon the classification of people into groups that are more than creatures of politics and institutions: race, nationality, religion, gender, sexual orientation (insofar as sexual orientation is believed to be inborn), and physical handicap. What is the common denominator of these groups? We may use the sociologists' label "ascriptive group," and emphasize among ascriptive groups those that have a physical manifestation. The label, however, misses the most important point. The groups that hold center stage in the politics of groupism are groups that can plausibly be thought to receive much of their reality and distinction from forces beyond the institutional constructions of politics. Although they may be the victims of politics and institutions, they are not merely their products.

To recognize this recurrent element in the politics of groupism is to understand why "class" cannot be the next "suspect classification" alongside race, gender, and physical handicap. For class is a social reality that is very directly the product of politics and institutions. The subversion of class differences may require changes in the economic and political structure of society. The incorporation of marginalized and persecuted groups into the established structure may simply not suffice.

Within such an imaginative world, the elites of the marginalized, pre-political groups will demand, in the name of the groups they represent, a more equal incorporation into the established structure. This assimilationist impulse may alternate with a secessionist threat: withdrawal from the larger society into a separate social world. Thus, American black leaders have from time to time turned their backs upon the ideal of more equal incorporation into American society in favor of the effort to build a separate African nation. Even when sincerely and passionately intended, however, the secessionism is likely to lack practical reality. In practice, it becomes a foil for the real thing, its opposite.

As the main beneficiaries of the politics of groupism and of its legal expression – the doctrines of substantive equal protection and anti-discrimination – the elites of each of the marginalized groups are easily cajoled and coopted into the elite institutions of the present social order, supposedly representing the rank-and-file of the groups they have in fact left behind. Something will have been gained, by the attenuation of prejudice in national life. Something will also have been lost. At the end of the day, each of the disadvantaged groups may find itself deprived of its natural leadership. The leadership may be caught between the blandishments of comfortable cooption and the pretenses of virtual representation.

The politics of groupism and its legal counterparts in the doctrine of substantive equal protection exaggerate the distinctions, and understate the similarities, in the social experiences of oppression and voicelessness. They fail to seek the common roots of the evils they address in connected institutions, institutionalized practices, and enacted beliefs. The distinctions of race and gender are real but they are also relative. The evils on which they focus are greatest when the denial of respect and of voice converges with the realities of economic and educational exclusion. They are one thing when combined with these realities, and another when disconnected from them. To address them, we must recognize both their common qualities and their shared roots. We must reconstruct economic institutions to moderate the hierarchical segmentation of the laborforce. We must reconstruct political and social institutions to favor the self-organization of civil society, the political mobilization of the citizenry, and the rapid resolution of impasse among branches of government.

To this end we must try to develop practices of economic and legal understanding that enable us to recognize the contingency of our institutions as well as their constraining force. Then, the sterile alternation between assimilation to the established structure and secession from it in the political imagination of groupist politics will give way to politics seeking to reimagine and reconstruct the structure. Such politics go forward on the maxim that to every advance in the incorporation of the marginalized into active and productive life there must correspond some change in social arrangements.

From the failure to recognize the commonality and the causes of the suffering to which it responds comes a fourth characteristic of the politics of groupism: the groupist politics of rights-conscious indignation meet their match in the counterpolitics of resentment. In the United States rightwing populist politicians and publicists successfully address the white male working class as a "minority" in the sense of the politics of groupism. These agitators have their counterparts today in almost every Western industrial democracy. Experiencing itself as a mass of angry outsiders, and victimized by elites in the seats of economic and political authority, this majoritarian "minority" can be maneuvered into support for an attack upon the state and a surrender to the business interests. Such counterpolitics of resentment have remained unimportant only in those countries where social and cultural homogeneity is greatest, the welfare state most successful in moderating economic insecurity, and the tax system most invisible (because most reliant upon indirect taxes).

Thus, the causal complaint against the style of pessimistic progressive reformism exemplified by the doctrine of substantive equal protection begins with the discovery of the troubling difference between those who need it and those who benefit from it. The complaint develops into an understanding that these legal politics draw their life from the social politics of groupism. Groupism helps divide each of the benefited groups internally, and inflames the counterpolitics of frustration by working-class people whose sufferings and anxieties it is unable to address. The result is to impede more inclusive popular alliances and to block the imaginative tools for developing the reconstructive programs needed to generate and sustain such alliances.

These defects of the legal politics of pessimistic progressive reformism are likely to be least pronounced when the effort at reform from the commanding heights of the judiciary works in implicit alliance with grassroots movements in civil society. The judicial initiatives help broaden the space on which social movements can operate; reallocations of right may tilt the scales in local conflict and national politics. Conversely, social movements may help inspire and guide such judicial initiatives as well as increase the pressure upon the resistant political branches of government.

The partnership between the federal judiciary and the civil-rights movement in the development of equal-protection and antidiscrimination doctrine offers an example. Researchers have shown that very little happened to change the realities of racial segregation in the ten years following *Brown v. Board of Education*. Nevertheless, the latent alliance between progressive judges and grassroots agitators seems to have helped shape and accelerate the longer sequence of civil-rights conflicts and achievements. The same can be said today of the association between feminist movements and the judicial development of women's rights.

In each of these instances we find a connection vital in any transformative practice: the connection between state-oriented politics at the top and society-based politics at the bottom. The trouble, however, is that there is nothing in the theory or practice of rationalizing legal analysis that would limit its reforming work to this favorable circumstance. From the standpoint of legal doctrine, the alliance appears as an accident rather than as a condition or a goal. Were we to think of it as either a goal or a condition, we would find ourselves forced to ask which institutional arrangements best ensure its realization. We would need to discover which ways of thinking about law help make rights redefinition at the top sensitive to social movement at the bottom.

I can now take the causal complaint to a third and final level. The trouble with substantive equal protection, and with the style of progressive politics it exemplifies, is that it deflects attention from the institutional structure of society to which our interests, ideals, and group identities remain fastened. Practices and institutions are not the whole story of exclusion and voicelessness; but they are the part of the story that the law can most effectively address. Consciousness and culture count as well; but legal thought does most to change them when its proposed images of human association come embodied in the flesh of practical arrangements. Prejudices about race and nationality, gender and sexual orientation, age and infirmity, are not fictions; but they become immensely more potent when bound up with the institutionally based realities of economic and educational disadvantage, of social disorganization and political demobilization.

Consider, for example, the hierarchical segmentation of the laborforce in contemporary industrial societies and the existence in some of these societies – the United States foremost among them – of a structural underclass. Many different institutionalized practices, imagined and reproduced in law, join to support this social reality: the distinction between permanent and temporary workers, or workers and subcontractors, enabling firms to deal with the business cycle by maintaining a two-tier workforce;

the power of firms to exert tight control over their investment and production strategies by relying upon internally generated investment funds and by invoking the property norm to deny responsibility to many groups of potential stakeholders; the marriage between a form of private property that makes concentration of ownership or control seem the indispensable instrument of economies of scale and ways of designing organizations and machines that sharpen the contrast between task-defining and task-executing activities; the steep social and cultural hierarchy of the school system and the ability of the professional–business class to abandon the public schools to their fate by linking privileged schools to privileged neighborhoods or by opting into a parallel system of private schools; the rules governing the *inter vivos* and hereditary transmission of wealth, enabling people to inherit differentially from their parents rather than more equally from society; the design of a tax system that while maintaining a pretense of progressive redistribution fails to achieve significant redistributive effects and, through its unpopularity, helps prevent the redistribution that might occur more effectively on the spending rather than the revenue-raising side; the ostentatious separation of welfare assistance to the underclass from economic help for the broad working-class majority; the abandonment of civil society to the organizational devices of traditional contract and corporate law, facilitating the division between the organized and the unorganized and setting the stage on which the big organized interests can make deals among themselves; the arrangements for electoral politics discouraging civic engagement by enabling money to buy attention and turning electoral choice into an interruption rather than a consummation of everyday decisions; and the forms of constitutional organization favoring compromise over experiment, and impasse over compromise. Although these practices and institutions reinforce one another, they form part of no indivisible system, nor could we ever infer them from abstract institutional conceptions such as "capitalism" or the market economy.

The problem with the legal program of pessimistic progressive reformism lies in much more than its failure to challenge these institutional sources of oppression and exclusion. As an exercise in practical reform, this program helps disconnect the elements of disadvantage and the agents of transformation. As a representation of law, it pays for the reallocations of right it achieves by conferring a halo of reasoned authority and necessity upon the institutionalized structure of society. As a form of social imagination, it leaves us without a language in which to describe and discuss the alternative futures of society. For each of these futures arises through some interaction between change of established practices and institutions and change in people's understanding of their interests, ideals, and identities.

Deepening and generalizing the causal skepticism: law under two political economies

I now extend this argument by developing it in the context of a view of the place of law in two contrasting political economies: the dualist and the corporatist. The point is to suggest how the doctrine of substantive equal protection and the law of antidiscrimination exemplify a certain aversive and misdirected relation of legal reform to social tension that is characteristic of law in the age of rationalizing legal analysis. The limits of this misdirected and aversive approach turn out to be the limits of pessimistic progressive reformism and of its law. The contrast between dualism and corporatism is neither exhaustive of the political-economic options in the rich industrial democracies nor inclusive of the choices made by any particular country. It nevertheless designates a difference of directions that is real. On the basis of this difference we can retell a starkly simplified but nevertheless revealing story about the failures of law and the illusions of legal doctrine.

The United States is the country most closely committed to dualism in political economy. The dualistic political economy is characterized by an especially stark contrast between capital-intensive mass-production industry, with its vanguard of knowledge-based and flexibly organized enterprise, and a second economy of labor-intensive shops and services, as well as, by a parallel segmentation of the laborforce, between a relatively privileged, skilled or semiskilled working class and an unskilled, unstably employed underclass; by a rejection of the legitimacy of pervasive governmental intervention in the economy as well as of government-brokered deals among organized interests; and by a transparent distinction between the parts of the welfare state responsive to the broad working class and the parts dealing with the underclass. In such a circumstance, resistance to redistributive taxation will be great; and it will be all the greater if the tax system pretends to produce a redistribution it cannot accomplish. A striking trait of the dualist political economy is that the working class (self-described in the United States as the middle class) is, although relatively privileged, persistently vulnerable. Not only does it compete with the underclass for the attention of government, but it also lacks any richly defined package of labor and social entitlements protecting against economic insecurity. The disappointment with politics and the hostility to governmental action help prevent the emergence of alliances and programs that might change the circumstances of the working class. They perpetuate a politics of frustrated and self-defeating resentment in which each part of the popular majority believes itself to be the victim of the other parts.

A dualist political economy has a reciprocal relation to social and cultural pluralism. Deep divisions of group history, identity, and consciousness help create such a dualism. The institutional arrangements of dualism reinforce these divisions, anchoring them in the relentless pressures of everyday life. The second relation – the one going from dualism to the divisions – entangles racial divisions in class divisions: in the United States, as in other societies that have some of the features of dualism, the underclass is largely composed of racial minorities as well as of single mothers and their children.

The first relation – the one going from the divisions to dualism – recalls the recurrence of a shameful burden. When slavery was abolished, the more enterprising slaveowners abandoned their slaves to migration and subsistence farming. When fordist mass-production became the heart of the industrial system, the more successful industrialists created a relatively stable and reliable laborforce, and abandoned the rest of the working class to its own devices. When high-skilled manufacturing and services began to displace fordist mass-production, its creators and financiers focused their attention upon a working elite of educated and adaptable workers, and left the others to the care of the state and the pressures of an unforgiving labor market.

There has been overwhelming continuity in the social and racial composition of the marginalized sector of society. Prejudice, whether state-supported or not, has been constantly rekindled by the exclusions and the anxieties endemic to this divided structure. The white male worker, competing with underclass and female laborers and threatened by economic insecurity, social closure, and political despair, in his sense of masculine self-reliance and capacity, has been, and remains, prey to every prejudice about race, gender, and sexual orientation. The prejudice has many lives and many wellsprings. However, it makes no more sense to see and to understand it apart from the real structure of social division and hierarchy than it would be to study a planetary atmosphere apart from the planet it surrounds.

The most intense and distinctive concern of legal thought under the regime of dualism becomes the law of antidiscrimination. In the United States, this law has found its most ambitious expression in the constitutional doctrine of substantive equal protection. The problems with which anti-discrimination law deals are real, but they are also limited and superficial. Law and legal thought develop as if they gave the highest priority to addressing the divisions and disadvantages of dualism, only with the institutional causes and constraints left out, and the attention directed to prejudice rather than to structure, although prejudice and structure are in fact closely linked. It is true that the divisions and exclusions of dualism represent, under a dualist political economy, a pervasive source of frustration of the exercise of rights. Given the spirit of contemporary law, they therefore become the privileged target of reform. What is remarkable, however, is that so intense and overpowering a concern should nevertheless remain so narrow in its concerns and so selective in its judgements.

To the questions "Why so selective and, in particular, why so anti-structural?" there are two basic answers. The first answer is that the priority given to prejudice over institutions merely expresses the dominant politics of groupism. To explain that priority, we must explain these politics. The second answer is that, for all the reasons explored here, rationalizing legal analysis is institutionally blind. These two answers are closer to each other than they appear to be. The anti-institutionalism of the method of policy and principle has many sources and ramifications. It is, among other things, both a cause and a consequence of the emptying out of politics and political debate, an imaginative expression of the burden weighing upon democratic experimentalism in public life and public discourse.

The relation of antidiscrimination and equal-protection law to the exclusions and subjugations of a dualist political economy is characteristic in its selectivity. It is characteristic of the way rationalistic legal doctrine imagines social life. The law gives a real response to real problems, yet also one that stops at the threshold of structural change and structural reimagination. The halt may be justified by the objection that judges, bureaucrats, and other official law appliers should not and cannot serve as the agents of structural change. However, this objection arises, the next part of this book argues, from an impoverishing, inhibiting, and superstitious obsession with adjudication as the central task of legal analysis. Within that view, judges are the real thing, and even nonofficial legal analysts and theorists picture themselves as judges when they talk about law. In this way the antistructural imagination gains a second lease on life.

The same quality of an arrested and misdirected response reappears in the work of law under a corporatist political economy. Corporatism, in a loose and inclusive sense, exists beyond the frontiers of countries like Austria that have traditionally been identified with corporatist institutions. In a more universalist and egalitarian form, we find it in the Scandinavian social democracies and in the Netherlands. In a form more respectful of inequality, and more reliant upon the family and the firm as sources of assistance and instruments of control, it appears in Germany, France, and Italy. When the aim is to understand the different forms and genealogies of the welfare state, these two variants are best treated as distinct types, each with its own agenda of problems, constraints, and opportunities. However, in this discussion of aversive social reform in law and legal thought, we can either disregard the differences between them or use these differences to illustrate a shared problem.

The decisive feature of the corporatist political economy is the combination of a market-limiting establishment of social rights with a politics-shaping practice of negotiation among the large organized interests of society. The principal subjects of group negotiation are the funding and the scope of social and economic rights. Each individual enjoys a package of benefits and entitlements that remains relatively insulated against the pressure of market competition and the downswings of the business cycle. These insulated and rights-based advantages include claims to health and education, compensations against physical and economic risk, care for the young, the old, and the sick, and restraints upon dismissal from work for those who do hold jobs.

In the full-fledged social democracies these social rights are more lavishly defined, more equally distributed, and more effectively independent of status and job than in the more hierarchical and statist societies of Central and Western Europe. The most passionate defenders of the European idea have understood that the social and imaginative cohesion of the community depends upon bridging the gap between these two types of corporatist political economy by giving a secure economic foundation to the promises of a more inclusive social democracy. In both types, however, we can find the same developed dialectic between rights remaining within the active, day-to-day reach of market-oriented activity and rights shaping the market from a place outside it. This dialectic is the specific form, under corporatist social democracy, of that most distinctive and universal dialectic of contemporary law: the contrast between rights of choice and rights withdrawn from choice for the sake of choice.

Government brokers deals among the organized interests of society about the content and the funding of the package of social rights as well as about the macroeconomic aggregates on which this package depends:

wage and price, and even savings and investment levels. These "social contracts" reconcile promises of rights with economic realities, and police the boundaries between the market sphere and the domain of market-insulated safeguards. Once again, the fuller social democracies differ from their less social-democratic counterparts in the inclusiveness with which the partners to the social contract represent the general working population. In the more unequal and status-oriented versions of the corporatist political economy a large part of the population remains excluded from the negotiating entities and disfavored by the negotiated deals. The resulting division between the organized and the unorganized reproduces under corporatism some of the features of dualism. The similarity becomes stronger when industry comes to rely upon disenfranchised migrant workers, or workers in poorer countries, and to treat them as the second, expendable part of a two-tier laborforce.

Both social rights and social contracts depend upon a widespread belief in the importance and legitimacy of manifest governmental presence in the economy. With this creed comes an advance of insight into the political constitution of legal relations, private as well as public. The campaign of legal thought since the nineteenth century to rid itself of the superstitious belief in the existence of a natural, prepolitical form of the market economy, of free civil society, and of representative democracy finds sustenance in this enacted idea. The practical consequence for party politics is that governmental policy has more room to maneuver than it enjoys under dualism. Political debate is less likely to become entangled in the opposition between faith and disbelief in government. The practical consequence for legal reform is that redefinitions of social rights can be fought out more evenly on the terrains of private as well as public law.

The trouble with corporatism lies in the limit it imposes upon advance in the core area of the democratic project: the area of overlap between the conditions of material progress and the conditions of individual emancipation. The social contracts of the corporatist political economy are constantly at risk of degenerating into a system of hierarchically arranged group prerogatives, as the new regime of social rights turns backward to the *ancien régime* of group-specific privileges and disabilities. The result is a heavy constraint upon practical innovation operating, simultaneously, as a constraint upon equality.

Packages of social rights under this political–economic regime entrench what would otherwise be transitory compromises against both economic and political challenge. These entrenched entitlements will characteristically extend outward beyond the economic and educational equipment for effective individual action. They will include the privileges each segment of the laborforce enjoys vis-à-vis its immediate superiors and underlings as well as the claims each section of business has upon the favors of the state. Because the instruments of individual agency become conflated with the prerogatives of status, the room for economic innovation narrows. Because the distributions of political and of economic influence never completely coincide, no set of deals will be able to match equally both sets of influences. Some will regard themselves as losers and strike back by withholding labor, capital, or votes, as their interests and powers may dictate, undermining the cooperative practice of social contracts with a costly social war of attrition. Because group interests are unevenly organized and represented, the unorganized or the less organized will become the orphans of the regime. The more complete social democracies will limit this inequality by disconnecting rights from jobs, but in so doing they will also increase the charge of welfare entitlements upon the whole society – a charge to be measured in the chilling of innovation as well as in the cost of entitlements. Because the social rights include group habits as well as individual instruments, the social contracts defining them will withdraw a broad array of affairs from the open agenda of politics, and narrow the range of experimental openness in policy and politics.

At the heart of practical progress lies the paradoxical relation between innovation and cooperation. Both are necessary to practical progress. Each needs and jeopardizes the other. Economic growth is the most important, but not the only, area in which to investigate these paradoxical relations. Once we pass beyond the early stages of resource scarcity and technological simplicity, innovation in techniques, organizations, and ideas soon overrides the level of savings as a constraint upon growth. Economic innovation depends at every level upon social cooperation: cooperation at the workplace among workers and between them and their supervisors; cooperation among firms – suppliers, customers, and even competitors; cooperation between firms and governments, at least in the production of basic physical, social, and human capital; and cooperation in the larger society among classes and businesses competing for the attention and favor of government. Nevertheless, every innovation threatens the arrangements, relationships, and expectations in which cooperative practices at any of these levels are embedded. Conversely, any cooperative practice, once so embedded, threatens to strangle innovative breakthroughs. The central problem of economic growth, and of practical progress generally, is the design of institutions moderating the reciprocal interference, and exploiting the mutual reinforcement, of cooperation and innovation; it is the advance toward cooperative arrangements that are less likely to hold innovative action hostage.

Reconsidered in this light, the trouble with dualism is that it leaves the need for cooperation unfulfilled or fulfills it only by the clumsy and costly devices of economic coercion. The trouble with corporatism, however, is that it rigidifies, as social contract and social right, a particular system of cooperation, imposing severe limits upon innovation. Instead of withdrawing from the agenda of short-term politics only those assurances of capacity needed to make economic and political self-determination effective, it takes out of the agenda a whole world of social arrangements. As a result, it places a heavy burden upon political and economic experimentalism.

We now have all the elements with which to understand the most distinctive concerns of rationalizing legal analysis under a corporatist political economy: flexibility and lawmaking from the bottom up. These are to be the antidotes to state-defined vested rights and state-orchestrated co-operation, just as, under dualism, substantive equal-protection and antidiscrimination law are made to serve as cures for selected forms of social apartheid. As before, the legal response to the social problem is both real and superficial, both intense and misdirected. The fancy theoretical form of the response is the interest in law beyond the state, law made from the bottom up, self-regulation and "autopoiesis." The humdrum practical form is the emphasis placed upon the "principle of subsidiarity," according to which power should devolve so far as practicable away from the central governmental authority and downward toward the individual, the family, the firm, and the local government. Each higher level takes over only those responsibilities the immediately lower level cannot effectively discharge.

To devolve power without organizing and reorganizing society is to let power accumulate in the hands of those who already enjoy it. It is to leave the petty despotisms of civil society without correction from afar or from on top. More generally, it is to diminish the complexity of fora and forces at different levels, with its promise of challenge and variation. A telling example of the problem is the system of worker self-management and worker ownership, instituted through the forms of the traditional property right.* If we begin with the simple form defined by respect for the present distribution of

---

* See the later and fuller discussion of the workers'-ownership and self-management system on pp. 157–61.

jobs and for the inherited idea of a unified property right, commitment to our initial goals of efficiency, equality, and participation will drive us to relax each of these two assumptions in turn. Once we reach the point of imposing restraints upon alienation, accumulation, acquisition, and payout of resources, we discover that, to operate effectively, the unreconstructed version of worker ownership, as the transfer of traditional consolidated property from one type of owner (the capitalist-investor) to another (the worker-proprietor), gives way to a more complex vision of powers of command divided and shared among the worker-proprietors and outside entities. Moreover, if we are to avoid the rent-seeking and dogmatism of centralized command economies, these outside entities cannot be simply governmental bureaucracies. They must themselves be independent and competitive funds, enjoying some of the components of what we now call property. To democratic governments must fall the residual but decisive role of setting the ultimate limits to variation and inequality in the decentralized allocation of productive resources. At the end of the day worker self-management and ownership understood as the mere transfer of the property right shall have been replaced with worker self-management and ownership interpreted as another name for a democratized market economy. Such an economy fragments property rights and vests their different components in distinct sets of rightholders.

In the absence of institutional innovations such as these, subsidiarity and devolution suppress transformative opportunity. The turning of transitory compromise into vested right continues to take place, if only in more decentralized settings. The campaign against rigidity misses its target. The spiritual counterpart to this practical abdication is resignation to a form of social life in which people give up on politics and seek solace and redemption in the "pianissimo of personal life." They hope to become big by making politics little, but their hope is misplaced.

To escape the fate of misdirection, law and legal thought under corporatism would have to confront and reimagine the practical institutional forms of their decentralizing and antistatist ambitions. Rationalizing legal analysis cannot, however, accomplish this objective without a revolution in its methods. Until he places the relation between institutions or practices and ideals or interests at the center of his concerns, the legal analyst remains doomed to live at the surface of social phenomena, where perverse consequences overtake good intentions.

The practical political failures of rationalizing legal analysis

You can now see more comprehensively what the discussion of substantive equal protection has already suggested. Rationalizing legal analysis does indeed express the possibilities and the limitations of an institutionally conservative reformism. In particular, it draws meaning, authority, and energy from the service it may render to a pessimistic progressive reformism: one using the retrospective idealization of law as a basis on which to improve the situation of the most vulnerable, those most likely to have suffered defeat and subordination in lawmaking.

In serving this family of reform politics, however, rationalizing legal analysis also throws light upon their limitations, both as forms of political practice and as varieties of political imagination. The more deeply we understand the relation between the political project and its legal instrument, the less reason we have to put faith in either.

The central defect of rationalizing legal analysis as political action lies in its failure to reach the deeper sources of disadvantage and exclusion in the institutions and practices of society. When it reaches them at all, its focus remains so narrow and its vision so superficial that the campaign for improvement often produces perverse and paradoxical results. To this basic flaw are connected all the other deficiencies of the method of policy and principle as practical reform: the initiating role assigned to the collective, shamefaced Bonapartism of the jurists, who hand down legal benefits from on high to people in their capacities as isolated victims rather than channeling them through the forward-looking devices of group organization; the emphasis upon the components of the experience of subjugation that are least immediately and transparently linked to the institutional structure of society such as discrimination motivated by the physical characteristics of different groups; the selective blindness to connections among the different sources of disadvantage and among the disadvantages of different groups; the frequent inversion of the relation between the amount of help needed and the amount of help given; the deepening of divisions between the elites and the rank-and-file of the benefited groups as well as between the groups that are and are not selected for help; the uncritical attitude toward the institutional context in which we are to realize programmatic aims such as decentralization and devolution of power; and, more generally, the anxious and obsessional redress of social evils that we cannot effectively alleviate without reordering our institutions, practices, interests, and ideals.

As political imagination, rationalizing legal analysis suffers from the impulse to suppress and to freeze the internal relation between institutions or practices and interests or ideals. It works by bestowing an idealizing image upon the practices and the institutions defined in law, and finds in the retrospective improvement of law the excuse for this uplift. The consequence is to leave unexpressed, unexplored, and unresolved the internal instability characteristic of programmatic positions in modern law and politics: the tension between recognized interests or professed ideals and their established institutional vehicles.

To the response that we can hope to play this internal relation out in other fields of discourse, the answer is that to play it out at all we have to do so in legal form. It is as law that the institutions and practices holding our interests and ideals hostage live in detail. It is in legal thought that we give a textured – and fateful – account of the relation between social arrangements and the conceptions of interests and ideals making sense of them. The greatest imaginative cost of the canonical style of legal reasoning is negative: it fills up the imaginative space in which another way of thinking might take root, and it does so in the crucial testing ground on which authoritative ideals meet practical realities.

Any proposal for the redirection of legal analysis, however, confronts the objection that it may require measures exceeding what judges can legitimately and successfully accomplish. We cannot progress in understanding the potential of legal analysis until we expunge the idea that judges, or others like them, are the primary agents of legal thought. We must demote the judicial role, assigning it a specialized, exceptional, and secondary responsibility. The civic body as a whole must become the primary interlocutor of legal analysis. The first role of the jurist should be to serve as the technical assistant of the citizen.

THE FOURFOLD ROOT OF RATIONALIZING LEGAL ANALYSIS: THE COMMANDING ROLE OF THE JUDGE

The historical context of an obsession

The limitations of rationalizing legal analysis find an omnipresent excuse in the constraints of the judicial role. Like its immediate predecessors, rationalizing legal analysis has been primarily meant for judges or for those who, as bureaucrats or as expert but unofficial legal analysts, stand, practically or mentally, in the place of judges. Even when contemporary theories of the "legal process" have turned the judiciary into but one of a system of legal agents, it has remained the first among equals, at the apex of the pyramid of "reasoned elaboration," just as legislation has been relegated to a residual status, a last-ditch instrument to be used when the powers of rational deliberation fail. Every proposal for the reform and redirection of legal analysis can be met by the objection: What could judges do with such a method? The conversation-stopping question "How should judges decide cases?" has remained the central question in the theory of law.

The query about the judicial decision deserves no such privilege. The privilege masks indefensible, antidemocratic precommitments, and its persistence helps arrest the progress of legal theory. In particular, the privilege has served as both cause and consequence of the failure of contemporary legal thought to move from its ever present concern with the effective enjoyment of rights to its undeveloped appreciation of the alternative institutional pathways for developing the exercise of rights in free societies. The judicial obsession has helped cast an antiexperimentalist spell upon legal thought, seducing it into the betrayal of its primary vocation in a democracy. We need to demote the question "How should judges decide cases?" to specialized and secondary status, as a question requiring special answers but leaving the field open for practices of legal analysis directed to other ends. The central end is the working out, in imagination and in practice, of the interaction between ideals or interests and institutions or practices through the detailed medium of law and legal thought. Before probing, however, the relation of rationalizing legal analysis to the exemplary status of the judge, it is useful to remember some puzzling features of the history of this status.

Dispute settlement has been, together with conquest and defense, the paramount source of government, for no aim has been more fundamental in the history of society than the effort to establish and sustain order, threatened by conflict, usurpation, and revenge. To our modern eyes, therefore, the early forms of government often appear to be judicial. This impression, however, conveys a half-truth: we conflate the inclusive practice of pacification and judgement by such protostate institutions with the specialized although ambitious work of modern judges. The most important point to understand about those early institutions is that they worked against a background of customary law, over parts of which sacred law or kingly intervention might be superimposed.

Customary law takes shape around a series of interlocking continuities: of law with the actual expectations and claims that people make upon one another according to the social roles they occupy; of normative standards with routinized behavior and belief; and of the acts by which people define what the law is with the acts by which they apply it in particular cases. The cumulative effect of these continuities is to naturalize society: by placing most social arrangements beyond the reach of effective challenge and revision, they become in practice the natural order of things. Even in late medieval Europe the emerging centers of government remained divided between *jurisdictio* and *gubernaculum*. *Jurisdictio* restated a common, customary law in the course of applying it. Princely *gubernaculum* intervened to manage crisis and dispose of resources and manpower without seeking to disturb the naturalized order of society. When such an enacted sense of naturalness has to coexist with an awareness of differences among ways of life in distinct societies, it turns into a richly defined conception of collective identity: Roman customs defining what it means to be a Roman.

Only fitfully and ambivalently did the common law of England or the *ius commune* of continental Europe develop in sharper contrast with social custom. Procedures emerged to conduct dispute settlement. Jurists started to think of their law as a product of history evolving in historical time. Societies began to assert greater powers to remake themselves through the artifice of their laws.

Adjudication and rational reconstruction

Now look ahead to the work of modern judges and the place of the modern judiciary. The judicial application and elaboration of law take place against a backdrop in which law is recognized to be made, and is made in fact, by nonjudicial agencies. In a democracy the political branches of government must count heavily among these lawmakers. Yet the power of the judges as elaborators of law seems to exceed what their occasional responsibilities as custodians of constitutionally entrenched individual rights can explain. Comparative historians of modern law have shown how, from around 1800, judges came to assume, even in continental Europe, greater responsibilities for the revisionary interpretation and reorganization of law. They did not remain the passive slaves to the original lawmakers that many of the radical reformers and democrats of the early nineteenth century wanted them to be. Codification often slowed the growth of judicial power. The prestige of academic jurists and private jurisconsults modified it. It, nevertheless, continued. Today, in a country like Germany, the techniques of the interpretation of law have become much more similar to those of, say, American judges than the divergent histories of the two traditions might lead us to expect. Historians have nevertheless failed to explain why judges have continued to climb the ladder of lawmaking power even where the traditional legal culture seems hostile to their claims.

We can find an answer in the reciprocal adaptation of institutional realities and spiritual preconceptions in these judge-promoting states. Rule-of-law ideals and administrative efficiency alike require that law be formulated as a body of rules and doctrines conferring typical, stable claims upon broad groups of role-occupants: citizens, taxpayers, consumers, and workers; creditors and debtors; spouses and children. Imagine that there are divisions among the interests and the ideologies producing this body of law but that the divisions are not so deep, nor the governing elites so fragmented and sectarian, that they cannot leave their agreements relatively incomplete and rely upon special cadres of officeholders to complete them. One way to understand rationalizing legal analysis and the significant judicial power that it both grants and conceals is to say that it serves as the instrument by which the lawmaking elites in the political branches of government transfer the responsibility for completing their agreements to judges and other professional law appliers. The ostentatious devolution of power to law appliers, through the use of vague rules and standards, is simply the extreme case of an inveterate habit. However, the judges could not be effective in this work of making patent the hidden social logic of what may appear to be ramshackle compromises if they were to deploy the methods of the political branches. Nor, by deploying those methods, could they reconcile the responsibility of refining law with the task of respecting and securing rights in particular cases. Thus, rationalizing legal analysis, like its nineteenth-century predecessors, serves as the discursive tool of an institutional fix.

As the divisions and the alternatives presented in democratic politics sharpen, the expedient of treating the law as a series of incomplete agreements, with an inner logic capable of being made patent retrospectively, loses its purchase on reality. There is no developing rational scheme that different fragments of law may be seen to exemplify. Rather than being a problem for democracy, the absence of such a latent scheme is, in a sense, a precondition of democratic vigor, for democracy expands by opening social life up to conscious experimentation. For the same reason, the devolution of law-completing and law-reconstructive responsibility to an insulated band of experts in rational deliberation makes no sense. Such an expertise properly belongs to citizens. Any pluralistic and democratic society may have good reason to leave some of its agreements incomplete, but only a democracy in the grip of antidemocratic superstition will entrust to a cadre of juristic mystagogues the task of elaborating these agreements in the light of systematic conceptions of right or welfare supposedly latent in those bargains.

Reconsidered from this angle, rationalizing legal analysis and the connection it establishes between adjudication and the rational reconstruction of law appear to depend upon a telling combination of circumstances. There must be enough practical experimentalism about social life to make deliberate lawmaking the main source, rather than the marginal corrective, of social arrangements. However, there must not be so much democratic experimentalism as to render suspect the passage from the prospective history of law as compromise among contested interests and visions to its retrospective history as the systematic embodiment of connected policies and principles. Democracy and democratic experimentalism are what this transaction constrains. Such a society continues to cling to a powerful residue of the old naturalization of social life under the aegis of customary law – and of the latter-day counterpart to this naturalization in the idea of a self-evident system of arrangements and rights for free economic and political life.

Rationalizing legal analysis draws much of its force and meaning from the largely untested belief in a natural correspondence between the method of legal reasoning and the responsibilities of judicial decision. The institutional and ideological constraints upon the judicial role in a democracy and the effort to expound law as connected principle and policy seem to reinforce and to justify each other. Once we have decided that judges should apply a method of reasoned elaboration, and interpreted reasoned elaboration as the rationalizing reconstruction of law in the vocabulary of impersonal policy and principle, we can then assign to every other agent of the legal system – the administrative agency, the private rightholder, and the legislature – a suitably loosened variant of reasoned elaboration. At last, we come to the residual, reason-resistant practice of electoral party politics, the last refuge, rather than the first source, of lawmaking. The judge stands at the center of this imaginative system because he is supposed to be the embodiment of reason in law.

Putting adjudication in its place

A threshold objection to this exemplary link between legal reasoning and the judicial decision is that being a judge is an institutionally shaped role rather than a social activity with a permanent core and stable boundaries. It is a role whose contours vary from one society and from one time to another. A simple thought experiment makes the point. Should the work of settling disputes of right among individual litigants and the work of reorganizing organizational practices that frustrate the enjoyment of rights (as through complex enforcement) be carried out by the same institutional agent, as it now more or less is, or should it be divided up and assigned to two different agents? In one case, the judicial role, as now understood in the United States, might have to continue expanding. In the other case, it might have to contract. No methodological program can remain indifferent to the institutional setting of its execution.

Two realities sunk in historical variation and contingency – the practice of legal analysis and the situation of being a judge – cannot be made any less variable and contingent by being somehow superimposed, as if they naturally went together and belonged to each other. Yet this arbitrary equation helps shape the program of rationalizing legal analysis.

Once we recognize the strangeness of this familiar identification of legal reasoning with judicial decision we can also begin to appreciate its consequences. These fall into two broad classes, of which the second and less tangible is by far the more important. The first set of consequences is the exorbitant influence exercised on the practice of legal analysis by the ambitions and anxieties of a special cast of characters: the judges, the bureaucrats, and the private jurists. These jurists stand in the imaginative position of judges, or whisper, figuratively or literally, into their ears.

These characters want important work to do, as we all do when we are serious. They also want to reconcile the importance of their work with the limiting claims of democratic legitimacy and practical efficacy. Rationalizing legal analysis can be understood as simply the most recent solution to this problem. Because it is reconstructive and revisionary, and can result in the reinterpretation and reassignment of rights, it creates an opportunity for important work. Because it claims to interpret law, or to elaborate it under rational guidance, and because it avoids the reimagination and remaking of institutional arrangements, it respects practical limits to the power of experts and democratic limits to the authority of unelected officials and professionals. In all these respects, rationalizing legal analysis neatly parallels the forms of policy analysis and prescription deployed by policy experts in and out of office. It tracks the essential logic of the social-democratic compromise, with its hospitality to tax-and-transfer and its abandonment of structural challenge.

The trouble lies in subordinating what legal analysis can do for the republic and its citizens to what it can do for the jurists by reconciling their ambitions with their anxieties. The "status group" stands in the way of the more general mission, imprisoning a larger task within the confines of special concerns. This imprisonment will impose an intolerable cost if its effect is to arrest the democratic project. It will arrest the project if it denies us the instruments with which to identify and to resolve the unstable relation between assumptions about institutions and practices and definitions of interests and ideals. This unstable relation lies at the heart of each of the familiar programmatic positions – conservative, centrist, or progressive – in contemporary democratic politics.

Thus, we come to the second, more elusive and more important class of consequences of the single-minded fascination with judges in legal thought. The effect of this fascination is to usurp the imaginative field in which more constructive and reconstructive practices of legal analysis might develop. The standard of serviceability to judges imposes a paralyzing constraint upon the reinvention of legal analysis: any more ambitious and transformative style of analysis will seem merely to increase the already excessive powers of judges.

Leave analysis to the judges, the answer may go, and deal with the internal relation of interests and ideals to institutions and practices by all the other readily available varieties of political argument, outside legal discourse. The trouble is that this internal relation is played out most importantly when it is played out in detail. At the indispensable level of detail, it lives in the law. The law does not describe behavioral regularities and social arrangements; it selects those arrangements from which claims, backed by state power, will flow. Legal doctrine, in turn, relates these power-giving and power-denying arrangements to conceptions of human connection: pictures of the possible and desirable forms of association in the different domains of social experience.

If the large-scale institutional and imaginative alternatives expressed as comprehensive ideologies have lost their seductions, and the great transformative projects they put forward have collapsed in failure and disappointment, the alternatives continue to live in the small. Nowhere does institutional detail meet imaginative conceptions more fully, and nowhere does their meeting have greater importance for people's powers and incapacities, than in law and legal thought. The lawyers have control, intellectual as well as practical, over this vital stuff. We dare not abandon it to them lest they represent it in a way motivated by the self-regarding reconciliation of the desire to do important work with the need to avoid embarrassment in the eyes of democracy.

This relation among law, lawyers, and citizens is typical rather than anomalous. As state-oriented politics in the rich industrial democracies narrow in scope, as philosophy relinquishes the claim to subversive and reconstructive authority, the struggle over the fundamentals disappears from the central arenas of politics and philosophy. What was withdrawn from the main staging ground of politics and culture reappears, however, under the disguise of technical expertise, in the practice and discourse of the professions. For the democratic project to advance, the specialized disciplines and the professional practices must somehow return to the central conversation of the democracy the larger agenda they helped take away from it. They must return it enriched, and they must return it in a way recognizing the inevitability of specialized knowledge and technical expertise, while transforming the relation of experts to citizens.

The jurist, no longer the imaginary judge, must become the assistant to the citizen. The citizen rather than the judge must turn into the primary interlocutor of legal analysis. The broadening of the sense of collective possibility must become the controlling mission of legal thought.

How should judges decide cases?

Suppose, then, that we treat the question "How should judges decide cases?" as a special question, requiring a special solution. Suppose, further, that in offering this special answer we take care to avoid the illusions of rationalizing legal analysis, its illusions about analogy, about arbitrariness, and about reform. We should define the method in a way that respects the human reality and the practical needs of the people who come into court without harnessing them to a glittering scheme for the improvement of law. We must be sure that our judicial practice leaves open and available, practically and imaginatively, the space on which the real work of social reform can occur. We must eschew dogma and accept compromise in our account of the practice as well as in our understanding of the society to which the practice contributes. We should try to remain close to what judicial decisions in contemporary democracies are actually like.

The view of legal analysis in an adjudicative setting I now offer deflates the vast intellectual and political hopes of rationalizing legal doctrine. It is less ambitious within adjudication, however, only because it is more ambitious outside it. Moreover, it has the virtue of realism: it describes the mass of actual judicial decisions much better than does the canon of rationalizing legal analysis. That it should be superior to its established rival even in this respect is striking when we remember the tendency of any discursive practice to become a self-fulfilling prophecy and the susceptibility of any discursive practice to be influenced by a prestigious conception of its work. The theory of it enters into the thing itself. That the program of rationalizing legal analysis should exercise some influence upon judicial practice, especially in the higher courts, is predictable; that this influence should nevertheless remain so limited is revealing.

The heart of most legal analysis in an adjudicative setting should and must be the context-oriented practice of analogical reasoning in the interpretation of statutes and past judicial decisions. This analogical reasoning must be guided by the attribution of purpose to the interpreted materials, an attribution that can often remain implicit in situations of settled usage but that must be brought out into the open whenever meanings and goals are contested. Purposes need to be explicated when they are contested in fact, in the larger experience of society and culture and in the life situations of the litigants, rather than merely by the advocates in court.

The practice of purposive analogical reasoning should, however, differ in two crucial respects from the method recommended by rationalizing legal analysis and its supporting cast of theories. First, it should acknowledge no drive toward systematic closure and abstraction: the conceptual ascent of purposive judgements toward prescriptive theory-like conceptions of whole fields of law and social life. Second, it should attempt to avoid any rigid contrast between the prospective and the retrospective genealogies of law: between law as it looks to those who struggle, in politics and public opinion, over its making and law as it looks after the fact to its professional and judicial interpreters. The purposes guiding the analogist must be just as eclectic in character as those motivating the contestants in original lawmaking. They range from the triumph of one group interest over another to the force of one set of anxieties in relation to a countervailing set of fears.

What matters is for the judge to form a view of these purposes that is continuous with the real world of discourse and conflict from which that fragment of law came. Moreover, the view should recognize the contestable and factional quality of each of the interests, concerns, and assumptions to which it appeals. They count not because they are the best and the wisest but because they won, and were settled, earlier down the road of lawmaking. Deference to literal meanings and shared expectations is simply the limiting case of a more general commitment to respect the capacity of parties and movements to win in politics, and to encode and enshrine their victories in law.

The transfer of this commitment to a system of judge-made law, such as the Anglo-American common law, presents special problems. For here there never was a moment before and beyond the rationalizing and retrospective discourse of specialized lawyers in each historical period. The key point is that a common law after democracy and within democracy must mean something different, and develop in a different way, from a common law outside and before democracy. To be tolerable within democracy a common law cannot represent the cumulative discovery and refinement of a natural and stable world of custom by a group of legal wise men. Nor can it be the basic system of private-law categories defining the necessary legal forms of free economies and societies. It exists on sufferance as a body of historical compromises that the people choose occasionally to revise. From the perspective of democratic beliefs and practices, we can no longer interpret the body of statutory law in the light of common-law ideas and analogies, nor acquiesce in the strict construction of statutes in derogation of common law. We should reinterpret the common law in the context of democratic experimentalism as a penumbra of arrangements and assumptions that the democracy has not yet disturbed and may not always need to displace. We strengthen its continuing vitality and authority by bringing to its case-by-case development the assumptions and analogies active in the political making, and the judicial construction, of statutory law. In this way we make it ours rather than expecting it, through its immanent development, "to work itself pure."

The context-oriented practice of analogical reasoning, with its respect for literal meanings and settled understandings, its refusal of conceptual ascent, its commitment to seek guidance in the mentalities and vocabularies of the real political world from which laws come, and its recognition of the contestable and factional character of the interests and concerns at issue, is also an incomplete practice. It is incomplete even as a method of judicial decision. To understand why it is incomplete and to grasp the implications of its incompleteness we must recognize that two large ideals bear upon its work and modify its course. The first is an ideal of concern with the litigants as real people, with their vulnerabilities and expectations. The second is an ideal of commitment to make adjudication serve the larger goal of advancing the power of a free people to govern themselves. We are often lucky enough to serve these ideals by clinging to the standard methods of judicial decision. Sometimes, however, loyalty to the ideals requires us to break with this standard practice. From such a departure for the sake of the ideal of human concern arises the deviation of equity. From the departure for the sake of the ideal of popular self-government comes the deviation of judicial statecraft.

In every culture a large part of moral life consists in the claims and expectations people make upon one another by virtue of their respective roles. The role-dependence of our ideas of reasonable and fair behavior holds as much for chosen as for ascriptive roles. Although you would hardly guess it from the moral writings of the philosophers, role-related expectations are the major field on which behavioral routines meet prescriptive beliefs. They are therefore the primary residue of customary law in modern society.

In a democracy whose arrangements have some measure of reality, because it is neither prey to extreme inequalities nor subject to colonial rule, the law will usually conform to such preexisting claims and expectations. To be sure, the law may also be used to change them and therefore to resist them. In the conditions of democracy, however, that is most likely to happen when there is already a conflict of moral and political sensibilities, opening a space in which the legal initiative takes hold.

Thus, the standard contextualist and analogical method of judicial decision will usually be able to placate the role-based popular code of fairness. The judge succeeds in bringing moral expectations established in the social worlds of the litigants to bear upon the purposive practice of analogical judgements. At times the law will openly invite him to do so through its use of open-ended standards like reasonableness, unconscionability, and good faith, or through trade practice and commercial usage. More often he will be able to act without explicit invitation, as part of the justified effort to read and elaborate law in the context of the social and cultural worlds that produced it.

Sometimes, however, the judge and the litigants will not be so lucky. The modest, sensitive, good-faith interpretation of the law will result in the case at hand in a stark contrast between the legal mandate and the moral outcome. This contrast may be the direct and foreseeable result of the law that people wanted to make. They may, for example, have reformed family law in ways designed to overturn role-based expectations in present family life. Alternatively, there may be no way to bridge the gap between law and custom without threatening, or appearing to threaten, some part of the institutionalized structure of society.

The problem is then not that the division between custom and law was itself intended but rather that it cannot be escaped without dramatically expanding the stakes in the conflict. For example, if, out of respect for the ideal of human concern, we were to use the doctrine of economic duress in contract law to void all contracts concluded between members of different social classes, we would find ourselves with a roving mandate to subvert and reconstruct the social order.

There are circumstances in which judges may and should wield a fragment of such a mandate so that the political branches and the citizenry can do so as well; I discuss them soon under the exception of judicial statecraft. For the most part, however, such work lies beyond what judges can effectively or legitimately accomplish. If they insist upon undertaking it, they risk being driven by the need to reconcile ambition with modesty to a clumsy and haphazard reformism, as productive of mischief as of good.

There will, however, be situations in which a large gap does open up between law and custom. The gap may not be itself the legal project nor its foreseeable consequence. Judges can fashion an ad hoc remedy, leaving the institutional structure of society untouched and unthreatened. Here is the opportunity for equity. The microexceptionalism of equitable adjustment is the one-time remaking of rights in the context of roles, the anomalous sacrifice of law to custom. It is an attempt to diminish the quota of cruelty in everyday experience, and to do so not on an aggregate scale but in the dimension of an event and an encounter. The humanity of the judge responds to the humanity of the litigants. Such a stopgap should enjoy no afterlife and exert no influence. It makes an exception to standard judicial practice, but an exception properly included within a larger view of the practice.

The ideal of popular self-government usually finds its best judicial defense in the modesty of the standard practice for all the reasons explored in my earlier discussion of the infirmities of judicial vanguardism. The shamefaced Bonapartism of legal elites, claiming to defend the people from their own ignorance, anger, and selfishness, does not have an encouraging record. Even if it chooses wisely the line of democratic advance, it discovers more often than not that its shortage of power and legitimacy keeps it from dealing with the institutionalized structures from which most disadvantage and exclusion result; that the flight from ultimate causes is soon attended by their sanctification; that its benefits get misdirected to the undeserving segments of deserving groups; that its high-handedness and haphazardness help keep the disadvantaged disorganized and divided; and that the practical effects are often as paltry as the corrective intervention is noisy. Moreover, to use any particular case to push history forward may often violate the ideal of human concern as well as the ideal of popular self-government by subordinating the problems of the litigants to the ambitions of a black-robed providence.

The arguments of this book have nevertheless also shown there to be circumstances in which the judges may properly take it upon themselves to cut through a Gordian knot in the law with their swords of constructive interpretation. They may do so under the promptings of the ideal of popular self-government. The basic condition justifying these acts of judicial statecraft is that there be an entrenched impediment to the enjoyment of rights, especially the rights composing the system of popular self-government. To call the obstacle "entrenched" is to say that it resists challenge and defiance by the ordinarily available devices of political and economic action, and that its victims consequently find themselves unable to escape it by their own efforts. There are then two principal variants.

The obstacle may be one that is diffuse in the experience of certain groups although triggered by particular practices. The political branches of government fail to respond, often because the antidemocratic taint touches the arrangements concerning their formation, such as voting practices or access to the media. The remedy may be a bold remaking of law, whether constitutional law or ordinary law. Such an arrogation of tribunician power amounts to a gamble for support. The prospects for its efficacy as well as the case for its legitimacy (efficacy and legitimacy overlap) are therefore greatly strengthened when the reformers below can appeal to a broad-based current of opinion in society. It is also reinforced when the reformers act as the partners of organized movements in the departments of social life in which they intervene. The partnership of the American federal judiciary with the civil-rights movements, and then, more tentatively, with the feminist movement, during the heyday of progressive jurisprudence, provides the most familiar examples.

Alternatively, the obstacle may be localized in the power structures of particular organizations or social practices. The corruption of the ideal of popular self-government may seem less evident. In its more subtle and limited form it may nevertheless be all the more insidious in sapping the capacity for individual as well as collective self-determination. The solution then lies in the structural but episodic intervention of complex enforcement.

So long as we fail to establish a distinct branch of government to perform this role, with more democratic accountability and greater investigative, technical, financial, and administrative resources than the traditional judiciary now enjoys, there will be no institutional agent well suited to the performance of this mission. Better an ill-suited agent, however, than none at all. Judges may often be the best agents around. At least they may be the only willing agents.

They will then have to test how far their power and authority as well as their wills and imaginations enable them to push the work of structural but episodic intervention. They will need to do the job in full awareness of the constraints their incongruity as agents imposes upon the execution of their self-appointed task. They will have reason to be both skeptical and humble. They will understand, in this variant of judicial statecraft as in the other, that it is one thing to call the spirits and another for the spirits to come.

KENOSIS: ESCAPING THE MISDIRECTIONS OF CONTEMPORARY THEORY

Theory as obstacle

Before turning to the constructive implications of this discussion of rationalizing legal analysis for the work of legal thought outside adjudication, there remains one more obstacle to overcome: the misdirections into which the most influential modern approaches to the understanding of law lead us. Wherever rationalizing legal analysis flourishes, the schools of jurisprudence become its operational ideologies. Thus, in the United States today theories of the legal process, of political right, and of economic efficiency offer alternative proposals to ground and refine the vocabulary of policy and principle. I have already shown how in each instance the theorist claims part of the rationalizing scheme to be there already latent in extant law and received legal understanding and part to be properly added, or completed, through the improving work of reasoned and retrospective elaboration. The criticism of these ideas is best accomplished by criticizing their real object, rationalizing legal analysis, refined or unrefined.

Other ideas, however, stand in the way. These ideas address more broadly the nature of law, and the relation of law to forms of social life and to systems of social thought. Over the last several generations, four such families of ideas have shaped, with varying force, our views of what we can do with law and legal thought: the belief that the indeterminacy or manipulability of legal doctrine is the central problem in legal reasoning, connected with the attempt sometimes to radicalize and at other times to tame the element of discretion in legal reasoning; the attempt (by theorists like Kelsen and H.L.A. Hart) sharply to distinguish the analytic representation of law from the inside practice of legal doctrine, and thus to escape the entanglement of theory in ideology; the functionalist view of law as the surface manifestation or the responsive tool of practical, functional requirements of social life; and the historicist or culturalist conception of law as the outward manifestation of the making and life of a people, according to which each legal order represents the mould of a distinct national existence.

We must rid ourselves of these approaches because each of them, tainted by illusion, directs us away from the discovery of transformative opportunity. By suppressing insight into the possible, each disorients our understanding of the actual – of existing societies and their established law, and of what legal thought is and can become.

The radicalization of indeterminacy

No obsession has enjoyed greater staying power, or exerted broader influence, in the history of modern legal theory than the concern with the relative indeterminacy or manipulability of legal doctrine. Since the late nineteenth century the criticism of the dominant styles of legal reasoning has taken predominantly the form of an effort to recognize a greater element of doctrinal elasticity and judicial discretion. The effort to rescue and restabilize the method of rational reconstruction in legal thought, of which the appeal to connected policy and principle is the most recent form, has operated by a series of maneuvers of confession and avoidance: abandoning some of the earlier position while clinging to a more defensible residue. Remarkably, these developments have occurred with equal force in both common-law and civil-law countries. They have even resonated outside these now universal legal traditions in the internal debates of Islamic, Jewish, and Hindu law.

The final outcome of this progression has been the radicalization of the indeterminacy thesis by the most determined opponents of rationalizing legal analysis. From the starting point of the given legal materials and with the help of the available methods of legal argument and the established canons of interpretation, we can characteristically infer, with similar plausibililty, opposite solutions to particular problems. Thus, we choose what we claim to discover. Faced with this claim, the standard-bearers of mainstream legal thought can see themselves as the defenders of reasonable moderation and moderate reasonableness against the excesses of rationalism and the extravagance of skepticism, against the mindlessness of law as analogy and the irresponsibility of law as ideology.

The radicalization of indeterminacy is, however, a mistake; not merely a mistake about law and language but also a mistake about the relation between what the radical indeterminists mean and what they say. Emerging as the all but inexorable outcome of a long progression of ideas, the radicalization of the indeterminacy thesis makes us realize that something has long since gone wrong in the terms of this discussion.

Imagine the following conversation between the would-be radicalizer of indeterminacy and the last-ditch defender of rational reconstruction. The defender says: "Do not accuse me of a naive belief in a plain-meaning theory of language or in a self-evident correspondence between words and things. I merely assert that it is possible to convey meaning on the basis of engagement in a common world or a shared tradition even though the world or the tradition may be divided and discontinuous and even though it may include only part of what we and our interlocutors are, experience, and value. In fact, some of you have developed enlightening accounts of the hidden forms of consciousness that make it possible to fix and convey meaning. I merely disagree with you in the evaluation of them, and I hope to improve them by bringing them into the light of reflection and conversation. Surely you, radical indeterminist, agree that it is possible to convey meaning, for here you are arguing with me." The radical indeterminist then answers: "You fail to understand me. I never intended to deny the possibility of transferring meaning. I want to contest the institutional and ideological assumptions upon which the transfer takes place. My aim was political before it was linguistic."

Now, however, we can see the problem with the conversation. The thesis of radical indeterminacy turns out to be in large part a metaphor for something else: a planned campaign of social and cultural criticism. The trouble is that it does nothing to equip us for this campaign or to illuminate its aims. It is a dead-end. It tempts the radical indeterminist into an intellectual and political desert, and abandons him there alone, disoriented, disarmed, and, at last, corrupted – by powerlessness.

Marginality tilts the scales. The radical reformers of the eighteenth and nineteenth centuries wanted to bind judges hand and foot to prevent the subversion of legislated programs and the usurpation of democratic power. The radical indeterminists have no organic links with parties or movements, nor can they imagine themselves or their allies in the seats of powers. They would like to believe that it hardly matters who wins and loses in the politics of the state and codifies political triumphs as law. Once the law gets into the hands of the interpreters – so they imply – everything will begin from scratch as if nothing had happened before.

We cannot, just by saying so, turn a political defeat into a word game. We must sacrifice the metaphor to the campaign, and recognize that law can be something, and that it matters what it is. Having rejected the radicalization of indeterminacy as a misstatement of radical intentions, we must then go on to repudiate the central role of the problem of determinacy and discretion in legal theory.

The project of a pure theory of law

A second influential misdirection in legal theory is the project of producing an analytic representation of law that can disengage itself from both normative controversies about what the content of law should be and causal–empirical controversies about the causes and consequences of different rules and doctrines. Although this ambition has exerted influence from time to time in the history of legal theory, it achieved its most uncompromising expression in Kelsen's "pure theory of law." Put aside the theory of legal reasoning in Kelsen and his more qualified English counterpart, H.L.A. Hart, and consider the central idea of an analytic description of law disentangled from ideology and sociology.

Much of the drive to disentangle has come from a desire to create a vocabulary for talking about law that would be free of the idealization of law produced by the practice of rational reconstruction in legal doctrine. From this impulse of desanctification arises some of the force that the idea of pure analysis in law continues to hold even today. However, the effort at disenchantment in the pure analysis of law has been rendered sterile by its association with a pseudoscientific prejudice: the search for intellectual universality and invulnerability through immunity to normative and empirical controversy. Give no hostages, or as few as possible, to programmatic commitment and empirical conjecture, they think, and we shall be stronger. In this way they have emasculated themselves, and deprived their campaign for the desanctification of law and legal doctrine of any productive outcome it might hope to achieve.

It is illuminating to compare their strategy to the direction taken by mainstream economic theory since the rise of marginalism and the development of general-equilibrium analysis. Economics has also sought to avoid wedding itself to controversial empirical and ideological assumptions. (Compare to Marx's economics, which, beginning from the same starting points, went in the opposite direction, and proved both productive and wrong-headed as a result.) It has paid for its methodological immunity by its explanatory sterility: the analytic machine generates empirical conjectures only when fed descriptions and explanations from outside and policy conclusions only when supplied with programmatic direction from outside. However, it is always tempted to veer away from this methodological austerity. Succumbing to this temptation, it repeatedly smuggles in, through the back door, the precommitments it claims to have thrown out through the front one; now, more dangerously, because undisciplined by explicit theory and argument. Such a social science is doomed to an eternal infancy.

Mainstream economics, nevertheless, enjoys a twofold advantage over the project of pure analysis in legal theory: the great explanatory power of its empirical residue – the psychological schema of maximizing, self-interested behavior – and the extraordinary versatility of the mathematical apparatus that can be brought to bear in the elaboration of that schema. For lack of such compensations, pure analysis in law degenerates into empty triviality.

Behind the misjudgement about invulnerability lies a mistake about the relation of method to conception. We have no way to judge the value of an analytic vocabulary for the descriptive representation of law – or of anything else – except by its usefulness to a particular explanatory or programmatic endeavor. More reality, more of it than rationalizing legal analysis and its supporting theories can countenance, is what we need and what the pure analysts are unwilling to give us.

The functionalist approach to law

A third misguided approach is the functionalist, evolutionary, and deep-structure explanation of law and legal history. Its most influential leftist form is orthodox Marxism, carried over to legal theory. Its most wide-spread conservative expression is a style of functionalist economic and sociological explanation of legal change that sees legal institutions as driven by convergence toward a system of best available practices. Today these two traditions are sometimes scrambled in the idea of "stages of capitalism," each with its built-in legal expression, only with the transformative sequel of "socialism" missing.

The functionalist element in this approach is the belief that the emergence and diffusion of legal arrangements can be explained by their consequences and, in particular, by their (unique) capacity to fulfill inexorable requirements of practical social life. The evolutionary element is the idea of a progression or convergence, if not along a single pathway, at least toward a common outcome. The deep-structure element is the notion that the key entities possessing the explanatory functional advantages are supposedly indivisible systems of arrangements such as "capitalism" or the "market economy," driven forward by lawlike forces.

The functional explanations would lack their distinct character and controversial force if they were not associated with the deep-structure assumptions. Our way of thinking about law in society would be very different from this one if, for example, we thought that the functional advantages select from the institutional and ideological materials that happen to be generated by many loosely linked sequences of conflict, innovation, and jumbling; that institutional orders are divisible so that revolutionary reform – the piecemeal change of a formative structure – is the standard mode of their transformation; that the pull of function interacts with the push of contingent sequence, leaving a large and indistinct realm of possibility within which the will and the imagination can maneuver; and that society can be so arranged as to strengthen or to repress this power to surprise and to remake.

The criticism of the functionalist, evolutionary, and deep-structure approach to law turns into the criticism of the social theory from which it arises. I have pursued this polemic elsewhere, and tried to show that, taken to the hilt, such a criticism leads not to agnosticism but to a different style of theoretical imagination, one decoupling explanatory ambition from the vindication of historical necessity and putting insight on the side of transformative freedom.

One feature of the application of the functionalist and deep-structure method to law deserves special emphasis. For it shows how the necessitarian functionalist method misses what is most interesting about the history of law. It demonstrates how the self-subversive work of modern legal thought has itself helped discredit and dissolve the marriage of functionalist explanation with deep-structure assumptions in the whole field of social and historical studies. This feature is the correspondence between (1) belief in the reality and indivisibility of supposed institutional systems – capitalism or the market economy – as the ultimate protagonists of the functionalist trial-by-evolution and (2) belief in the existence of a definite system of rights – especially contract and property rights as well as rights of property against government. Such rights are taken to be both the outcome of the functionalist evolution and the necessary form of the market economy or of "capitalism." In such a view, differences – among capitalist societies or market economies – must be cast as minor and transitory variations on the same evolving themes.

However, just as the history of economic activity has demonstrated with mounting clarity that similar economic results can be produced by divergent economic institutions, so the history of law and legal thought has shown that the same institutional conceptions – like "market economy," "capitalism," or "private property" – can be translated into alternative sets of legal–institutional arrangements, with decisive consequences for the character of social life. Each of these two lines of discoveries has slowly become more familiar. Only because we fail to connect them and to draw out their joint implications does the functionalist-necessitarian approach retain even today a semblance of plausibility.

If, for example, a mixed form of public–private corporate control ("township–village enterprises") appears in China, we are more likely to view it as a passing adaptation of market principles to Chinese circumstances if we begin with the preconception that the market economy evolves toward a well-defined set of best available practices. We are less likely to do so if we think of existing institutions as a small subset of a much larger, indistinct set of possible forms. These contrasting beliefs will not only color our interpretation of developments; they will also encourage or discourage the developments from occurring in the first place.

Conversely, the multiplication of successful institutional heresies around the world – and the discovery that well-chosen heresy is often part of the price of success – makes it increasingly less possible to think of the institutional anomalies as deviations from a standard model of economic and political organization. We begin to think of each of the deviations as possible starting points toward something else, as experiments that are born out of haphazard compromise and that risk miscarriage along the way, but that also contain the potential to begin an alternative trajectory of national development.

Moreover, what is successful in the short run may prove, at the next stage, to impose a costly constraint. For example, an elitist and authoritarian partnership between business and government in the north East Asian economies may have proved successful in sustaining economic growth in a world of semiskilled mass-production. It may nevertheless prove insufficient and damaging when industrial evolution calls for higher levels of flexibility, knowledge, and workteam self-direction.

We must act upon conjectures of what makes continuing success possible, and prevents a national economy from settling into a rigid character unresponsive to changes in the economic fortunes of the world. One key to such continuing power lies in the ability to reconcile cooperation with innovation, and to develop the cooperative arrangements minimizing impediments to innovation. We therefore have a practical

stake in learning how to disassemble and recombine property rights so
that economic agents may gain more access to productive resources while
enjoying less opportunity to veto other people's experiments. We may, for
example, want a property regime that favors cooperative competition
because it recognizes multiple claims to productive resources while denying to a residual "owner" the right to be a decision-maker of last resort.

Reconsidered from the standpoint of such concerns and discoveries,
the functionalist explanation of law turns out to be many-sided and incomplete, and its moves toward necessitarianism and convergence are
revealed to be a false start. Moreover, we have an interest in its being false
and therefore also in acting as if we knew for sure (which we do not) that
it is. The "natural selection" of institutional arrangements works with the
materials that many particular histories happen to have generated; the outcome results from some rough-and-ready compromise between
preexisting interests or superstitions and desired powers or advantages;
the test of failure and success measures an available something against an
available something else; the choice of economic institutions is compli-
cated by its being, at the same time, the choice of a form of life; the
short-term triumph diverges from the long-term potential; deviations from
standard models of organization may be either local adaptations or alternative beginnings; and our ideas about alternatives – especially our ideas
about their specific legal forms – influence our capacity to champion and
establish them.

Legal thought has not been merely the passive victim or beneficiary of
these discoveries; it has been their coauthor. Since the heyday of nineteenth-century legal science it has helped undermine what it set out to
vindicate: the conception of a built-in legal content to the idea of a free
economic and political order. By its cumulative erosion of the conception
of a predetermined system of property rights in particular, and of rights of
individual and collective self-determination in general, it has destroyed
some of the assumptions upon which a functionalist necessitarianism
about institutions relies.

The historical–culturalist approach to law

A fourth misdirection is the historicist and culturalist treatment of law as
the unique expression of the life of a people, the voice of a national tradition. The exemplary expression of this approach is Jhering's *Spirit of
Roman Law*. Its influence, although qualified and fragmentary, is all
around us. Sometimes the functionalist and historicist approaches have

combined, as when different and nearly unalterable national political cultures are held responsible for making the race to functional advantage run on distinct tracks: one set of corporate forms suitable to the Americans, another to the Japanese, and another yet to the Germans. The form of life, unique and organic, manifest in legal detail and developed as legal tradition, becomes in the strong historicist view the central topic of legal study and the chief protagonist of legal history.

The idea of law as the expression of a unique form of life drastically exaggerates the unity and continuity, and understates the made-up character, of the cultures manifest in law. For example, having understood the contemporary Japanese life-employment system and its supporting labor-law practices as the creatures of a conflict-averse culture, we may be surprised to discover that this system is a relatively recent invention of conservative statecraft by entrepreneurs, politicians, and bureaucrats; that it followed several generations of bitter industrial conflict; and that one of its conditions and byproducts has been a marked division between the secure and the insecure segments of the Japanese laborforce.

The whole of a culture – say, of the ancient Romans or the contemporary Japanese – turns out to resemble this example, repeated a thousand times over in a thousand details of social management. Institutions become a second-order fate, but only after having been shaped and stabilized by a surprising history of fighting and compromise, of halting insight and armed illusion. People forget the sufferings and sorrows of this war, and reimagine them as culture.

Underlying this fact is a persistent feature of our relation to the institutional and discursive contexts in which we act: there is always more in us than there is in them, more powers of insight, desire, and association than they are able to countenance or to prevent. Consequently, people have a two-sided consciousness in even the most entrenched and all-inclusive society and culture. They never surrender completely to the routines and pieties that seem to have mastered them. They secretly entertain a mental reservation. If the established order suffers a trauma, they may suddenly cast aside what they seemed, so completely, to have embraced.

The dual structure of consciousness has a significant consequence for the interpretation of law and legal history. It lends extraordinary interest to the exceptions, the countervailing solutions, the residues and "mistakes," of every legal order. For these signs of past or rejected solutions, of subordinated interests, and roads not taken, form material with which the hidden, contrary side of the divided consciousness can work. Each of them becomes a possible starting point for more general alternatives in law. Thus, from having been intellectual and political embarrassments, they become intellectual and political opportunities.

The mistake of historicism has, in the course of recent history, become more mistaken for reasons related to the mounting case against functionalist necessitarianism. The worldwide emulation of cultures, and the relentless pressure to pillage and recombine practices from all over the world for the sake of practical success, increasingly eviscerate the customary content of national identities. These identities become abstract: disengaged from any stable set of customs clearly marking the boundaries between one form of life and another. The will to difference outlasts actual difference, and becomes, through the weakening of difference, all the more intransigent. Real customs can be compromised; abstract collective identities cannot. Historicism, from being an illusion, becomes a danger, lending prestige to the self-deceptions of nationalism.

Kenosis

After we have rejected these several misdirections in legal theory, do we need a general ground on which to stand? A comprehensive normative and explanatory theory of law requires nothing less than a systematic doctrine of society and personality capable of both explaining and proposing. It is foolish to make dogmatic pronouncements about the impossibility of "grand" theory and to identify the possible futures of speculative thought with its familiar past. In other books I have tried to show that the instruments are already at hand with which to explain ourselves without discounting our freedom, with which to recognize the formative influence of imaginative and institutional structures while discarding the determinist baggage that has ordinarily accompanied the idea of discontinuous structures, and with which to advance the democratic project by reimagining many of its practical forms and unexamined assumptions. There is a future for social theory beyond the marriage of functionalist explanation with deep-structure assumptions, just as there is a future for democracy beyond social democracy, and the first of these two futures can help show the way to the second.

It is just as dogmatic, however, to insist upon a systematic discourse of explanations and ideals as the sole possible path of progress in our imagination of society. This book tries a different tack, one closer to the arguments and conflicts in which people actually engage. It seizes upon a particular problem – how to understand an influential practical discourse, rationalizing legal analysis, and, having understood it, what to turn it into. The argument begins in the middle of the stuff – the institutions and ideologies surrounding us – and seeks guidance from the family of political ideals that now enjoys greatest authority throughout the world – the democratic project. It works from the bottom up and from the inside out. Faithful to this spirit, its attitude to general theoretical misdirections such as those criticized in this section is like the attitude the patristic theologians labeled *kenosis*: emptying out. The intended product of *kenosis* is readiness. The empty space is to be filled by ideas as we need them and by deeds as we can do them. Self-consciousness can make do, as it ordinarily must, for system.

LEGAL ANALYSIS AS INSTITUTIONAL IMAGINATION

Aims of a revised practice of legal analysis

Implicit in my discussion of rationalizing legal analysis is a series of connected standards by which to guide and to assess the redirection of legal thought outside adjudication. These standards converge to yield the idea of legal analysis as institutional imagination.

Thus, the method we need should be free of the taint of institutional fetishism and structure fetishism. Institutional fetishism is the identification of abstract institutional conceptions like the market economy or representative democracy with a particular repertory of contingent arrangements. Structure fetishism is its higher-order counterpart: the failure to recognize that the institutional and imaginative orders of social life differ in their entrenchment as well as in their content: that is to say, in the relation to the structure-defying and structure-transforming freedom of action and insight they constrain. The method should help us identify and resolve the internal instability characteristic of programmatic positions in contemporary law and politics: the conflict between the commitment to defining ideals and the acquiescence in arrangements that frustrate the realization of those ideals or impoverish their meaning. Consequently, it should seize upon the internal relation between thinking about ideals or interests and thinking about institutions or practices. When so doing, it can gain energy and direction from a larger conception of the democratic project as well as from more particular professed ideas and recognized interests, for the democratic project, properly interpreted, is both our most powerful family of ideals and our most promising way to reconcile our devotion to these ideals with the pursuit of our material interests. To these ends, the method should make good on the capacity of law and legal thought to move at the level of full detail in representing the relation of practices and institutions to interests and ideals and in connecting the realities of power to the discourse of aspiration. To mobilize these resources, it must rid itself of the antianalogical prejudice; of the illusory belief in rational reconstruction as the necessary and sufficient antidote to arbitrariness in law; of the confusions and equivocations of conservative reformism, particularly in the variant of pessimistic progressive reformism; and of the obsession with judges and the ways they decide cases. It must elect the citizenry as its primary and ultimate interlocutor. It must imagine its work to be that of informing the conversation in a democracy about its present and alternative futures.

Mapping and criticism

These aims come together in the practice of legal analysis as institutional imagination. This practice has two, dialectically linked moments: mapping and criticism. Give the name *mapping* to the suitably revised version of the low-level, spiritless analogical activity, the form of legal analysis that leaves the law an untransformed heap. Mapping is the attempt to describe in detail the legally defined institutional microstructure of society in relation to its legally articulated ideals. Call the second moment of this analytic practice *criticism*: the revised version of what the rationalistic jurists deride as the turning of legal analysis into ideological conflict. Its task is to explore the interplay between the detailed institutional arrangements of society as represented in law, and the professed ideals or programs these arrangements frustrate and make real.

Mapping is the exploration of the detailed institutional structure of society, as it is legally defined. It would be naive positivism to suppose that this structure is uncontroversially manifest, and can be portrayed apart from theoretical preconceptions. The crucial point of mapping is to produce a detailed, although fragmentary, legal–institutional analysis replacing one such set of preconceptions by another.

The perspective to be adopted is the standpoint of the second moment of the revised practice of legal analysis I am sketching: the moment of criticism. Thus, the two moments connect closely; they are related – to use one vocabulary – dialectically and – to use another – internally. Mapping serving the purpose of criticism is an analysis exhibiting the formative institutions of society and its enacted dogmas about human association as a distinct and surprising structure, and, above all, as a structure that can be revised part by part. The established system of such arrangements and beliefs both constrains the realization of our professed social ideals and recognized group interests and gives them much of their tacit meaning.

The preconceptions to be replaced negate the possibility or the significance of criticism. Such preconceptions present the greater part of any extended and received body of law and legal understandings as an expression of a cohesive moral and political vision, or of a set of practical necessities, or of a lawlike evolutionary sequence.

One set of such anticritical abstractions exercising especially great influence in contemporary law and legal thought is the second-order Lochnerism explored earlier. Remember that the earlier, cruder, repudiated Lochnerism is the contrast between a law that is just there, prepolitically, as the built-in legal structure of an accepted and established type of economic and governmental organization – call it liberal capitalist democracy or whatever – and a law that represents the unprincipled, faction-driven, redistributive intervention of government in this core legal structure. That is the Lochnerism American notables – and their European counterparts – rejected, although they still have not rejected it completely and unequivocally. The Lochnerism that survives, generating a steady stream of abstractions that prevent the work of mapping–criticism, is the Lochnerism meant to distinguish concessions to factional interest or outlook from expressions of impersonal moral and political vision or practical necessity. The expressions must be rescued from the concessions, and it is on the basis of invocations of the former and denunciations of the latter that rationalizing legal analysis does its work.

The language of contemporary politics commonly superimposes such reassuring ideological abstractions, more or less directly, upon low-level promises to particular organized interests. At every turn it becomes impossible to tell whether the abstractions serve as an ideological disguise for the pursuit of the interests, or whether, on the contrary, the pursuit of the interests is being disoriented by the abstractions. What we chiefly lack is what should be the very heart of political discourse: the middle ground of alternative trajectories of institutional and policy change. To help develop this middle ground is one of the tasks of the combined practice of mapping and criticism. A requirement for the accomplishment of this task is that we resist the impulse to rationalize or to idealize the institutions and the laws we actually have.

What type of insight may one hope to develop through the practice of mapping? Consider the example of the relation of the traditional property right to the many exceptions that begin to surround it. The property right, bringing together many faculties assigned to the same rightholder, is the very model of the modern idea of right, and the central mechanism for the allocation of decentralized claims to capital. Yet we find in contemporary legal systems many areas of law and practice that settle matters in ways departing from the logic of this property entitlement. In agriculture, for example, there may be a partnership between the government and the family farmer decomposing the property right and limiting the absoluteness of the property owner's right in exchange for varieties of governmental support. In the defense-procurements industry, and even more under the conditions of war capitalism, a similar decomposition in the form of collaboration between public power and the private producer may occur. In the development of contemporary capital markets we see a continuous creation of new markets in particular faculties abstracted out of the comprehensive property entitlement. The situation then begins to look like this: the main mechanism is surrounded by a growing number of exceptions. However, even if traditional property had been eviscerated more than it in fact has been, it would continue to occupy the vital role of holding the space that any other generalized form of decentralized allocation of capital would hold. It holds the place that would be occupied by the alternative method of decentralized capital allocation already prefigured in the current exceptions to the unified property right. This is a typical example of the type of combination of sameness and variety one might hope to discover through mapping.

The second moment of this revised practice of legal analysis is criticism. Criticism explores the disharmonies between the professed social ideals and programmatic commitments of society, as well as the recognized group interests, and the detailed institutional arrangements that not only constrain the realization of those ideals, programs, and interests but also give them their developed meaning.

The relation between criticism and mapping can now come more clearly into focus. Mapping provides materials for criticism, and criticism sets the perspective and the agenda for mapping. Nothing in my account of the revised practice of legal analysis defines the extent to which criticism can itself be informed or guided by a more context-independent type of moral and political argument. Rather than addressing that issue now, however, it is enough to recognize how little we need a prior and confident view of it to begin revising the practice of legal analysis in this way and to begin practicing the revision. The reoriented approach may prove compatible with a broad range of positions about our ability to connect with a less history-bound mode of judgement. Moreover, the new practice may itself have something to teach us about the relative merits of different views of authority beyond context in moral and political disputes.*

Consider now some lines along which we might work out the anti-rationalizing response to the circumstance of contemporary law and legal thought. The first task – the task of the mapping moment – is to understand the existing institutional situation as the complex and contradictory structure that it really is, as the strange and surprising settlement that you could never guess from abstractions like "the mixed economy," "representative democracy," or "industrial society." In this view, the jurist should work as an enlarger of the collective sense of reality and possibility. He must imitate the artist who makes the familiar strange, restoring to our understanding of our situation some of the lost and repressed sense of transformative opportunity.

The focus of mapping is the attempt to construct a picture of our institutions – of the government, of the economy, the family – out of the stuff of law and legal doctrine. It is a hard task; the material wears no particular picture on its face. What kind of picture do we want? First, we want a view that defines itself by contrast to the rationalizing account. This account – remember – wants to present the stuff of law as tied together in a way that justifies most of it while rejecting a minor part of it. Rational reconstruction in law justifies and interprets the greater part of the law and of the received legal understandings either as the expression of an evolving system of moral and political conceptions or as the outcome of inexorable functional requirements. Affirmatively, the view we want is the view serving the purposes of the second moment of this analytic practice: the moment of criticism, when we focus on the disharmonies of the law and on the way in which the ideal conceptions, expressed in policies and principles, or the group interests represented by programs and strategies, get truncated in their fulfillment and impoverished in their meaning by their received institutional forms.

Throughout this book I have already offered a number of examples of the mapping exercise: the partial alternatives to the unified property idea that we can already witness in current law and practice; the relation of traditional rights adjudication to the structural but episodic intervention of complex enforcement; the disharmonies of substantive equal protection

---

* See the later discussion of the campaign to split the difference between rationalism and historicism, pp. 170–82.

and of the related law of antidiscrimination; and, more generally, the dialectical organization of contemporary law in each of its branches as a duality of rights of personal choice and popular self-government and rights designed to ensure the reality of individual and collective self-determination.

Do we need a full-blown theory, a practice of social explanation, a set of programmatic ideas, and a conception of the relation between programmatic thinking and social explanation to inform mapping? The answer is yes and no. We need such ideas fully to develop and elucidate the revised practice of legal analysis. But we need not have such a theory to begin the mapping.

We already have two points of departure at hand. One starting point is the effort to radicalize the professed social ideals or party programs, to take them beyond their existing institutional constraints, and to change their meaning in the course of doing so. Another point of departure is the negativistic work of demolishing the rationalizing conceptions and interpretations of contemporary law.

Thus, this mapping involves no naive acceptance of the low-level, analogical, glossatorial picture of law as an unshaped, undigested heap. It demands a radical redrawing of that picture from the standpoint of the precommitments of criticism. The moments of mapping and criticism form a dialectical unity. We can nevertheless claim for the low-level, analogical conception of law certain advantages. It presents extant law and received legal understanding free – or freer – from the rationalizing spell and from the special outlook of the Madisonian notables, ever anxious for a view of law on which, as judges or publicists, they can act with the least embarrassment.

Is criticism more likely to occur under conditions in which mapping dominates the legal culture, or in situations in which rationalization does? To answer this question, we must begin by remembering that mapping and criticism are indissoluble; they are aspects or moments of the same practice. Just as mapping provides materials for criticism, it is already done with the interests of criticism in mind. Moreover, as a practical matter, the formation of such a transformative analytic practice is possible only in the historical circumstance in which we can rebel against runaway rationalization. For, even as rationalizing analysis in law, and in the corresponding areas of political and social thought, mythologizes our institutions, it also generalizes our ideals. It thus sets the stage on which the mapper–critic can go to work.

IMAGINING THE ALTERNATIVE
FUTURES OF A FREE SOCIETY:
EXTENDED SOCIAL DEMOCRACY

The idea of alternative institutional futures

Imagine the practice of mapping and criticism put to work on the stuff of contemporary law and legal thought. Suppose it carried forward many stages into the future, with all the intermediate, transitional steps missing. We would come up with several alternative conceptions of the desirable sequel to social democracy, as it is currently understood and partly practiced in the North Atlantic world. Here are three such conceptions, sketched with a degree of simplicity, and of remoteness from present arrangements, that may help suggest the promise of diversity hidden under the mask of conformity. None of these three programs fits on our current spectrum of right and left, a spectrum organized around orientations increasingly less pertinent to present concerns. The real division between radicals and conservatives has become less the difference between statist and antistatist commitments than the contrast between those who want to realize contemporary party-political programs within the limits of the inherited governmental and economic institutions and those who propose to revise those institutions and to redefine their programmatic commitments as a result.

The familiar versions of rightwing and leftwing party programs combine a commitment to economic competition, in one instance, and redistributive and participatory aims, in the other, with an acceptance of established economic and governmental arrangements. The trouble is that, once these arrangements are left unchallenged, the distinctive programmatic aims of the right and the left cannot be taken very far; they turn into tilts of emphasis that, although capable of helping or harming people in the here and now, fail to present clear alternatives for society. If we accept the established institutional framework, we cannot take the familiar divisions between right and left too seriously; we must discount and retrench their programmatic commitments.

Suppose, however, that we show ourselves willing to find alternatives to the unified property right the better to achieve a higher reconciliation between decentralized economic decision-making and economies of scale. Or imagine that we commit ourselves to seek redistributive goals through economic reorganization rather than through tax-and-transfer schemes that attempt, retrospectively, to compensate for the unequalizing operation of the economy. Then, we shall have radicalized rather than retrenched our programs. Whether we radicalize or retrench, we shall have abandoned our traditional view of the line between right and left. In particular, we shall have rejected the way of drawing the line that tracks attitudes toward markets and toward their displacement by governmental enterprise, allocation, and regulation.

The fragility of conventional ideological distinctions between the right and the left should hardly cause surprise, for these distinctions mark variants of what can justifiably be described as the dominant political program of the modern age. This program seeks to find the arrangements capable of exploiting the overlap between the institutional conditions for the enhancement of the productive capabilities of societies – through accelerated innovation and recombination – and the institutional conditions for the emancipation of individuals from entrenched social roles and hierarchies. According to a widespread view, the major task of political philosophy is to find a standpoint – deeper or more neutral – from which to adjudicate among conflicting doctrines, outlooks, and interests. However, the first job of political philosophy may be, instead, to sweep away false, superficial ideological contrasts, the better to probe the ways in which we may diversify our unified, dominant political program. It is a first step toward exploring the alternative and divergent routes that lead beyond that program. The diversity of the futures of democracy is not the problem; it is the task and the solution. We need ideas that help us create ideological conflicts we can take more seriously before we claim to settle ideological struggles that are not, in fact, what they seem.

Each of the three futures of a free society I now discuss is a deliberately faraway image of one possible path for the advancement of democracy. Each describes a distinct way of continuing the now arrested development of legal thought, by turning its central concern with the effective enjoyment of legal rights into a motivated institutional tinkering. I picture each of these paths at a point remote from our present arrangements the better to bring out its distinctive nature. However, the direction matters more than the distance. We can connect each back, through numerous transitional steps, to the here and now. We can in turn represent each of these transitional steps as both a series of institutional innovations and a set of class or group alliances; innovations and alliances are just the reverse sides of each other.

There is, nevertheless, a crucial asymmetry in this correspondence. We build group alliances by trying to change social arrangements, both through the use of governmental power and through the self-transformation of civil society. Successful institutional innovations then turn what had up till then been tactical partnerships between different groups into lasting mergers of group interests or group identities. For example, a successful postfordist industrial reconstruction, breaking down the barriers among traditional mass-production industry, the economic rearguard of under-capitalized shops and services, and the economic vanguard of skill-intensive, flexible production would lay the basis for a more inclusive popular alliance in the rich industrial democracies than now seems feasible.

However, if social alliances need institutional innovations to be sustained, institutional innovations do not require preexisting social alliances. All they may demand are party-political agents and institutional programs, having those class or group alliances as a project – as a project rather than as a premise. If institutional change and group alliances were not asymmetrically related in just this way, the problem of willed structural change in history would remain insoluble: the dialectic or the drift of history – the one, unbelievable; the other, unreliable – would have to provide what conscious politicking would be powerless to accomplish. For the group alliances and antagonisms prevailing at any given time tend to presuppose and reinforce the institutionalized structure of society. Thus, for example, the industrial working class, headquartered in mass-production industry, imagine their enemy to be the underclass of temporary workers, who compete with them for both the semiskilled jobs of traditional industry and the welfare favors of the state. They seek to defend their place rather than to change it. The spark of movement must come from political action equipped with institutional imagination.

Thus, the discussion of the passage from the present policy debate to the missing programmatic conversation at the beginning of this book describes early moves in the same conversations whose later moves I now seek to explore. Legal analysis as institutional imagination is simply the practice of these conversations, continued, as they can and should be, in the detailed materials of law.

Just as each of the three futures of a free society can be connected back, through transitional steps, to the here and now, so each represents the choice of a different form of life: one encouraging some forms of individual and social experience while discouraging others. Contrary to the claims of those who would starkly separate impartial right from factional good, there is no set of institutions that is neutral among forms of life. The mirage of neutrality gets in the way of the practical pursuit of relative openness to diversity of experience as a positive but partial attribute of a social order.

The relation between institution and spirit, between practical arrangements and forms of life, is the key to the way I represent each of these three futures of a free society. Thus, in each instance, the discussion begins with the evocation of the animating and distinctive spirit, goes on to outline the specific institutional arrangements and forms of law, and concludes by addressing the basic practical and spiritual problems we can expect that direction of institutional change to present. Far from being fatal objections to each of the programs, the problems are its life. By managing them, each program defines, more fully and realistically, its character.

These faraway programs are neither predictions nor blueprints. They are simply institutionally imagined enlargements of our familiar repertory of social options, thought experiments in the service of tinkering, carried a few moves ahead of where we normally carry it in the day-to-day of political and legal argument. Their speculative development is no substitute for the patient work of tinkering in the here and now of pressing constraint, immediate need, and haphazard opportunity. Nevertheless, by such an enlargement of the political and legal imagination we can struggle more resolutely against fate and drift, and weaken the power of our circumstances over our minds. We can see more clearly the choices concealed by our present commitments, and join the tactical to the visionary.

The direction of extended social democracy

One trajectory for the deepening of democracy may be labeled extended social democracy. Of the three pathways to the reconstruction of democracy that I outline it is the one requiring the least break with established and inherited institutional arrangements. It therefore also most closely approaches, in its spiritual message and moral demands, a sensibility dominant today in the rich industrial countries. If this line of development has less interest than the other alternatives as a political innovation, it has proportionately greater interest as an extension of tendencies at work in the industrial democracies of the present day.

The core conception animating extended social democracy is the belief that the privileged arena of experience is the life of the individual: the ability of the individual to define and to execute his own life projects. Politics – the politics of governments and political parties – stops being the plausible source of great changes and hopes. It runs –when successful – on a narrower course; its aim becomes to ensure the efficiencies, the equities, and the decencies making individual action effective.

The law and institutions of extended social democracy

One set of institutional techniques defining extended social democracy has to do with the commitment to neutralize the background of inherited advantage and inequality among individuals. Not only must the hereditary transmission of property be greatly restricted but individuals must also be given a social endowment – a package of rights and resources – securing them against extreme economic insecurity and affording them the means with which to open up a path of their own in the world. Some of the contents of this individual endowment account may be spent freely by the individual, whereas others, regarding his early education, his pension and unemployment guarantees, or his health protections, fall under strict rules or require, for the suspension of these rules, the intervention of social trustees.

The form of governmental finance most effectively funding the operation of the government under extended social democracy is a universal and direct consumption tax. This tax falls on the difference between income and savings or investment, allowing for a generous exemption for modest consumption and a steeply progressive rate for the taxable portion of the consumption bill. Such a tax has two consequences favorable to the social and economic aims of extended social democracy. First, it turns taxation into the ally, rather than the enemy, of saving and investment. If there is a real problem of underconsumption, it can be addressed directly by a countervailing macroeconomic policy. Second, it applies to what a social democrat should most want to tax: the hierarchy of standards of living and the individual appropriation of social resources. To be sure, it becomes possible in principle for the austere to accumulate wealth and, thus, economic power. Two different and complementary ways of controlling economic power respond to the aims of extended social democracy: the fragmentation of economic power through facilities for decentralized access to capital; and the outright taxation of wealth. The wealth tax and the consumption tax together provide extended social democracy with its fiscal program. They may have to be supplemented by a comprehensive flat-rate value-added tax, which, being the least regressive or disruptive of the indirect taxes, assures the government the substantial revenues the direct, redistributive taxes may be insufficient to provide.

A second, overlapping set of institutional techniques in the repertory of extended social democracy has to do with the requirements of flexibility and accelerated innovation in economic life. Extended social democracy values the opening of opportunities for independent economic initiative both for its contribution to material progress and for its boost to the definition and execution of life projects. Two forms of governmental engagement illustrate the commitment to a qualitative rise in the range of opportunities for entrepreneurial creativity and individual action.

By one such engagement the government would help provide small and medium-sized firms the means with which to establish regimes of cooperative competition. Firms competing in some respects are able to cooperate in others, pooling financial, technological, and commercial resources and thereby ensuring their access to economies of scale. Mixed public–private banks and technological assistance services would count among such forms of support for interfirm networks. These constructive efforts would be animated by the attempt to expand the space for a style of production giving a central role to group learning. Learning is one thing democracy and economic innovation have in common.

By another such engagement the government should make available to people opportunities for ongoing education and retraining throughout adult life. The needed resources may be part of each person's social-endowment account. They are as much a contribution to the capacity for individual self-determination as to the conditions of permanent innovation in the economy. Opportunities for constant retraining, reinforced by guarantees against economic insecurity, make possible a quickened experimentalism in economic life. They enable people to dispense with the costly and inhibiting principle of job tenure.

The common coin of both the equality-expanding and the innovation-favoring techniques of extended social democracy is a vast enlargement of the responsibilities of education. A remaking of popular education is a requirement at once of the capacity for individual self-determination and of the practice of economic innovation and recombination. The content of education should suit these objectives. Its aim must be to develop generic practical and conceptual capabilities. The school must stand on the side of possible humanity and society against familiar experience and established order. The primacy of educational concerns represents one of the commitments shared by all varieties of the deepening of democracy.

These campaigns for an extended social democracy are most likely to be waged in the conditions of a corporatist political economy. For corporatism helps consolidate many of the practical and ideological tools needed to build extended social democracy: highly organized labor and entrepreneurial groups, fora for the social negotiation of national economic strategies, and a widespread social acceptance of the propriety and utility of active governmental intervention in the development of national strategies of economic growth.

At the same time, however, corporatism produces an impatience with the pathology of rigidity. Transitory advantages secured by organized groups quickly become, under a corporatist regime, vested rights. The entire social order begins to resemble a gigantic aggregation of group-specific privileges. The price rigidities and veto powers these privileges imply shackle innovation in every domain of practical life. Moreover, because these privileges are unevenly distributed, rigidity becomes injustice.

Thus, extended social democracy, facilitated by a corporatist style of political economy, becomes, at the same time, the antidote to the characteristic stickiness of entrenched and unequal group interests under a corporatist regime. The impulse toward greater flexibility appears, in extended social democracy, as the expression of an impulse both to loosen and to equalize the dense system of group deals and prerogatives, of political rents, covert subsidies, and effective disabilities characterizing the industrial democracies of the present day, especially those that have gone furthest toward adopting corporatist practices.

From a broader perspective, it is as if the program of extended social democracy represented a synthesis between the pretended liberalism of an earlier day and the social-democratic compromise developed since the time of the Great Depression and the Second World War. However, it is less a midpoint between those two political orientations than a movement creating the conditions for a fuller realization of liberal claims. This effort to make the world safe for the liberal teaching about the common ground of economic progress and individual freedom requires the reshaping of institutions traditionally associated with the liberal cause. The search for the common ground between material progress and individual emancipation progresses through cumulative and directed tinkering with the practices and institutions by which, in the past, we have tried to secure this common ground.

The legal ideas with the greatest affinity to extended social democracy are therefore those emphasizing the continuous creation of law from the bottom up, by social organizations. Not only does the legal doctrine of extended social democracy develop the theory and practice of intermediate organizations, operating on the ground between government and the private actor, but it also gives special importance to associations lying in between a contract and a corporation. The world of extended social democracy should see a proliferation of many forms of joint venture in the use of productive resources and the provision of technical and professional services: many activities now conducted within the straitjacket of a corporate form would be undertaken instead in the form of temporary and focused combinations of people and resources.

The other major frontier of the law of extended social democracy is the social endowment of the individual rather than the practice of decentralized initiative. The individual must enjoy a set of protections and immunities relatively insulated from the risks of short-term political conflict. The practical kernel of the metaphysical language of fundamental rights in the Anglo-American tradition retains its force: to call a certain safeguard a fundamental right is to say that we should not expose it to frequent danger and disturbance in the normal course of political conflict. The safeguard becomes a fundamental right in fact when it gains some measure of immunity from such risks.

Not everything in the social endowment of the individual deserves to be treated as a stable and sacrosanct right. At one pole of the spectrum of force, clarity, and stability in the definition of entitlements are the basic guarantees against public and private oppression, the core liberties of expression and association, and the entitlements of participation in civic life. Even these entitlements, in their practical ramifications, shade into zones in which the relativity of rights to resources makes contextual qualification unavoidable. Thus, freedom of expression may require governmental activity ensuring to a broad range of organized and unorganized movements of opinion access to the means of mass communication. However, no one, and no group, can have a certain and indefeasible right to a particular portion of media resources. At the opposite pole of the spectrum lies the definition of the actual sums available to protect the individual against catastrophic risk and to fund his ongoing and lifelong education. In between these two extremes, many claims will share something of the force of the definition of a fundamental right with something of the relativity of the investment of social resources in the satisfaction or the development of the right.

Thus, the legal theory of extended social democracy looks for entitlements mediating between public and private law, and between contract and corporation. Similarly, in its demarcation of the prerogatives of the individual, it works out the doctrine of hybrid entitlements, clearly marked and unconditionally exercised in some respects, but subject to controversial, ad hoc redefinition in other respects. These hybrid forms, growing directly out of the law of the welfare state, express the idea – so basic to contemporary law even in the existing social democracies – that individual and collective self-determination depend upon empirical and therefore defeasible conditions.

The spirit and champions of extended social democracy

The spirit of extended social democracy is one of radical individualism. Politics should become little so that individuals may become big. The quest for the sublime – restless experimentation with the frontiers of experience – should take place on the scale of individual biographies. When we transpose this quest to politics, so the doctrine of extended social democracy teaches, danger and disappointment result. Great projects of reconstruction and regeneration regularly end in dreary authoritarianisms, cutting off opportunities for economic and cultural innovation, to the benefit of self-serving and sanctimonious elites.

This idea lends some weight of authority or, at least, inevitability to shared habits of life: in particular, to a life in which the focus of energy remains in the world of family and leisure; the most vanguardist and rebellious forms of culture take on a dream-like character as if they were festivals of the spirit incapable of finding a home in the workaday world; and private consumption, ever more varied and refined, appears as the prosaic material counterpart to this high-flown and ecstatic narcissism of the spirit. To enjoy these experiences of quiet decencies in public life and quickened anxieties and joys in private life remains a mark of economic and cultural privilege. Ordinary working people continue to face the grinding demands of poorly paid and unstable work while finding solace in the remnants or beginnings of community life. The ambition of extended social democracy is to give everyone the opportunity to share in the opportunities of a private experimentalism.

It is a telling fact about the spiritual direction and political tendency of the rich industrial democracies that the preference for this version of the advancement of democracy should have taken root most strongly in the social-democratic parties, the very movements with the most pronounced collectivist heritage. Slowly and gradually, these parties have broken their privileged links with the organized working class, active in mass-production industry. They find this traditional constituency to be a shrinking part of the population, stuck in a declining sector of the economy, and perceived by others and ultimately by itself as just one more faction, with factional interests, rather than as the bearer of universal popular interests. When the labor and progressive parties sever their favored links with these working-class organizations, they often believe themselves to have no alternative but to turn to the generic "quality-of-life" concerns of the professional–business class.

Although this class may represent but a small portion of the population, it is a portion enjoying cultural ascendancy, especially over the vast masses of propertyless and powerless whitecollar workers, in services, shops, and offices, who imagine themselves members of a "middle class" to which all but the richest and poorest belong. The impoverishment of the vision of alternative routes of institutional change, aggravated by the necessitarianism of traditional leftist theory, revenges itself on the social-democratic parties of the present day. Unable to imagine a trajectory of economic growth and institutional change that would break down the barriers between mass production and other sectors of the economy, these parties also fail to build the political and social alliances that such developmental pathways both require and produce. In this circumstance extended social democracy revokes what would otherwise appear to be its abdication of transformative ambitions: it renews the life of the democratizing impulse even in the midst of the ruin of the alliances, strategies, and programs sustaining classical social democracy.

The internal instability of extended social democracy

Consider now two basic obstacles to the development of the program of extended social democracy. These obstacles are not fatal objections to the program; they reveal part of its distinctive agenda of problems. A cumulative sequence of changes – of ideals and interests as well as of institutions and practices – develops by the way in which it responds to such problems. The understanding of the difficulties of extended social democracy has a special interest: of the different routes to the radicalization of democracy, this one is the closest to established arrangements in the North Atlantic world. By addressing its anticipated problems, we can develop a deeper understanding of some of the practical and spiritual problems of these existing societies. Extended social democracy represents the hypothetical development of tendencies already at work in an actual world: the projection of these tendencies enables us to explore them disentangled from many of the countervailing forces now concealing their character and consequences.

The first category of obstacles to the execution of the program of extended social democracy includes a series of variations on the theme of internal instability: like its standard social-democratic counterpart, this program suffers from a recurrent tension between its egalitarian and participatory commitments and its institutional conservatism. We can retrench the commitments, giving up the large part of them that we cannot hope to realize within the institutional framework. Alternatively, we can radicalize the commitments, transgressing the institutional boundaries, and prepare to rethink the commitments in the light of the changed arrangements.

The most general example of this internal instability in the program of extended social democracy is the tension between the political energy required to inaugurate such an inclusive series of reforms and the suppression of political energy that seems required to uphold the program. The essence of extended social democracy is the effort to close the door on the history of great collective conflicts engaging the use of governmental power, and the substitution of this history by the strivings and experiments of individuals. Once aroused, however, and sustained over the long period required to carry through an agenda of fundamental reform, political energy is likely to change the aims in the pursuit of which it had been enlisted. It awakens people to the power of aspirations they can realize only through group effort and in group life. Moreover, the integrity of the social-democratic design, in each of its detailed provisions, is sure to require continuing vigilance. Unexpected and unforeseeable dangers will arise – novel forms of inequality or unfamiliar conspiracies of group interest – for which novel solutions, requiring political action, may be needed.

If continuing political energy is to be maintained, both the guiding objectives and the practical forms of extended social democracy may have to shift. In particular, we may need arrangements – such as mandatory voting, public financing of campaigns, free access to the means of mass communications, and closed-list electoral regimes – that work, in concert, to heighten the level of political mobilization in society. Once established and effective, such arrangements soon invite parallel changes in the constitutional organization of government and in the public-law framework of civil society.

These additional shifts would use the appeal to plebiscites and referenda, the power to call anticipated elections, and the multiplication of branches of government to ease and accelerate the practice of fundamental reforms. They might also provide civil society with a public-law framework for its organization: creating associational forms readily available to people on principles related to jobs (unions and professional associations), home (neighborhood associations) or shared purpose and experience (common-interest organizations), inclusive organizations within which competing tendencies would compete for place just as political parties compete for position in the structure of government. The accumulation of such reforms, however, would soon reshape both the distinctive practical instruments and the defining spiritual direction of extended social democracy.

A second example of internal instability in the program of extended social democracy has to do with the reconciliation of its commitment to equality of opportunity with its devotion to flexibility in production. This reconciliation may require both the development of new forms of association between public power and private producers, and the creation of new means for the decentralized allocation of capital, breaking the limits of traditional property rights. The decentralization of access to resources may be vital to both flexibility and equality. Such decentralized access may need to be squared with economies of scale, and to be preserved by a scheme for continuing redistribution in the face of reemergent inequality. The classical image of small-scale property – petty-commodity production in one terminology and the yeoman republic in another – suffered from a vitiating instability. Either it would give way to rapid concentration, as successful producers devoured their failing competitors, or it would be overridden by the egalitarian interventionism of a redistributive state.

If the reformers are to reconcile a broad range of scale in the aggregation of economic resources with the need for large investments in capital goods as well as in infrastructure and in people, and join effective limits upon inequality of economic power to a broadening of freedom of initiative, they may have to tread a path of cumulative institutional innovation. Firms developing among themselves networks of cooperative competition may require legal forms standing someplace on the continuum from contract to the corporation. Public enterprises and public banks, freed from the onus of short-term profit-making, may be required, alone or in association with private producers, to make long-term strategic investments. They may help support the establishment of cooperative-competitive networks of private firms, and develop, in partnership with them, a technological vanguard capable of producing, in customized fashion, the machines and the inputs that the rearguard of the economy can assimilate. The partnership of public and private may in turn require the development of organizations intermediate between government and the private producers, with attributes of both. These organizations would be protected against direct political control and charged with the task of administering or distributing productive resources, under regimes of temporary or conditional property rights.

Such innovations put to the test the relative institutional conservatism of extended social democracy. They suggest the need to change the institutional form of representative democracy and of the market economy and to open the door to a continuing series of reforms in the inherited framework of political and economic organization.

Little politics for big people?

Turn now to a spiritual problem afflicting the progress of extended social democracy. The sense of the program is that politics should become little so that individuals may become big. The problem is that after politics shrink, individuals may end up shrinking as well. As the state withdraws to the performance of residual coordinating responsibilities, the focus of energy is supposed to shift to individuals, and to the activities by which they form and execute their own life plans. People should nourish strong and distinct desires and undertake innovations in practice or in sensibility from which collective benefits may result and exemplary influence may radiate.

Desire and striving, however, are relational in character: they normally seek expression in ways of living together. If extended social democracy succeeded in its professed aim of creating strong individuals, the qualities of individual experience would soon become attributes of group life. People will want to establish practices or communities in which the visions and impulses they value may be prominently expressed. However, as their desires come to seek expression in shared forms of life, the de-energized world of extended social democracy would prove a disappointment. Such desires would go in search of alternative social futures, including the futures explored in the other two routes to the radicalization of democracy discussed here.

One way or another, politics, having cooled down, would begin to heat up again. The biographical space would prove too confined a terrain on which to try out a distinct way of being human. But every foray into a collective space reintroduces conflict – political conflict – over the relative influence that different visions and interests should be allowed.

There are two ways in which the search of strong individual impulse for a collective voice may be interrupted. Each such form of interruption presents the spiritual problem of extended social democracy in a different light. People may renege on the demand for a distinct form of group life because they have not in fact developed strong and distinct visions and desires. Politics will then remain little only because individuals have themselves been belittled.

Alternatively, individuals may entertain strong desires of a very particular and compromising sort – narcissistic or self-referential desires, entrapping them within a labyrinth of subjectivity and turning them inward toward experimentation with their own tastes and feelings. The possibility of such desires offers an apparent exception to the relational character of desire. It is, however, a troubled exception: its flaw lying as much in the inhibiting character of the experience it makes available as in the mutilating partiality of its scope.

Narcissistic and self-referential impulses are unable to make good on the reconciliation of the twin conditions of self-assertion: our simultaneous need to engage with others and to control or overcome the threats of subjugation and depersonalization with which every such engagement confronts us. Experience with such desires may serve a purpose of destabilization and self-subversion, dialectically related to a larger plan of freedom. Nevertheless, such experience offers us no real promise of movement toward greater freedom and self-possession.

Thus, politics must once again grow lest individuals shrink; or strength of striving must tend to diminish in proportion to the scope of politics; or the coexistence of heat in biography with coldness in history must be sustained by the ascendancy of self-referential desires. Here, as in its vulnerability to the tension between ideal aspirations and institutional conservatism, the deficiencies of extended social democracy mirror and accentuate the frailties of an established form of life while broadening the reach of its most seductive ideals.

IMAGINING THE ALTERNATIVE FUTURES OF A FREE SOCIETY: RADICAL POLYARCHY

The direction of radical polyarchy

The radicalization of the democratic project can be pursued in a second direction – radical polyarchy. Radical polyarchy represents a more decisive departure from the form of social life established in the contemporary industrial democracies than does extended social democracy. Yet there is nothing in its defining conception or distinctive techniques that cannot be built out of readily available institutional and ideological materials.

The basic idea of radical polyarchy is the transformation of society into a confederation of communities. These communities should not be shaped on primarily ascriptive lines, according to inherited race or religion. Instead, they should draw on the forces of shared experience and commitment.

Inheritance of race or religion may play a role in the self-definition of many such groups – only an illiberal dogmatism would wage war against the community-defining powers of religion and race. Nevertheless, communities, in this view, must be inventions more than destinies, marriages (in the modern, post-romantic way) rather than tribes. Such communities must be neither all-inclusive nor rigidly exclusive. They must never encompass the whole life of their members, who must, on the contrary, pass from one community to another in different aspects of experience. Moreover, they should, most of them, remain open to people whose abilities, ambitions, or commitments converge.

Thus, radical polyarchy represents a liberal communitarianism. The starting point of its doctrine is that, for us, democrats and moderns, faced with the real problems of industrial societies, only a liberal communitarianism can be either realistic or appealing. The communitarian element lies in the conviction that the most important action in society takes place within settings of group life rather than in the biographies of individuals or the histories of societies. Creative diversity is, characteristically, diversity in forms of group life; and only against the backdrop of strongly marked but open-ended communities can true individuality develop. The liberal element results from the refusal to credit the reactionary and despotic idea of all-enveloping communities, especially when based upon "natural bonds," prior to conscious effort and election.

All the characteristic problems of radical polyarchy have to do, in one way or another, with the tense relation between its liberalism and its communitarianism. However, the advocate of radical polyarchy considers these problems part of an unavoidable price. We must pay it to escape the deceptions and disappointments that result when the communitarian ideal serves as the instrument of a backward utopianism mythologizing the past to reverse the ills of a supposedly individualistic society, or when it imparts a softening nimbus to unchanged structures of power.

By the first perversion, communitarianism becomes a rejection of modernity and complexity and therefore also of individuality and subjectivity. By the second perversion, communitarianism turns into a way of generalizing the blend of unequal exchange and sentimentalized allegiance marking so much of experience in hierarchical societies. Thus, the corporatist communitarianism propounded in interwar Europe by the Catholic Church and centrist reformers, and embraced by ideologists as diverse as Durkheim and Santi Romano, came to grief on its unresolved ambivalence about the established economic arrangements and the existing corporate forms.

Illiberal communitarianisms understand community to be organized around shared experiences and merged identities. For them, community is defined by contrast to conflict, including conflict of interest or experience. Radical polyarchy, on the contrary, treats community as the diluted version of love – an area of heightened experimentalism and reciprocal involvement, with the defenses among people lowered. Such a communitarianism is not the simple antithesis of conflict; it incorporates conflict into its normal life. Both the institutional and the spiritual problems of radical polyarchy follow from the relation between its liberalism and its communitarianism.

The law and institutions of radical polyarchy

Radical polyarchy works with institutional techniques of devolution of power and organization of civil society. It wants to devolve central state power to local or specialized communities. It wants civil society to be organized, or, rather, to organize itself, so that it can effectively receive and exercise these devolved powers. The link between devolution and organization is what chiefly distinguishes the program of radical polyarchy from the traditional liberal or centrist ideas it superficially resembles. The basic institutional principle is that to every stage in the devolution of power there should correspond an advance in the organization of civil society.

Devolution of power goes forward by giving ever greater faculties of initiative to the organizations closest to the settings in which people live and work or to the contexts in which they organize around shared concerns. Thus, one form of devolution is the impulse to break up large productive units into smaller, more flexible and participatory components, combining these decentralized units within networks of cooperative-competitive firms. Another form of devolution is the development of a system of worker-controlled and worker-owned firms. Worker ownership and self-management as well as cooperative competition, making possible a higher reconciliation of smallness and flexibility with economies of scale, are two distinct paths toward the devolution of economic power. Although they operate through partly incompatible techniques, they overlap in their political sense, and they raise similar problems.

A second instance of devolution of power is the strengthening of local government. As the objectives of radical polyarchy advance, distinct places may acquire increasingly distinct characters. As a result, the conception of local government may outgrow its territorial meaning. Local citizenship may be granted even to people who are more distant but who, for one reason or another, are in close communion with the citizens of the place. Moreover, a structure of local or neighborhood associations, made available by (public) law, may parallel the governmental structure, creating a more complex and deliberately pluralistic and even conflictual relation between the apparatus of local government and the organization of people in local society. Both local governments and social organizations in local society may in turn hold property interests in productive resources. They may also develop arrangements for the selective turnaround of troubled or resource-starved firms. Such arrangements may ease the terms on which capital becomes available to economically promising or socially significant businesses, and determine the circumstances and the ways in which failing firms should be rescued and reconstructed.

Yet a third instance of devolution would transfer power to specially interested and organized publics. Among such publics may be alliances of parents, teachers, and local governments responsible for a confederation of schools, or alliances of physicians, hospitals, firms, a local government, and patient representatives engaged in supervising health care.

The devolution of power by such devices gives increasing density to the associational life of society. Thus, systematic devolution superficially resembles the principle of subsidiarity embraced by the centrist and Christian-Democratic parties of contemporary European politics: the idea that a higher level of government should exercise power only when that power cannot effectively be exercised by the entity closest to the life of the individual. What distinguishes devolution under radical polyarchy from the principle of subsidiarity as well as from the naive forms of libertarian liberalism is a militant suspicion of inherited institutions and hierarchies. To devolve power to existing firms, communities, and associations in an unevenly and hierarchically organized society without reorganizing the society is merely to abdicate power to those already organized and privileged. The key objection to a conservative liberalism has always been its uncritical reliance upon the idea of a pure prepolitical space that will open up if only we can push back the heavy hand of governmental interventionism. By contrast, the political and legal theory of radical polyarchy recognizes that every social world is controversial, contingent, and, above all, constructed through politics. In that recognition lies the meaning of the link between devolution and reorganization.

For devolution to advance, civil society must be reorganized in a way satisfying two fundamental requirements: that no group be persistently and significantly disadvantaged in its level of association and that the whole organizational order resist a recentralizing impulse. That is why each of the preceding examples of devolution suggests a sequence of reforms in the arrangements governing production, local government, or the provision of welfare needs.

Such reforms do not imply an abrupt and comprehensive switch to a novel set of institutions. They do suggest a cumulative loosening of the inherited institutional forms in the direction of decentralized self-government in production and exchange, community life and welfare distribution. Such a reform program emphasizes a type of law produced from the bottom up by self-directing networks of groups rather than imposed from the top down by a central government. This type of law resembles public law in that it provides a setting for collective action among collective agents. However, it recalls private law in that it remains open to diversity and divergence. Among its characteristic strategies are the dismemberment and regrouping of previously unified packages of rights and the creation of parallel structures in the organization of some segment of society.

Both cooperative competition among confederations of firms (for reasons already shown) and worker ownership and management (for reasons yet to be explored) require a disaggregation of the traditional property right. They decompose the constituent faculties of the unified property right and vest those faculties in different rightholders. The rightholders enjoy these distinct rights at the same time and in the same productive resources. We need the disaggregation and recombination of the property right in one instance to reconcile small scale with the efficiency of large magnitudes and, in the other instance, to prevent (as I shall soon show) the economic regime of worker-owners from destroying itself.

An example of the strategy of parallel structures is the coexistence of empowered local governments with empowered neighborhood associations – two parallel tracks of local territorial organization, one inside and the other outside government. The point of the parallel structures is to leave open an alternative route to the expression of discontent and the practice of experimentalism. The two structures may be partners, or they may be rivals. Where one is closed to a particular social movement, the other may be forced open. What unites the technique of parallel structures with the strategy of dismemberment and recombination of rights is the practice of a tinkering designed to make society more hospitable to tinkering, of a decentralized and even anarchic sort.

The spiritual paradoxes of a liberal communitarianism

Consider now the characteristic spiritual and practical problems the development of radical polyarchy must face. Both the former and the latter have to do with the difficulty of reconciling the liberalism of radical polyarchy with its communitarianism, the commitment to ongoing experimentalism with the persistence of devolution.

The central spiritual problem of radical polyarchy is the tension between the chosen, constructed, and partial character of the decentralized organizations to which this program devolves power and the attributes of group life commanding attention and allegiance. The power of tribal feelings seems connected to their "natural," unchosen quality as well as to their disengagement from practical chores. Such prepolitical groups evoke the power of the family bond, beckoning the individual into a world of fleshy destiny and dependence. Can organizations that envelop only part of the life of each of their members and remain bound up with practical concerns and responsibilities nevertheless remain a focus for devotion and connection?

This problem of the spiritual potency of chosen bonds in turn connects with a second problem, the ability to contain the expansionist tendencies of strongly felt group ideals. Suppose the decentralized organizations of radical polyarchy do succeed in becoming and remaining magnets of social energy, enclaves of distinct forms of life and densely overlapping bonds among their members. Will people not inevitably assert these distinct varieties of experience, wanting to see them mirrored in the life of the groups around them? After all, the reproduction of oneself, of one's own experience and commitments, is the most primitive and universal ideology, lurking under the disguise of more refined and elaborate pieties.

We seem here to face a paradox neatly paralleling the conundrum of big individuals and small politics under extended social democracy. If the communal bond is strong under radical polyarchy, it can be expected to generate controversial and expansive group ideals, and to cause a conflict that must end with the triumph of some programs and sensibilities over others. On the other hand, if people are happy to restrain their visions within their enclaves, we may doubt whether these visions were ever strong.

There is an exception to the relation between the strength of forms of group life and their expansionism: groups with a natural character, like families, races, or inherited religions. For such groups there may be some uncontroversial marker of inclusion, some built-in restraint upon expansion.

However, it is precisely such natural markers of group membership that a liberal communitarianism must relegate to an accesssory role.

Both aspects of the spiritual problem of radical polyarchy – the power of chosen attachments and the self-restraint of strong ideals – depend, for their management, upon a measure of success in changing the quality of the communitarian experience. To the extent we understand community and live it out as a merging of interests and identities by opposition to other communities, both facets of the problem become more acute. We may, however, tread another path: the downgrading of the bond to the group and the upgrading of the reciprocal involvements among its individual members.

Real allegiance, in this view, is something we give to incarnate people, not to tribes or organizations. Each community, rather than accomplishing a merger of individual identities, presents simply a zone for heightened reciprocal engagement in some practical sphere of social life. The regulative ideal is not the relation of the child to his unchosen biological parents, a blind destiny that may be humanized, but the relation of a man or a woman, in marriage, to the spouse that he or she chose.

The decisive issue is the plausibility of extending to broader reaches of social life the psychological experience of attachment without tribalism. Here, as always, it would be foolhardy to predicate a political program upon success in achieving a drastic and sudden change in our present dispositions. It is also unwise, however, to disregard the subtle and pervasive interactions between practical arrangements and subjective experiences. The major practical conundrum of radical polyarchy closely follows its spiritual problems.

The practical dilemma of devolution and inequality

The core practical problem the execution of radical polyarchy must face is a dilemma of devolution and inequality. After presenting this dilemma in its most general and abstract form, I explore its application to the debate about worker-managed and worker-owned firms.

Suppose that the rules of devolution and organization defining the programmatic aims of radical polyarchy represent a relatively stable, once-and-for-all fix, to be changed only rarely and with great difficulty. There is a constitution of communities and of intercommunity relations, whether or not this constitution finds expression in forms that we would today recognize as constitutional. By this horn of the dilemma, we can change the rules of devolution of power and organization of civil society only fitfully and with great difficulty. Moreover, new and unforeseeable varieties of inequality will continue to emerge no matter what the rules of political and economic devolution may be. Some groups will prosper and expand, under whatever restraints those rules may impose upon them. The only guarantee – if it is one – against reemergent inequality would be an ongoing redistribution by a higher-level authority. However, if such a redistributive practice were tightly bounded by rules, it would also confront the problem of unforeseen and reappearing inequality. If, on the contrary, the redistributive practice allowed for a broad margin of discretionary administration and reinterpretation, the higher redistributive authority would have dealt with the perils of inequality by relinquishing some of the commitment to devolution.

The relation of reemergent inequality to a rigidly rule-bound structure, viewed through the lens of a self-restrained, antirevisionary practice of rule interpretation, deserves further analysis; it throws a surprising light upon the connection between property and rules. The classic idea of property relies upon the conception of rigid boundaries demarcating a zone in which the owner (rightholder) can use his property as he will, with minimal regard to the effect of its use upon others. The true social meaning of the consolidation of all the different faculties composing property into a unified right lies in the attenuation of social interdependence in the practical decisions of economic life. Only on this basis can labor be bought and sold, and its product saved up to buy more labor.

Understood in this way, unified property loosens its connection to the primitive notion of control over things, and merges into the classical idea of rights. For what are rights, as viewed by classical liberalism, other than clearly demarcated zones of discretionary action? Within the boundaries of the right, the rightholder does, more or less, as he will, free to discount or disregard the consequences of the exercise of the right for others. Beyond the boundaries of the right, his every action becomes open to a calculus of consequences and interdependencies.

Some of the most famous controversies in the history of modern legal thought dealt with the consequences for the system of public and private rights of the unavoidable collisions among supposedly indefeasible rights. From these controversies we should have learned two lessons of continuing importance to the reorientation of legal analysis. The first lesson is that no single, closed, and coherent system of rights can be inferred, by any analytic procedure, from the idea of the market economy. The second lesson is that no real version of the market economy, of the property regime, or, more generally, of a pluralistic society can abolish conflict.

Moreover, the intractable conflicts will deal with central issues, such as the contrasting claims of capital and labor, rather than with minor problems of adjustment or definition.

The exemplary significance of traditional property or classical rights in turn relies upon a practice of rule interpretation hostile to the frequent revision of received interpretive understandings. Such a practice clings to the ground of established analogy and familiar gloss. Otherwise, the brightline boundaries around the zones of entitlement would prove to be subject to a permanent second-guessing, according to the outcome of a contest among moral and political visions conducted in the form of an analysis of extant norms.

A rigid fix on the rules of devolution and organization, required to entrench the goals of radical polyarchy, depends upon the maintenance of a definite scheme of property, rights, and rules, sustained by an anti-revisionary interpretive practice. Such a scheme is impotent to guard against a trend of inequality or expansion, unless it is either qualified by an ongoing redistribution subversive of its decentralizing goals or supplemented by restraints upon the alienation of property, the rearrangement of resources, and the accumulation of capital. Such restraints would be so severe that they would condemn the society to poverty.

The inequalities thus produced will be all the more formidable because they will not have to face the counterweight of strong governmental power. A strong state is one that is able to formulate and implement policy at some remove from the dominant interests, especially the dominant economic interests, of the society. Although Marxism has accustomed us to think of the state apparatus as the long arm of these interests, it is also the great lever of their transformation. In its absence, entrenched inequalities and the arrangements producing them become naturalized. They take on the appearance of an inescapable fate because there is no practical political instrument with which to change them.

Consider now the other horn of the dilemma of devolution and inequality under radical polyarchy. Suppose that we can change the rules of devolution and organization easily and frequently, or that a higher redistributive authority, not itself rightly programmed by relatively unchanging rules, can correct the emerging inequalities. Then, we shall have dealt with the problem of reemerging inequality but only by compromising some of the constitutive aims of radical polyarchy. The redistributive agency will be a central government; so will the forum in which people discuss and change the arrangements for devolution and organization. As these arrangements become, under radical polyarchy, the shapers of people's life chances, the conflict over their content takes on decisive importance. Influence in that conflict becomes, under this modified version of radical polyarchy, a magnet of ambition and anxiety.

The sense of the dilemma of devolution and inequality is that the program of radical polyarchy cannot easily free itself from the taint of the conservative liberal belief in a space of free human action that we can open up by cutting off the heavy hand of governmental interventionism. The acknowledgement of the link between devolution of power and organization of civil society does not suffice adequately to deal with the interference between these two sets of institutional commitments. The organizational initiatives needed to contain inequality turn out to qualify devolution, unless we accept severe restraints upon both the accumulation of wealth and the change of position under radical polyarchy. These restraints would not merely make people poor; they would prevent them from becoming or remaining free. The dilemma of devolution and inequality suggests the internal fragility of a liberal communitarianism.

The admonitory example of workers' ownership

The complaint presented by this dilemma may seem too speculative to matter. It nevertheless comes to life when we consider in detail the instrument or variant of radical polyarchy that comes closest to contemporary debates: the regime of worker ownership and worker management. Consider a simple thought experiment designed to explore the limitations of the traditional, unrevised version of workers' control. The experiment shows that the economy of worker-owned and worker-managed firms fails on grounds of both efficiency and democracy unless it moves progressively away from the simple idea of transfer to the laborforce of an enterprise of the traditional property rights enjoyed by the individual capitalist. Each departure from this simple model generates an additional series of difficulties, which must be managed by movement yet further away from the simple version.

In the end, the transformed regime of workers' control – the one promising to combine democratic legitimacy with economic effectiveness – requires a continuing interaction between the firm or its workers and centers of initiative and power outside the firm. The workers do not succeed to the traditional property right; only to some of its components. Traditional property is not merely transferred from one rightholder (the capitalist) to another (the worker); its constituent faculties are disassembled and reassigned among a variety of rightholders, who come to hold limited and superimposed rights in the same productive resources. This revised version of worker management abandons a simple scheme of economic devolution for the sake of a more realistic and attractive vision of economic progress and democratic flexibility. The thought experiment about workers' control rings the changes on the dilemma of devolution and inequality, suggesting the impossibility of reconciling, in this, the most familiar terrain of polyarchy, strong devolution with equality, flexibility, and efficiency.

Consider first the simplest case of the regime of workers' control, defined by the full application of two restrictive assumptions. The first such assumption is the principle of respect for the basic distribution of jobs and resources existing at the time of the regime change. Workers acquire full property rights in the firms in which they happen to work at the time the new system is inaugurated. The second restrictive assumption is the principle of respect for the traditional system of property rights. What each worker acquires is the full-blown and fully alienable private property. The right is vested in the individual worker, and from it derive all more particular claims both to an income stream from the gains achieved by the firm and to the exercise of control over management. The image is one of a regime produced by the simple transfer of otherwise unrevised property rights: the individual worker inherits, through the providential intervention of reform, the same unified package of property rights that might otherwise be held by the traditional capitalist or the entrepreneurial state.

The unrevised version of the worker is as arbitrary in its distributive consequences as it is self-destructive in its internal operation. The initial acquisition of property rights under such a regime is a game of economic musical chairs. Some workers work in capital-intensive industries; their jobs are tied to rich hoards of resources. Others labor in capital-poor jobs. Still others may be jobless at the moment of the great reform. Yet at the instant of the regime change each will inherit much, little, or nothing according to the place he happens to occupy in this scheme of relative favor. Existing disparities of circumstance, dividing workers from one another, would suddenly freeze into vested rights. It seems strange that a reform animated by a vision of social justice and regeneration would be strong enough to produce a striking change in the economic organization of society and yet resign itself to such a crazed assignment of rights and resources.

Moreover, this arbitrary scheme would soon undo itself. Some of the worker-owned firms would prosper while others would fail, often because of remote economic events bearing little relation to the merits and faults of the workers themselves. Acceptance of the traditional regime of property rights would ensure a rapid process of reconcentration and inequality both among firms and among individual workers. Successful firms would buy up their less successful competitors. Individual workers would soon sell their shares in the firms like peasants given a plot of land, and little else, under a primitive plan of agrarian reform.

No time would pass before jobs had been separated from property and a two-tier laborforce of propertied workers and wage earners had developed. Some workers would continue to work in firms in which they held no ownership quotas. Others, having sold their quotas, or never having owned them in the first place, or having owned them in firms that failed or were sold out, would find themselves searching for jobs in an interfirm market for wage labor. Nothing would have changed in the basic principles of economic order except that the move to worker ownership, instituted in the spirit of polyarchy, would have weakened the central government and its compensatory welfare programs.

Consider now a first level of departure from the self-defeating restraints of the simple regime. This second variant maintains the assumption of traditional property rights but relinquishes the assumption of respect for the distribution of jobs at the time of the regime change. When we establish the regime, we reserve funds to compensate those who hold relatively less capital-intensive jobs or no jobs at all. The priority use of these funds is to give the individuals disfavored by the preexisting job distribution the training and the capital they need to advance within the hierarchy of economic advantage.

The corrective redistribution, however, could not be limited to the moment of the regime change; it would need to enjoy a persistent life, for all the forces driving toward recentralization and inequality that operate under the simple case would continue to work under this revised regime. It would be paradoxical to the point of irrealism for a social reform to be strong enough to challenge the distribution of economic opportunity while remaining indifferent to the distributive sequel of the great reconstruction. The same forces and commitments that brought about the reform in the first place would struggle to extend and perpetuate its work.

To continue the redistributive practice after the inauguration of the regime is, however, to trespass against the other restrictive assumption of the simple case: the maintenance of traditional property rights. It is also, in the language of the dilemma of devolution and inequality, to restrict devolutionary ambitions for the sake of egalitarian commitments. If the

redistributive practice takes the form of a discretionary and episodic correction of emergent inequalities, it circumscribes traditional property
rights without effectively replacing them. If, as seems more likely, the
redistributive activity becomes heavily rule-bound, it gives rise, over time,
to an interdependency of sources of economic authority within the firm
and outside it. Such an interdependence will manifest itself in a complex
coexistence of different types of property rights, vested in different
categories of rightholders, of which the workers will be merely one.

Thus, we arrive at a second moment of distancing from the simple
form of worker ownership. Now, we begin to relax the second assumption – of respect for traditional property rights – as well as the first
assumption – of respect for the preexisting distribution of jobs. To prevent
rapid reconcentration and entrenched inequality, we impose restraints
upon the exercise of property. The key restrictions are inalienability of
ownership quotas and limits to the power to buy other firms with accumu-
lated gains. Inalienability may work by vesting the property jointly in the
collective laborforce or by prohibiting separation of jobs from ownership
quotas. (For every such variation on inalienability there is a familiar
counterpart in the history of the attempts by the reformers of
agrarian–bureaucratic empires to stabilize agrarian reform.)

The functional equivalent and complement to restraints upon
alienability is the imposition of limits upon successful firms in their accumulation of retained earnings for the purpose of enhancing their own
productivity or buying up other firms. The acquisition of other firms may
usher in an entrenched hierarchical division between worker-owners and
propertyless wage laborers. However, even the untrammeled investment
of the firm in itself can support an extreme and irreversible inequality of
economic position and opportunity. The workers in each firm may simply
prefer to invest in ever stronger increments to the productivity of their
own labor through technological improvements. Instead of buying up
other firms and reducing other workers to the dependent status of wage
labor, they may progressively increase the distance between the technical
instruments of their own work and the means at the disposal of other
workers in other firms. They may refuse to hire new colleagues, or hire
them only rarely and on the basis of favor and connection. We therefore
need restraints upon accumulation to complete the work of restraints
upon alienation, although, to some extent, the two categories of restrictions may be interchangeable.

The effect of such limits upon traditional property, however, is to give the
worker-owners an incentive to waste the value of the firm, by subordinating

its future interests to the immediate consumption of gains. They will want to distribute to themselves as much of the earnings of the firm as possible. Here we have a danger that is more than hypothetical: it turned out to be the fatal flaw in the Yugoslav self-management system. Restraints upon alienation and accumulation, needed to prevent economic oppression and wage labor, in turn encourage wastage of the assets. But how can an external authority – or a set of rules standing in the place of such an authority – police effectively against the twin contrasting perils of running up and running down the value of the firm, to the detriment of relative equality, flexibility, and openness in the dealings among firms?

The pressure to answer this question carries us to a fourth and final stage of distancing from the simple version of workers' control. The competing risks of asset wastage and entrepreneurial imperialism cannot be contained within the framework of traditional property rights – not at least without a pervasive interventionism that would undermine the workings of a market economy and mock the polyarchic commitment to devolution.

Radical polyarchy reconstructed

The radical polyarchy capable of managing these spiritual and institutional problems is a program that has succeeded in liberating its vision from the remnants of the nineteenth-century idea of "petty-commodity production": an economy of independent and small-scale firms, which, even when internally organized on cooperative principles, remain unable to cooperate. The maintenance of such a world against the forces of competition and concentration would require an ever-present redistributive interventionism. Such an interventionism would exercise an inhibiting and regressive influence upon production, and prevent this communitarianism from becoming truly liberal.

The idea of closed citadels of rights modeled upon traditional property must give way to the conception of multiple and superimposed entitlements, coexisting in tension. The power to make law, from the bottom up or by secession from the background legal order, must go hand in hand with a societywide structure of political and economic organization congenial to a persistent and decentralized experimentalism. Recognition of the need for such a structure is what chiefly distinguishes a corrected version of radical polyarchy from its unreconstructed counterpart.

For all its defects and dangers radical polyarchy remains seductive because it holds out the promise of generalizing a principle of social order that is already beginning to revolutionize how people work together in the most successful firms and schools throughout the world, in the experiences of postfordist flexible production and of skill-oriented cooperative learning. This family of forms of coordination flattens hierarchy, avoids fully articulate contract, and mixes cooperation and competition. By moderating the contrast between supervision and execution and enabling plans to be continuously revised in the light of experience with their execution, it encourages as well the ongoing revision of conceptions of interest and identity. It draws social arrangements closer to the procedures of practical reason, understood as an accelerated interaction between idea and experiment, between task-definition and task-fulfillment; between disaggregation and recombination; between assumptions and surprises.

At the same time it opens up a vast intermediate zone between the narrow terrains of arm's-length bargaining, or hierarchical coordination at work, on one side, and representative democracy, on the other side. We come to see and use the inherited forms of each of these devices of coordination as limiting cases of a less distinct and more inclusive repertory of practical experimentalism. In such a world we do not put the mythical figures of the selfless citizen of the republic or the other-oriented member of community in place of the real, anxious, interest-bearing and interest-pursuing individual. We try, instead, to broaden the scope of his activity by tinkering, cumulatively, with its setting of institutionalized practices and enacted beliefs.

The combination of practical advantage with democratic aspiration in this vision gains additional force from the intervention of a third element: the development of generosity in the moral history of contemporary humankind – a generosity fueled by the desire to imagine the otherness of other people rather than bound to the distancing techniques of an officious altruism. The violent clash of group hatreds, motivated in large part by the will to difference, asserted in the face of the waning of actual difference, and by the rage of collective impotence in the achievement of real difference, obscures another, more subtle and progressive development: the slow, halting growth of our power to recognize and accept the originality of other people. Many forces have contributed to this result: from the increasing influence of educated women to the ascendancy of psychologizing over moralism, and from the diffusion of learning about other people and their circumstances to the Christian–romantic residue in the formulaic stories of popular culture. The program of radical polyarchy promises to draw these intangible forces into the design of practical arrangements. The arrangements can in turn nourish the forces by multiplying opportunities for their expression in everyday life.

For all these reasons radical polyarchy contains a visionary message outreaching its institutional proposals. A test of the other two futures of the democratic project explored here – extended social democracy and mobilizational democracy – is their capacity to accommodate something of this very earthly utopian ideal.

IMAGINING THE ALTERNATIVE FUTURES OF A FREE SOCIETY: MOBILIZATIONAL DEMOCRACY

The direction of mobilizational democracy

Consider now a third possible direction for the radicalization of the democratic project: mobilizational democracy. For extended social democracy, the real action goes on in the life of the individual; it wants politics to become little so that individuals may become big. For radical polyarchy, the real action goes on in the communities and organizations – the distinctive forms of group life to which power increasingly devolves; it wants society to become a confederation of communities within which individuals can work and flourish as the communal beings they properly are. For mobilizational democracy, there is no privileged seat of the real action, or, rather, the favored theater is the whole of society; it wants to heat politics up, both the macropolitics of institutional change and the micropolitics of personal relations, and to loosen all factional strangleholds upon the key societymaking resources of political power, economic capital, and cultural authority. It refuses to abandon, or to narrow, the space of societywide politics.

The crucial empirical conjecture underlying the proposals of mobilizational democracy is the belief in a two-way causal connection between two potential attributes of a social order: the moderation of its entrenched divisions and hierarchies and the relative availability of its arrangements to challenge and revision. The basis of the connection lies in the non-naturalistic character of social facts. A set of social relations and arrangements becomes stable, real, and thinglike to the extent that it gets insulated against disturbance amid the ordinary practical and discursive conflicts of society.

Availability to challenge and revision should not be mistaken for a condition of permanent flux. The point is not that institutional arrangements constantly change – an exercise from which people would soon seek release – but rather that the distance between pursuing interests within a framework and changing bits of the framework as you go along diminishes. Change becomes banal, as the transparency of the institutional context of action, and its openness to tinkering, increase. This is no move from stability to instability; it is a shift in the quality of stability, a shift that merely moves forward in a direction in which market economies and representative democracy have already taken us.

The spiritual parallel to the empirical conjecture informing the program of mobilizational democracy is an effort to realize the pagan ideal of greatness – individual and collective empowerment in our modern vocabulary – that can be more readily reconciled with the Christian ideal of love, and with the egalitarian and solidaristic commitments that this ideal has helped motivate. In the doctrine of mobilizational democracy we find new reasons to affirm the connections among the three major complaints against modern societies: that we are too unequal, too divided from another, and too little. We discover that to redress the first two complaints we must redress the third.

In another direction, the causal conjecture strengthens the claim of the program of mobilizational democracy to advance the old radical-democratic hope of exploiting the area of potential intersection between the institutional conditions of practical progress – especially economic growth – and the institutional conditions for the emancipation of the individual from extreme and entrenched hierarchy. The cause of practical experimentalism – and its demand for a more inclusive freedom to tinker – is what these two projects have in common. Mobilizational democracy gambles on the affinity between the flexibility persistent economic and technological innovation requires and the human interest in a fuller experience of freedom.

The law and institutions of mobilizational democracy

Three sets of institutional reforms advance the program of mobilizational democracy, reconstructing the institutional forms of the state and of party politics, of the economy and the firm, and of civil society and its organizations.

The political program of mobilizational democracy consists in the reversal of the two sets of institutional techniques characterizing the dominant political and constitutional tradition of modern democracy: the preference for constitutional arrangements that slow down transformative politics through opportunities for impasse and requirements of consensus; and the adoption of practices that help keep the citizenry at a low level of political mobilization.

In lieu of the impasse-favoring or consensus-requiring arrangements, mobilizational democracy places constitutional techniques that facilitate the transformative use of political power and the decisive execution of programmatic experiments. Among such techniques may be the artful mixture of the characteristics of parliamentary and presidential regimes in ways that open up multiple paths to the winning of central state power; the priority given to comprehensive programmatic proposals over episodic legislation; the resolution of impasse over the adoption of such proposals through national plebiscites and referenda; and the vesting of power in different branches of government to call anticipated elections for all branches simultaneously.

In place of practices hostile to the political mobilization of the citizenry, mobilizational democracy favors a persistent heightening of the level of political mobilization in society. To this end, it employs, in the circumstances of contemporary polities, means such as rules of mandatory voting, electoral regimes favorable to strong parties, public financing of campaigns, and extended free access to the means of mass communication. The key conjecture animating these reforms is the idea of a causal connection between the energy level of politics and its structural content: there is no such thing as a low-energy politics that has as its content the frequent practice of structural reform. A program that wants to diminish the distance between the ordinary politics of marginal redistribution and the transformative politics of structural change must therefore insist upon a prolonged heightening of the level of political mobilization.

In the work of economic reconstruction, mobilizational democracy seeks to multiply the terms under which people have access to productive resources. It fosters regimes of cooperative competition among firms. It establishes organizations intermediate between the government and the firm, and with varying degrees of independence from both, and makes them responsible for the decentralized allocation of financial and technological resources under varied property regimes. These regimes should extend all the way from the single-minded pursuit of the highest rate of return for the use of resources to the intimate and preferential involvement with a confederation of firms. Such experiments in the coexistence, within the same economy, of different systems of contract and property law will regularly require the dismemberment of the traditional property right and the vesting of its component faculties in different kinds of rightholders. Among these successors to the traditional owner will be firms, workers, national and local governments, intermediate organizations, and social funds.

One of the preconditions for this quantum increase in economic flexibility is continuing reliance upon a package of guarantees against catastrophic economic insecurity and of claims to continuing reeducation throughout a lifetime. Here, mobilizational democracy, like radical polyarchy, meets the program of extended social democracy. Every extension of the democratic project requires that people be assured access to the practical and cultural instruments with which to contain insecurity and to form and execute their own life projects. These guarantees must be secured by law. They must be made effective by forms of corrective intervention that are both localized and structural, like the expanded practice of complex enforcement discussed earlier in this book.

The acceleration of politics and the quickening of economic innovation have their counterpart and their condition in the self-organization of civil society. Civil society outside the state must be both highly and universally organized for the political and economic institutions of mobilizational democracy to maintain their integrity. The traditional devices of private contract and incorporation are insufficient to accomplish this objective just as the traditional forms of unified property are incapable of reconciling greater decentralization and flexibility with the necessary scale and aggregation of people and resources.

Social experimentalism and human rights

These institutional innovations in the organization of the state, the economy, and civil society strengthen the intensity and widen the scope of practical experimentalism in all areas of social experience. Do they thereby threaten human rights? Mobilizational democracy seems to require that more be put up for grabs in politics. Respect for human rights, however, requires that something – if only the guarantees constituting the rights themselves – be withdrawn from politics.

To assess the realism of the danger to personal safeguards we must look beyond the speculative vocabulary of human rights to the practical problems this vocabulary conceals. Two substantial ideas combine to give salvageable empirical content to the otherwise elusive language of rights. One element is a technique; the other an objective for whose sake we properly deploy the technique.

The instrumental component in the idea of human rights is the withdrawal of certain matters from the agenda of short-term politics. In this sense, a fundamental right is simply an entitlement that has gained a measure of protection from disturbance in the course of ordinary political and economic conflict. Constitutional entrenchment – the need to meet the test of a qualified majority vote – is merely the most familiar form of such an immunity. The immunity is always relative: in the end, nothing can prevent the ideas and arrangements establishing rights from remaining hostage to the practical and ideological conflicts of politics. The cult of the constitution may increase the inhibition. So may a speculative doctrine of natural right. They do so, however, at a tremendous cost, including the cost to the very concerns to which rights talk responds.

What should be withdrawn from the agenda of short-term politics? Only if we subscribe to the fetishistic belief that a free society has a single, natural institutional form do we believe this question to have a self-evident answer. As we move way from this fetishism, we need to give the question an ever more explicit response.

Within the social theory informing the program of mobilizational democracy, the best answer is that the entitlements secluded against the risks of short-term politics should accomplish two distinct but related tasks. They should protect people against radical insecurities, including the risks of public and private oppression. They should also supply people with the economic and cultural equipment they need to define and execute their life projects. Some rights, such as access to original and continuing education, participate in both aspects of the fundamental immunities.

If people lacked protection in a haven of vitally protected securities, they would find the accelerated and expanded experimentalism of a mobilizational democracy too threatening. They would soon exchange its terrors for the first protective despotism or demobilized polity they could find. Viewed in this light, the relation of human rights to the stronger experimentalism it sustains resembles the relation of a parent's love to the child's willingness to risk adventure and self-transformation.

If people lacked the economic and cultural means with which to form and to execute their life projects, they would be unable successfully to use their greater freedom under mobilizational democracy. Their incapacities would soon undermine and pervert their liberties. Seen from this angle, the relation of fundamental rights to democratic experimentalism resembles the relation of vision to will.

Mobilizational democracy should therefore not be mistaken for a regime hostile to relative exemptions (for all exemptions must be relative) from the agenda of short-term politics. Instead, it thrives upon an indispensable dialectical relation between what is added to transformative opportunity and what is protected against transformative risk. For the sake of politics, as well as for the sake of individual liberty, some things must be denied to politics. We may wish that the content of this dialectical relation between the matters subject to (short-term) politics and the matters withdrawn from it were rigidly and permanently defined, but it is not and cannot be, because it has an empirical and experimental character.

Thus, just as we should not mistake the broadened experimentalism of mobilizational democracy for a quest for permanent flux in social affairs, so too we should not expect the acceleration of politics under mobilizational democracy to conflict with human rights. What we must renounce to achieve this objective is an illusion, although an illusion that has often been useful, for a while, to the cause of freedom. This illusion is the belief in an immutable foundation for human rights. One such foundation would exist if it were true that a free society has a single natural or necessary institutional form, or, at least, that free societies tend to converge toward such a form, and that a canonical system of rights is one of the constituents of this free order. These beliefs, however, are false. Freedom is not safe, nor can it develop, when hostage to false beliefs.

The brand of institutional fetishism defined by these illusions was one of the major elements of nineteenth-century legal science. Contemporary legal and political thought refuses fully to relinquish it. For although we rarely defend the idea of a predetermined institutional content for democracy, we fear that a candid recognition of the contingency of such democratic institutions as we possess will endanger the rights sustaining freedom. Freedom, however, gains nothing, and loses much, from being entangled with superstition. No matter what secular or sacred basis we claim for the rights we profess to support, we cannot avoid conflict over their content. By having sought to tie our hands with the restraints of institutional fetishism, we shall have distanced ourselves from the real driving force of practical freedom, the empirical relation between our economic and political experiments and the equipment we need to experiment securely and effectively.

Moreover, by having stepped away from this real guide, out of a respect for an illusory guarantee against the dangers of politics, we shall also have diminished the prospects for the emancipation of society from control by political and economic elites. For, according to the social theory informing the program of mobilizational democracy, there is a link between the insulation of institutional arrangements from challenge and revision and their power to generate and support rigid hierarchies of power and advantage.

Political virtue and political realism

Once we sweep aside the false objection of hostility to human rights, however, the real threats to the program of mobilizational democracy begin to come into focus. The spiritual and practical aspects of these dangers have a common source in the excessive dependence of the institutions of mobilizational democracy upon a permanently heightened level of vigilance and engagement. Mobilizational democracy is not another version of the authoritarian and utopian attempt to replace the incarnate, self-concerned, interest-pursuing individual, incurably ambivalent about society and politics, with the mythical figure of the selfless and transparent citizen. It seeks to broaden rather than to replace the normal activity of forming and pursuing interests.

If mobilizational democracy depended upon the radical-republican ideal of unconditional engagement, it would forfeit both its realism and its attractiveness. Its appeal would rest upon a one-sided and indefensible picture of human dispositions. In practice, a minority of talkers and self-promoters would find expanded opportunities for preferment while the majority would shrink from this oligarchy of busy-bodies, and seek to reestablish a social world centered on individual careers and family life. The majority would resist, and rightly so, the sacrifice of dense personal commitments and ambitions, of material pleasures and spiritual longings, to a single-minded devotion to national political projects and passions.

A general principle of programmatic argument underlies this crucial point. In considering the relation of institutional reconstruction to human nature, we must tread a path between contrasting errors. Yes, it is true that all facets of human experience are influenced by the institutional context of the experience. We cannot divide human life into two parts and claim only one of the two to be susceptible to political influence. Even the most intimate aspects of life – our most private sentiments of love and loathing – remain hostage to the organizational structure of society.

On the other hand, however, nothing enables us to change our dispositions suddenly and radically. A fatal objection to a program of reform is its dependence upon a scheme of drastic human regeneration. In the absence of any well-founded distinction between permanent or universal and variable or local human characteristics, we must prudently suppose that we shall remain similar, in behavior and longing, to what we are like now. It is not in the cards that, under any reconstructive scheme, we shall see privatistic concerns replaced by selfless civic devotion. What we can realistically hope for is that, under favorable institutional conditions, the range of our ordinary pursuit of private interests will broaden, and the contrast between realizing interests and challenging structures will diminish.

For all these reasons, mobilizational democracy should not depend upon the predominance of political passion over ordinary experience. Nevertheless, any lessening of vigilance or engagement poses peculiar dangers to this program. This risk has economic, temperamental, and spiritual dimensions. The economic risk is that a lull in the level of mobilization enables the governing forces to benefit their supporters in ways that turn temporary advantage into vested right. The freer scope of transformative experimentalism under mobilizational democracy may prove to be self-destructive if it eases the way for the collusion of political power and economic advantage.

The temperamental risk is that the talkers and self-promoters may do even better when general engagement retreats than they do when it advances. As people shrink from the boredom of constant meetings about everything and nothing, the small minority of the obsessively engaged may take over the participatory institutions, speaking for their absent, distracted, and sullen fellows.

The spiritual risk is that an ever wider gap will open between the dogmas of civic commitment on which the regime rests and the human reality with which it must live. In the darkness of this gap broader human concerns may be suppressed while pretenses of civic engagement begin to conceal narrow self-interest.

The most troubling question for mobilizational democracy remains its failure adequately to economize on political energy and political virtue. The regime is lost if it must choose between consuming people's attention and succumbing to their privatistic preoccupations.

THE CAMPAIGN TO SPLIT THE DIFFERENCE BETWEEN RATIONALISM AND HISTORICISM

The deflation of rationalism

The problems and opportunities explored in this redirection of legal analysis and this exploration of the alternative futures of democracy belong to a larger situation of thought in our time. The prestigious style of legal doctrine criticized under the name rationalizing legal analysis exemplifies a theoretical campaign contemporary intellectuals conduct in many fields of thought. Call it the campaign to split the difference between rationalism and historicism by deflating rationalism and inflating historicism.

By rationalism I mean the idea that we can have a basis for the justification and the criticism of forms of social life, and that we develop this basis through deliberation, which generates criteria of judgement cutting across our traditions, cultures, and societies. The gist of historicism is the idea that we have no standards of judgement with an authority transcending particular, historically located forms of life and universes of discourse. The flaws in rationalizing legal analysis turn out to illustrate the fundamental weakness in this larger philosophical campaign to deflate rationalism and to inflate historicism, and to find the imaginary middle point between them.

Legal analysis as institutional imagination represents a special case of a more general alternative to rationalism and historicism. The general answer, like the more focused one it generalizes, involves as well a revision of the question itself. The campaign to split the difference between rationalism and historicism can succeed only by radically shifting course in the methods it employs and the outcomes it justifies.

The widespread theoretical effort to find the middle point between rationalism and historicism often serves to justify a particular political program – the project of progressive liberalism, or of institutionally conservative social democracy. It is not clear at the start whether there is a more than accidental link between the methodological enterprise and the political program. The link, the following discussion suggests, is real although complex. My argument develops in three parts. First, I explore the structure of this effort to split the difference between rationalism and historicism, suggesting the legal counterparts to its main incidents. Then, I examine the way in which we would have to reorient this theoretical campaign to make sense of it and to allow it to achieve its professed objectives. Later, I consider the motivations, both impersonal or programmatic, and personal or existential, that could lead someone today, in a circumstance such as ours, to follow the path I advocate.

Begin by placing the contemporary campaign to split the difference between rationalism and historicism in a rudimentary historical context. Take rationalism, at the outset, to mean an attempt to find a basis of criticism and justification in a practice of deliberation producing standards that apply universally and cut across particular settings of conversation and forms of social life. The characteristic modern form of this rationalism seeks to identify a type of social organization that remains neutral with respect to the life projects of individuals and the outlooks of particular groups. We can also redefine this modern rationalism affirmatively as the effort to infer a blueprint of social organization from the abstract idea of voluntary society; that is to say, from the idea of a chosen association among free and equal individuals. This modern rationalism seems at every point either to remain too indeterminate to provide the guidance it promises, or to become determinate only by abandoning the neutrality it claims.

There is a premodern rationalism. However, it is very hard to say with assurance exactly what it is. Sometimes people speak of a doctrine of objective value. In what texts and what thinkers do we actually find this doctrine? There seems at first nothing in common between, say, the Aristotelian attempt to uncover a latent rational structure in our experi- ence of moral opinion, under the guidance of a theory of human flourishing, and the effort, exemplified by the philosophy of the middle and later Plato, to turn abruptly away from common moral opinion, out of respect for ideal conceptions presenting themselves to the imagination with an irresistible authority.

Premodern rationalism nevertheless has a distinct shape. This shape lies precisely in the oscillation between the attempt to impute a rational structure to the established social order and the available universe of moral opinion; and the countervailing effort to challenge opinion and order from an external, custom-transcending standpoint. The character- istic problem of the premodern rationalist is a familiar dilemma. The imputation of rational structure and authority to ordinary moral opinion always seems unjustifiably to privilege the ideas and the experiences of particular groups and cultures. The countervailing effort to break with this world of ordinary opinion always seems to have too controversial a justifi- cation to persuade us in fact to turn against the entrenched institutions and the accepted dogmas of society.

Here are two complementary stories relating the modern and the premodern rationalism. One is a story about the evolution of ideas. It finds the basic flaw in premodern rationalism in its inability to support a critical distance from our culture and its preconceptions, while still somehow responding to our given points of departure, in accepted belief and ordinary experience. Modern rationalism, with its characteristic drive toward impar- tiality of view, begins in an attempt to develop a less biased mode of moral and political judgement, grounded upon less controversial assumptions.

However, the latter-day rationalisms turn out to be always either non-neutral or indeterminate. They reach particular conclusions only by forfeiting their claim to neutrality. Sometimes, for example, they forfeit it by accepting current versions of the market economy or of representative democracy as reliable approximations to a system for summing up the choices of individuals; that is to say, as a practical embodiment of the perspective of impartiality. At other times they forfeit it by drastically reducing the complexity of the raw material – moral intuitions and personal wants – with which they work. In particular, they disregard the way in which desire and belief accommodate to practical arrangements and prestigious dogmas that, as longing and fantasy, they also challenge.

This internal story about the evolution of ideas needs to be complemented by an external story, a story about actual social experience. According to this external story, the driving force in the evolution of rationalism is the actual experience of the churning up, the recombination, and the reinvention of forms of social life, making us ever more aware of the extent to which ideal conceptions have roots in historically located practical arrangements. This experience of churning and recombination produces a keener awareness of the crucial and fragile link between ideal conceptions of social life and the practical arrangements that both constrain the more complete realization of those conceptions and give them much of their implicit meaning. What begins by suggesting different ways to realize the same ideals ends by exposing the complex and partly incompatible meanings we attach to those ideals. The result of this probing, stretching, and breaking is both to confirm and to discredit the responsiveness of our ideals to the inchoate yearnings and the forceful desires from which they draw life and to which they give shape.

The effect of institutional innovation upon our understanding of the content and authority of accepted social ideals undermines the pre-rationalist attempt to break away from ordinary moral opinion in the name of unquestionable moral insight or intuition. The same churning and recombination undermine the claim of any particular version of a market economy or a representative democracy to embody a reliable version of the idea of voluntary society. All this disappointment and discovery, repressed but not completely avoided, encourage the effort constantly to deflate the claims of rationalism and to meet the pressures described by the internal and external stories I have retold.

One way to characterize the counterpart to this deflation of rationalism in the history of legal ideas is to distinguish two types of legal rationalism contrasted earlier: nineteenth-century legal science and contemporary rationalizing analysis. The strong, nineteenth-century approach distinguished between a true or prepolitical law – the law of the private order of contract and property and of its proper relation to the limits of governmental action – and a soft, fake or politicized law, the law created by governments to intervene, for redistributive purposes, in the pure system of private and public rights. The weaker, deflated, and contemporary form of this legal rationalism gives up this distinction between political and prepolitical law. It nevertheless attempts to maintain the contrast between a law that is merely the product of factional fighting and a law embodying a public morality or a public interest.

As this idea of a suprafactional law in turn proves to be either non-neutral or indeterminate, many jurists retreat to a more disenchanted but also more tangible view of their task. They embrace pessimistic reformism, and reinterpret rationalizing legal analysis as a noble and necessary lie. They try to impose restraints upon the factional self-dealing that occurs through majoritarian politics. They seek to protect the groups that seem unable to protect themselves. Little by little, the impulse to limit this purifying and corrective intervention to what can plausibly stand as interpretation of law and accommodate to the established institutional structure of society changes its character. The desire to reiterate faith in the necessity and authority of present arrangements now weakens. What has increasingly taken its place is a frank recognition of the constraints, of power and legitimacy, upon the institutional roles the legal analyst can hope to occupy and the reconstructive work he can effectively undertake. So do the jurists harness an involuntary skepticism to a resigned benevolence.

The inflation of historicism

Consider now the transformation of historicism, the other pole from which the characteristic contemporary philosophical campaign begins. At the center of historicism is the thesis that the standards capable of justifying or criticizing a form of social life are the standards that this form of social life itself produces. No criteria of judgement cut across traditions or cultures. If we can move across traditions and cultures at all, we can do so only by choosing to be different people and to live a different life; there is no higher-order rationality. In contemporary culture, historicism takes a conservative and ironic form, recurring in many areas of thought. It says in effect: all that there are in the world are historically located forms of life and clumps of conversation; nothing else exists. Only those justifications are available that arise from taking a position within one of these forms of life or traditions of

talk. You must judge each such setting by its internal standards, or, if, excep-
tionally, you are willing to risk the authoritarian and obfuscating
consequences, by the imported standards of some other setting; no other
alternative is available. In this way the ironic, conservative historicist turns
on its head the claim of the ultimate groundlessness of each society and
culture. He makes this claim into a justification for reengagement in the
established tradition, with a defensive and ironic proviso.

One objection to such a historicism is that it presupposes the unavoid-
ability of a dilemma that the collective and individual history of moral
experience has often escaped: the supposed need to choose between a
moral and political conversation that is rich precisely because it is fully
embedded in a particular tradition and a conversation that is thin because
it tries to transcend all particular traditions. The belief in such a dilemma
fails to account for one of the most striking facts about this history of
belief and feeling: the occasional revolutions in moral and political sensibility. The most astonishing example of such ruptures is the rise and
propagation of the world religions, such as Christianity and Buddhism,
proposing views of how to live that violently contradicted the dominant
moral wisdom of the societies in which they spread.

A second objection to this conservative and passive historicism is that
it seems to run counter to many features of our contemporary situation.
What makes the search for justification urgent is precisely the sense that
we lack closed, uncontroversial traditions within which to stand. If we
had them, we would hardly need rationalism or historicism. It is precisely
the waning of these traditions, their recombination, their reconstruction,
their breaking up and jumbling together that inspires the search for justification and criticism, and provokes, by way of response, the invention of
fictive traditions and the will to collective difference. If traditions retained
the distinctness that this conservative historicism supposes, the debate
about rationalism and historicism would lose its sense.

A third objection to this historicism is that it imputes guiding force to
facts that seem incapable of exercising any normative authority: the facts
of continuity and consensus that the conservative historicist takes as
something in between an insurpassable horizon of justification or criticism
and a source of insight into a transhistorical moral order. Thus, the conservative historicist must characteristically attempt to inflate historicism
just as the rationalist deflates rationalism. The most common form of the
inflation of historicism is to treat the political traditions and institutions of
the contemporary Western industrial democracies as deserving special
respect as a source of moral and political guidance: not just because they

are ours but because they somehow incorporate or embody a claim of impartiality among individuals and their interests and ideals. The claim of privilege may extend to the intuitions, preferences, and beliefs likely to develop in these societies.

To identify the typical legal form of this inflation of historicism consider first a crude, undeveloped form of noninflated historicism. It is no more than a limiting case, an extreme position in contemporary legal thought, but it exercises far greater influence over everyday lawyers' thinking than over legal theory. It teaches that the law has to be interpreted against a background of the dominant moral and political ideas of society. There is a common culture, supplying all the instruments that we need to interpret and elaborate law when rule-guided inference runs out.

Thus, we can picture the relation of the legal analyst to his material as being uncontroversial in one of two opposite ways. It may be uncontroversial because we imagine him to be a kind of legal ethnographer, describing a common culture to which he need not submit. Or we may suppose the relation to be uncontroversial because we think of the legal analyst as quoting his own consciousness; he participates uncontroversially in a culture and speaks it as one would speak a natural language. The problem arises when we confront the actual fragmentation of this supposed culture: its failure to exist in a unitary form. It remains anchored in the conflicting outlooks of particular classes and communities. Moreover, people experience ambivalence between wants or intuitions that take the existing structure for granted, and longings or fantasies that presuppose its overcoming. The legal inflation of historicism is a way to deny this fragmentation or to circumvent its consequences. This inflation often begins as an effort to single out the authoritative part of the shared culture, the part that counts more, because it is somehow more impartial or embodies more fully the idea of voluntary society.

You can now begin to appreciate the general character of the philosophical campaign to split the difference between historicism and rationalism. When the philosophers and legal theorists seek this imaginary mid-point between rationalism and historicism, they look for something that retains part of the authority, the critical distance and push of rationalism, without making its claims to transcendence over context. That is what they want, and they want it most often to justify a version of the progressive liberal and social-democratic program. That is what they want, but can they get it?

Splitting the difference between rationalism and historicism in philosophy and social theory

One philosophical or social-theoretical form in which we encounter this philosophical movement to split the difference between rationalism and historicism is exemplified by ideas such as the American philosopher Rawls' conception of overlapping consensus in a democratic society or the German philosopher Habermas' notion of a framework of uncoerced conversation. The historicist factor in these ideas is the conviction that certain beliefs are authoritative just because they are the beliefs likely to thrive in a modern democracy. The countervailing rationalist element is the conception that a modern democracy is not just any society, but a society whose structure makes good on the promise of voluntary association, of association among free and equal individuals. The authority of the structure carries over to the authority of the beliefs that flourish within it.

The central flaw in this approach is its failure to question the authority by which the established organization of the government, the economy, and civil society represents the ideal conception of voluntary society. Which part of the structure should we take for granted and which part should we challenge? Until we are able to ask and to answer this question, we cannot really know what level of authority the beliefs flourishing within this framework should enjoy.

Splitting the difference between rationalism and historicism in legal analysis

The most important and detailed example in contemporary culture of the campaign to split the difference between rationalism and historicism is, however, not to be found in the writings of philosophers. It is rationalizing legal analysis itself. The rationalistic element in this reigning approach to legal analysis is the claim that we can rationally reconstruct the law as the partial expression of an intelligible and defensible plan of social life. This plan may conform to practical, functional requirements or it may bear witness to the progressive evolution of moral and political conceptions. The historicist element is twofold: first, the recognition of the historical specificity and distinction of each legal tradition; second, the call to the jurists to take heed of the circumstances of their time and place as they complete the plan implicit in the law through the improving work of rational reconstruction.

Rationalizing legal analysis gives a deeper sense to the splitting of the difference between rationalism and historicism. It lends a special authority to the law as it goes about its work of reasoned and retrospective elaboration. It gives the deeper sense and lends the special authority by representing the social, economic, and political arrangements in law as rough approximations to the ideal of a free civil society, a free market economy, and a free representative society – that is to say, to a social order in which everyone counts as equal. The institutional arrangements of such a society result from the exercise of individual and collective self-determination. Such a tradition is more than a tradition. Such a context is more than a context. Although particular, it has the practical and conceptual means with which to evade and correct its own particularity.

It is one thing to struggle for such an outcome through politics and thought. It is another to assume that it is already at hand. A major part of my purpose has been to explore the cost of this assumption and the way to avoid bearing it.

By understanding rationalizing legal analysis and its supporting theories as a certain way of splitting the difference between rationalism and historicism, we can generalize our insight into the failures of this approach to law. The law, we have seen, appears to the jurist as the result of two processions. On the one hand there is the procession of organized partisan and factional fighting within the groundrules of the democracy. On the other hand, in the spirit of rational reconstruction, there is the procession from a system of practical requirements or of normative conceptions. Once suitably reinterpreted, the law looks almost as if it had been made up according to a blueprint. If the law really is the product of such factional fighting, and if democratic politics are in earnest and do not operate as the unconscious or unwitting instrument of preset practical or moral imperatives, we cannot reasonably expect the law to display any such cohesive functional or ideal plan. At best it may contain, in varying proportions, the beginnings and residues of many such plans. The notables must intervene to complete stories merely suggested by the material they interpret and elaborate. They will need drastically to overstate the extent to which the law spells out such stories, lest their work appear an intolerable usurpation.

When we consider only the legal form of this attempt to split the difference between rationalism and historicism – the form taken by rationalizing legal analysis and by the theories that uphold it and propose to refine it – the vices of this campaign seem to be manipulation and vanguardism. However, once we recognize the legal project as a special case of a more general enterprise, comparing its legal and philosophical forms, we discover that there is a more basic problem. The dominant contemporary form of the campaign to split the difference between rationalism and historicism conditions our practical stake in the progressive reallocation of rights and resources on an idealization of the institutional order of society. It disarms us imaginatively in the criticism of that order. Nevertheless, our political programs and our spiritual ideals alike remain unavoidably engaged in the practical arrangements of society.

The campaign to split the difference between rationalism and historicism reoriented

In the light of this criticism, how should the campaign to split the difference between rationalism and historicism be reoriented? What different methods would it have to employ and what different outcomes would it have to produce to meet these objections? The beginning of an answer to these questions is an awareness that what I described as the unified practice of mapping and criticism is just a special case of such a reorientation of the campaign to split the difference between rationalism and historicism. This practice starts in the middle of the stuff, exploring and exploiting the disharmonies between professed party programs or ideal conceptions, and the institutional arrangements that both constrain their fulfillment and impoverish their meaning.

Reconsider in this light the criticism aspect of this practice of mapping and criticism. Begin with the idea that the raw material of criticism is a series of promises of happiness. Criticism is about promises of happiness. Promises of happiness are routes to the fulfillment, the reconciliation, and the correction of our strongest longings, according to conceptions that elicit faith and are not unequivocally disconfirmed by experience. These promises of happiness take two main forms. One such form is an existential project, a typical biography, a model of how to live in the world. Another form they take is a translation of the abstract, indeterminate idea of society into a series of detailed pictures of human association; conceptions of how people can and should deal with one another in different areas of social practice.

In circumstances of stability, the quiescent moments of history, each such conception of human association appears wedded to arrangements representing it in practice, and embedded in an uncontroversial domain of social existence. Thus, a particular ideal of private community may be exemplified by practices of family life, rooted in a particular world of family and friendship. If any part of this structure becomes unstuck, if we start to apply certain ideals of social life to areas of practice from which they were previously excluded, or to choose between alternative practical realizations of those inherited conceptions, we begin to discover hidden ambiguities in the ideals. We must then decide how to resolve the ambiguities and reinterpret the ideals.

You may well ask: Where is the energy for the transformation, and where is the authority for it? The rationalist characteristically supposes these to be two different questions. The historicist is more likely to think that they are really just the same question. Each of these two views holds part of the truth.

In the normal, stabilized situation, the logic of group interests, collective identities, and accepted ideas about social possibility enjoys a semblance of transparency and necessity. However, the semblance results from the absence of effective challenge to the surrounding background: the basic institutional arrangements and the enacted pictures of human association. In such a situation the energy comes from the definitions of individual and group interests, from the collective identities, from the conceptions of social possibility pursued within the constraints loosely set by established arrangements and beliefs.

Suppose, however, we begin to disturb this background. It always can begin to change, if only because a characteristic tactical ambiguity persists in our ways of defending current definitions of interests. We always have tactics for the defense of interests that keep the structure in place and other tactics that jeopardize and change the structure. Then, as this background structure begins to be challenged, people's confidence in the established definitions of interest, identity, and possibility also wanes. At such moments of challenge and agitation, ideals no longer appear to be costly constraints upon interests. Instead, people's conceptions of what their interests are begin to depend ever more explicitly upon stories they tell themselves about the alternative social worlds into which they might move. These stories supply alternative views about the directions in which they can develop their ideals as well as their interests.

According to a widespread view, the primary task of political judgement and political theory is to adjudicate – from some more impartial or otherwise authoritative standpoint – among the many conflicting programs and ideologies we confront in contemporary politics. An underlying theme in this book is that our problem is less that we have too many programs than that we have just one program: the only political program with authority in the modern world, the program of democratic experimentalism from the eighteenth century to the present day, the program that liberals share with socialists. Its central commitment is to lift the grid of social division and hierarchy weighing upon our practical, passionate, and cognitive dealings with one another.

We have two overriding reasons to pursue this project: first, to enhance the practical productive capabilities of society, the resources of restless practical experimentation and innovation; and, second, to diminish the extent to which participation in group life pins us down to mechanisms of dependence and depersonalization and thereby undercuts self-assertion, the effort to develop and sustain an individual presence in the world. The great gamble this modern political project makes is that we can devise and establish institutions enabling us to exploit the area of potential overlap between the conditions of these moral and practical goods: between the development of the practical productive capabilities of society and the creation of conditions in which individuals win freedom from circumstances of dependence and depersonalization. Our inherited conceptions of the divisions between rightwing and leftwing, or liberal and socialist, versions of this modern political program remain entangled in a dense brush of superstition about the possible institutional forms of political and economic pluralism. A task of criticism is to push beyond false or superficial distinctions between, for example, pro-government and anti-government commitments, so that new and more significant ideological conflicts can emerge.

In this book I have offered two main examples of such a practice of criticism. These examples connect in a way illuminating both the genius and the limits of contemporary law in the industrial democracies. The first example is the discussion of the constraints that institutional conservatism imposes upon the great animating idea of contemporary law and legal thought: the commitment to ensure the effective enjoyment of rights, and in particular of those rights sustaining individual freedom and popular self-government. The second example is the exploration of the alternative futures of democracy, each of which takes our interests and ideals beyond the institutional horizon within which we now keep them.

The spirit of this critical practice becomes clear by comparison to the current philosophical attempt to split the difference between historicism and rationalism. In contrast to that attempt it implies a critical attitude toward the existing and established institutional framework of society. It also requires a critical approach to the data of wants and intuitions. For one thing, a ramshackle and replaceable institutional structure helps shape these wants and intuitions. For another thing, they suffer a characteristic ambivalence. They fall in between desires or preconceptions preserving the institutional order and taking it for granted, and longings and fantasies seeking to escape this order. Finally, by contrast to the present philosophical campaign to split the difference between rationalism and historicism, this practice of institutional imagination suggests how to arrive at relatively more controversial and unsettling conclusions, starting from relatively less controversial points of departure: the established commitments of contemporary law or the fighting faiths of the great parties of opinion in politics.

The habit of retrospective rationalization – of law, politics, production, and history; the search for a speculative simulacrum of impartiality of judgement, teaching us how to deal out resources and rights within a structure left unchallenged; and the abandonment of this search in favor of a conservative embrace of yesterday's progressivism will not help us travel such a route. The working out, in imagination and practice, of institutional variations on the realization and reshaping of our interests and ideals is the discipline we need. It would be a lifeless discipline if it were not animated by the hope of continuing to live in history as a history of great practical and spiritual alternatives.

PROPHECY AND PROSTRATION IN LEGAL THOUGHT

The cult of state law and the quest for latent moral order

The practices of legal analysis explored, criticized, and redirected in this book give the most recent expressions to a very old marriage between two ideas. The first partner in this union antedates the state. It is the idea of a moral order latent in a form of social life, an order expressed in reciprocal expectations and claims, refined and reproduced through continuous conversation, penetrating and softening the realities of power and scarcity, and sustained by authoritative images of human association. Such images provide pictures of what dealings among people can and should be like in each domain of social experience. The second partner in the union has been statolatry: the cult of the state, of its reasons and its edicts.

From the marriage of the older belief in latent order with the newer statolatry comes a quest that has remained the unifying theme of legal thought ever since states emerged and jurists began to make sense of governmental enactments: the belief that a rational and defensible scheme of human life must, however incompletely and imperfectly, underlie the savage and surprising deeds of power. Democracy has had a two-sided relation to this marriage: if democracy has made power seem less terrible, it has also made more troubling the idea of a latent, unchosen order. The method of policy and principle in legal analysis, flourishing in democratic societies and spreading throughout the world from its favored position in the United States, is no more than a step in an historical sequence of discourses. In this sequence each succeeding style of discourse celebrates the marriage of state power with latent order and manages the subtle meaning of this marriage for democracy.

The history of legal thought has by now become so crowded by all the defenses, concessions, and compromises needed to uphold faith in this operation that we readily forget the rudiments of the undertaking. It is especially easy to lose sight of the continuing potency of the old idea of immanent moral order that the jurists of state-made law took over from the expounders of customary law. When the expressions of that idea in routinized social life began to weaken, the lawyers and the priests found new roots for it in the sacred laws of the major religious traditions.

The charms of the conception of immanent order continued until recently to be more palpable than they have now become. A young person being trained in legal doctrine in a peripheral part of the Western world in the second half of the twentieth century could still experience these charms almost undiminished, in the form of the long fossilized project of nineteenth-century legal science, perennially rehearsed in those faraway places. He could study Roman law through the unhistorical lens of the traditional Romanists, reading Savigny on possession as if the German bureaucrat and the Roman jurisconsults were nearly contemporary co-discoverers of the same moral order. He could be thrilled by the sense of participation in a form of consciousness that seemed both archaic and indispensable, preceding the social sciences, giving birth to them, and yet continuing to perform a mission they were powerless to accomplish. Identifying with the ancient priesthood of the jurists, he could see in their work a halting escape from the accidents, absurdities, and atrocities of history. We can laugh at him now, but we cannot so easily sever our anxieties from his sympathies.

The association of the quest for latent moral order with the cult of the state and its law had its progressive aspect in its corroding effect upon the belief in a natural, prepolitical system of social life. As the great lever of transformation, the state links social change with social will. The price of this appeal to the state, however, is high. It has been steadily increasing. We recognize only part of the cost of pietism about power.

We can hope to purge state-imposed law of some of its coercion and violence, subjecting it to the discipline of democratic accountability, and withdrawing from the agenda of short-term politics those rights that define and protect the means for individual and collective self-determination. Something of the terrors of coercion and violence nevertheless always remains in the law of the state. The quest for immanent moral order is as likely to conceal them as to improve them. This book, however, has emphasized a different side of the cost of our search for immanent order within governmental law: the immunization of the basic institutions of society, defined in law, against effective criticism, challenge, and revision. By embracing forms of thought, discourse, and practice – such as rationalizing legal analysis – that contribute to this immunization, we frustrate our interests, betray our ideals, and belittle our hopes.

Democratic experimentalism opposed to latent moral order

To avoid paying this price, it is not enough to cool the fervor of our statolatry by dissolving the bond between the cult of the state and its law and the search for latent moral order. We must go further and rid ourselves of the residue of the idea of latent order itself. In its place we should put a vision of the great constructive forces legal analysis as institutional imagination should serve.

One such force is practical experimentalism embraced to heighten our powers: of insight into our circumstances, and of emancipation from drudgery, infirmity, and insecurity. At the heart of practical progress lies the relation between cooperation and innovation. To progress in any department of practical life we must innovate and we must cooperate. Innovation both requires and threatens cooperation. It threatens cooperation by jeopardizing the stable loyalties, reciprocities, and expectations in which real human relations lie embedded and from which traditionalists have inferred the idea of immanent moral order. The overriding task in the design of arrangements conducive to practical progress is therefore always to imagine and establish the arrangements for cooperation, in the small and in the large, that are least likely to prevent permanent innovation.

The other great constructive force is the demand for personal freedom and self-assertion. It is much more than the need for safeguards against governmental oppression. It is the search for a solution – for better, not perfect or definitive solutions – to two intersecting problems. We both need other people and need to be protected from them. We must be able to participate wholeheartedly in particular societies and cultures, in particular forms of experience and consciousness, yet we cannot surrender our powers of desire or insight to any one of these versions of humanity or to any collection of them. Moreover, we must live in a way recognizing the truth that there is more in us, individually as persons or collectively as mankind, than there is in the institutional and discursive worlds we make and inhabit; that they are the finite and that we, with respect to them, are the infinite. As we free ourselves from entrenched structures of social division and hierarchy, we diminish the quota of dependence and depersonalization in group life and begin to heal the wounding conflict between the conditions of self-assertion.

As we diminish the distance between the routinized acceptance of an institutional or imaginative framework for human action and the exceptional remaking of the framework, we expand the prospects for wholeheartedness. We make wholehearted engagement possible with less prostration and illusion by changing the relation between structure-respecting routine and structure-defying transformation or transcendence. For these reasons, democracy matters to freedom interpreted in its largest sense as surfeit of being. It gives some partial answer to that great, hidden source of human sadness: the disproportion between the intensity of our desires and the indignity of the objects on which they must ordinarily fasten. We are ourselves the only proper objects of such desires, but not we as we are now, but rather we as we might make ourselves, we as original spirits who shall be able to give ourselves more fully to one another because we shall no longer be the hapless creatures of a destiny imposed by class and culture. To connect the conditions for the development of this freedom with the demands of practical progress through practical experimentalism is the true promise of democracy.

The essential requirement for the union of these material and spiritual forces to operate more quickly and more powerfully is that we be willing to tinker for their sake – with our practices and institutions, with our understanding of our ideals and interests, and with each in relation to the other. In legal analysis and in political economy – the twin disciplines of the institutional imagination – we must develop a conversation about tinkering, until, by dint of talking and thinking as motivated tinkerers, we gradually turn into both realists and prophets.

A parable: the Jews and their law

No religion gives a more central place to law in its system of beliefs than does Judaism. Here is a little story about the religion of the Jews and its possible future. In its content and implications it moves so far away from the established religion that it would be futile to defend it. Moreover, it violates a taboo – an intolerable one to whomever takes religion seriously – against the religious criticism of religion. The parable suggests a lesson about the religion of law in democratic societies.

Like Christianity and Islam, Judaism is an historical religion. It treats history as a scene of decisive action in which divine purpose and human action meet, not as an epiphenomenal backdrop to permanent spiritual reality. It takes the reality of the world and the individuality of people to go all the way down rather than dismissing them as illusions concealing the real thing. It represents the relation between God and humankind on the model of relations among people. The revelation of God in history resembles the mysterious and always partial disclosure of one person to another. The stories of religion contain truths deepening the truths prefigured in the stories we tell about ourselves. The personal counts for more than the impersonal.

At the center of the religion of the Jews lies monotheism, revealed in human history through a struggle between idolatry and iconoclasm. God elected the Jews for reasons no one can grasp, but the singularity resulting from the election belongs more to the plot than to the message. When God first made his covenant with the Jews through Abraham (Genesis 15 and 17) he said nothing about obedience to law. (God made the earlier covenant of Genesis 7 – the one for which he gave the rainbow as a sign – through Noah with all humankind rather than with the Jews.) He simply told Abraham to walk before him and to be perfect. He ordered the Jews to circumcise their male children, and the male children of the foreigners they bought, as a token of the covenant. He branded them before he gave them any rules. When God tested Abraham by instructing him to sacrifice Isaac, he was probing Abraham's faith – that is to say, his trust – and therefore also his hope, but he was not handing down law; he gave his order only to revoke it at the moment of its impending execution. God's demand was so perplexing that Abraham never mentioned it to the son he was about to sacrifice, preferring, as Kierkegaard suggests, that Isaac hate his father than that he hate God. Later, at Sinai, God gave rules. Here began an all-consuming interest in the law. However, the initial source of religious energy lay in an encounter that produced no law, in a covenant to be tested again and again in the light of a struggle between idolatry and iconoclasm, in a struggle between idolatry and iconoclasm to be fought out again and again in the light of the covenant.

In the aftermath of the destruction of the second Temple, the Jews abandoned the sacrificial-cultic element in their religion. They extended the basis for the rabbinical elaboration of the halakhah – a mixture of biblical precept and rabbinical exegesis and casuistry – that has been the mainstay of Judaism ever since.

The development of rabbinical Judaism, organized around the study and practice of the law, represented a great advance in the history of the religion. It wrested religious authority away from a caste of priests and a succession of prophets, and gave it instead to many loosely connected communities of discourse and to their leaders. In acting upon the commitment to reshape the prosaic details of social life, it offered men and women a practice and a discourse with which to connect, and to keep connecting, the sacred and the secular, sanctifying everyday experience and ordinary people. It began to teach people how to reconcile, as individuals and as communities, self-construction and forgetfulness of self. However, like any form of spiritual and social liberation, it contained a danger.

The danger lay and lies in the ambiguous relation of the halakhah to the covenant with God and to the always unfinished struggle between idolatry and iconoclasm. The cult of the law may manifest the covenant, or it may conceal it. It may quicken the contest between idolatry and iconoclasm, or it may freeze it. It may conceal the covenant and freeze the contest by placing a regime of rules – demanding but contained – in the uncontainable place of a personal experience: the lived analogy between the insatiable demands people make upon one another, and the insatiable demands God and man make upon each other. This twin insatiability finds its only effective response in mutual acceptance, and in the acceptance of our vulnerability to the refusal of acceptance by other people. Rules and rituals may help set the stage on which we can live out this ambition less distracted by fear and injustice and with greater clarity of intention and expression. However, people may begin to believe that if only they follow the rules to the hilt, they will be spiritually as well as socially safe. They may put conformity to law in the place of responsiveness to people and to God, holding God and people alike behind a screen of routinized practice. Thus, the ritual obedience to the law may itself become a form of idolatry, preventing Jacob from wrestling more directly with God. Soon even for the orthodox, or for the orthodox especially, the problem of iconoclasm and idolatry may come to seem an ordeal of the past.

During the long period of catastrophe and regrouping leading from the diaspora to the near extermination of European Jewry at the hands of the Germans, the Jews had a reason for single-minded devotion to the halakhah. The sacred law remained a chain of remembrance and identity, binding the Jews to one another and to their history and thus also, through the covenant, to God. Within the orthodox religion of the rabbis, a rich practice of commentary and conversation developed precepts for every realm of social life, informing analogies with conceptions (while avoiding runaway conceptual ascent) and finding reasons where there appeared to be only accidents. Outside the orthodox religion, in the climate of European enlightenment and its sequels, reformers and critics invoked latitudinarian interpretations of the law in the service of an effort to reveal the rational, ethical kernel in the shell of rule and ritual. As the Pharisees stood to the Sadducees, so do these humanist demythologizers of religion stand to the apparatus of latter-day orthodoxy. Thus, two divergent enterprises began, the one leading inward, toward conformity to the law as elaborated by rabbinical practice; the other outward, toward translation of the halakhic vocabulary into a moral language continuous with the concerns of modern humankind. Each of these enterprises distanced itself in its own way from the initial source of religious energy. Both Reform Judaism and Zionism promised, in their beginnings, to stay close to that source, even at the cost of outright desanctification of the law. Nevertheless, each later reverted to the easier path of latitudinarian interpretation of the law in the service of convergence with secular humanism.

Now, however, there is hope that the time of catastrophes in Jewish history may be coming to a close. God may therefore be about to weaken the grounds for the centrality of the halakhah. The task, as Jesus of Nazareth and other "marginal Jews" have said from time to time, is not to destroy the law but to fulfill it – the law of Sinai and the prophets rather than the law of the midrash and the rabbis. To fulfill the law is to put the love of God and the love of people at the center; it is to open ourselves up to all forms of prophetic insight into the transcendence of the person, made in the image of God, over finite circumstance, as well as into the conditions of reconciliation among people. We do not know who these prophets could now be nor what language they would now speak. Then again, we never know before the fact. Contemporary Jewish philosophers have said as much. Even they, however, have been reluctant to draw out the disturbing implications of their personalist teaching for the cult of the law. To the objection that to pursue these implications would be to invent a different religion, the answer is that the continuing dialectic of idolatry and iconoclasm in the light of the covenant *is* the religion if anything is. In an historical religion, when history comes to an end, prophecy and remembrance turn together toward the wholehearted acceptance of the present, and faith gives way to sight.

De nobis fabula narratur. We all hold the place of the Jews in a story like this one. The marriage of the cult of the state with the belief in latent moral order has turned our understanding of law more into a shield against the subversive, transformative, and redemptive forces of practical experimentalism and personal freedom than into an instrument for their development in the institutionalized life of society. However, we can put the shield down, and make it into something else. Our time of troubles is never over. Nonetheless, the long and partial peace is slowly destroying many of our pretexts for the idolatry of our institutions and for their idolatrous representation in legal thought and political economy. Although the institutional and imaginative paths along which the constructive forces can develop are always contestable and divergent, they are also, as the earlier discussion of the alternative futures of democracy shows, particular. Their particularity, and their connection back to our present circumstance through countless steps of transition, enable us to imagine them as law and to undertake them as politics.

The realist and the visionary

Lawyers have pictured law as reason encoded in the doings and dreams of power just as economists have seen actual market economies and their law as approximations to a pure system of rationality and reciprocity. They have sung for their supper by singing in their chains. Hope and insight may nevertheless succeed where indignation and history worship failed, and draw the lawyers and economists into the work of giving eyes and wings to the institutional imagination.

Our interests and ideals remain nailed to the cross of our arrangements. We cannot realize our interests and ideals more fully, nor redefine them more deeply, until we have learned to remake and to reimagine our arrangements more freely. History will not give us this freedom. We must win it in the here and now of legal detail, economic constraint, and deadening preconception. We shall not win it if we continue to profess a science of society reducing the possible to the actual and a discourse about law anointing power with piety. It is true that we cannot be visionaries until we become realists. It is also true that to become realists we must make ourselves into visionaries.

Many of the ideas in this book were initially presented as three Storrs Lectures at the Yale Law School, a Rubin Lecture at the Columbia Law School, and a Chorley Lecture at the London School of Economics.

Index

Printed in the United States
by Baker & Taylor Publisher Services